It
Business Dictionary

A Bloomsbury Reference Book
Originally published by Peter Collin Publishing

PH Collin

Peter Blanchard
Sylvia Berlincioni

Berlitz Publishing/APA Publications GmbH & Co.
Verlag KG, Singapore Branch, Singapore

Italian Business Dictionary

© 2005 Berlitz Publishing/APA Publications GmbH & Co.
Verlag KG, Singapore Branch, Singapore
© Bloomsbury Publishing 2003
© Copyright P.H. Collin 1995, 2002

Printed in Singapore by Insight Print Services (Pte.) Ltd.,
December 2004

ISBN 981-246-681-9
Cover photo © Photodisc/PunchStock

Text computer set by Bloomsbury

Preface

This pocket dictionary is designed for any business person, student or traveller who needs to deal with the language of business. It contains over 5,000 essential business terms in Italian and English with clear and accurate translations.

Abbreviations

adj	adjective
adv	adverb
f	feminine
fpl	feminine plural
m	masculine
mf	masculine *or* feminine
mpl	masculine plural
n	noun
v	verb

Prefazione

Questo dizionario si rivolge a studenti e uomini d'affari che utilizzino la lingua inglese in ambito commerciale. Contiene più di 5000 termini indispensabili con traduzioni chiare e accurate.

Abbreviazione

adj	aggettivo
adv	avverbio
f	femminile
fpl	femminile plurale
m	maschile
mf	maschile *o* femminile
mpl	maschile plurale
n	sostantivo
v	verbo

Contents

Indice

Inglese-Italiano
English-Italian

Aa

A1 di prima classe
abandon abbandonare *o* lasciare
abandon an action rinunciare ad un'azione (f)
abatement riduzione (f)
abroad all'estero
absence assenza (f) *o* mancanza (f)
absent assente
absolute monopoly monopolio (m) perfetto
accelerated depreciation ammortamento (m) accelerato
accept (v) [agree] accettare
accept (v) [take something] accettare
accept a bill accettare una cambiale
accept delivery of a shipment prendere in consegna un carico di merce
accept liability for something assumersi la responsabilità di qualcosa
acceptable accettabile *o* soddisfacente
acceptance accettazione (f)
acceptance of an offer accettazione (f) di un'offerta
acceptance sampling campionatura (f) per accettazione
accommodation address indirizzo (m) di comodo
accommodation bill cambiale (f) di favore *o* effetto (m) di comodo
according to conformemente a
account conto (m)
account executive direttore (m) del servizio marketing *o* direttore delle vendite
account for rendere conto
account in credit conto (m) in credito
account on stop conto (m) bloccato
account: on account in acconto
accountant ragioniere (m) *o* ragioniera (f) *o* contabile (m)
accounting contabilità (f)
accounts department reparto (m) contabilità
accounts payable conti (mpl) passivi
accounts receivable conti (mpl) attivi
accrual importo (m) maturato
accrual of interest maturazione (f) degli interessi
accrue maturare *o* accumularsi
accrued interest interesse (m) maturato
accumulate accumulare *o* accantonare
accurate accurato *o* preciso
acknowledge receipt of a letter accusare ricevuta di una lettera
acknowledgement conferma (f)
acquire a company entrare in possesso di una società
acquisition acquisizione (f) *o* acquisto (m)
across-the-board uniforme *o* indiscriminato
act (v) [do something] agire
act (v) [work] funzionare
act of God causa (f) di forza maggiore
acting facente funzione di *o* sostituto
acting manager direttore (m) facente funzione
action [lawsuit] azione (f) *o* causa (f)
action [thing done] azione (f)
action for damages causa (f) per risarcimento
actual effettivo *o* reale
actuals prezzi effettivi (mpl) di vendita
actuarial tables tavole (fpl) attuariali
actuary attuario (m)

ad valorem ad valorem *o* in base al valore di

ad valorem tax tassa (f) ad valorem

add aggiungere *o* sommare

add on 10% for service aggiungere il 10% per il servizio

add up a column of figures sommare una colonna di cifre

addition *[calculation]* addizione (f) *o* somma (f)

addition *[thing added]* aggiunta (f)

additional addizionale *o* supplementare

additional charges spese (fpl) supplementari

additional premium premio (m) addizionale

address (n) indirizzo (m) *o* recapito (m)

address (v) indirizzare *o* rivolgere la parola a qualcuno

address a letter *or* a parcel indirizzare una lettera *o* un pacco

address label etichetta (f) indirizzata

address list lista (f) di indirizzi

addressee destinatario (m)

adequate adeguato *o* sufficiente

adjourn aggiornare *o* rimandare

adjourn a meeting aggiornare una riunione

adjudicate in a dispute pronunciarsi in una vertenza

adjudication aggiudicazione (f) *o* giudizio (m)

adjudication tribunal tribunale (m) di arbitrato

adjudicator giudice (m)

adjust adattare *o* adeguare

adjustment accomodamento (m) *o* accordo (m)

administration amministrazione (f) *o* gestione (f)

administrative amministrativo

administrative expenses spese (fpl) di amministrazione

admission ammissione (f)

admission charge spese (fpl) d'ammissione *o* spese d'entrata

admit *[confess]* ammettere

admit *[let in]* far entrare

advance (adj) anticipato

advance (n) *[increase]* aumento (m)

advance (n) *[loan]* anticipo (m)

advance (v) *[increase]* aumentare

advance (v) *[lend]* prestare

advance booking prenotazione (f) anticipata

advance on account anticipazione (f) su un conto

advance payment pagamento (m) anticipato

advertise fare pubblicità *o* reclamizzare

advertise a new product reclamizzare un nuovo prodotto

advertise a vacancy pubblicare un'inserzione (f) per un impiego disponibile

advertisement annuncio (m) pubblicitario *o* pubblicità (f)

advertiser inserzionista (m) *o* chi fa pubblicità

advertising pubblicità (f) *o* reclame (f)

advertising agency agenzia (f) di pubblicità

advertising budget budget (m) pubblicitario

advertising campaign campagna (f) pubblicitaria

advertising manager direttore (m) della pubblicità

advertising rates tariffe (f) delle inserzioni pubblicitarie

advertising space spazio (m) pubblicitario

advice note bolletta (f) d'avviso

advise *[tell what happened]* informare *o* avvisare

advise *[what should be done]* consigliare *o* raccomandare

adviser *or* advisor consulente (m)

affidavit attestazione (f) ufficiale

affiliated affiliato *o* associato

affirmative affermativo

afford permettersi *o* avere i mezzi economici

after-sales service assistenza (f) post-vendita alla clientela

after-tax profit utile (m) al netto delle imposte

agency agenzia (f)

agenda ordine (m) del giorno

agent [representative] agente (m) o rappresentante (m)

agent [working in an agency] agente (m)

AGM (= annual general meeting) Assemblea (f) Generale degli Azionisti

agree [accept] accettare

agree [approve] approvare

agree [be same as] concordare o corrispondere a

agree to do something acconsentire a fare qualcosa o accettare di fare qualcosa

agree with [be same as] concordare o corrispondere a

agree with [of same opinion] essere d'accordo con

agreed convenuto o concordato

agreed price prezzo (m) concordato

agreement accordo (m)

agricultural agricolo o agrario

aim (n) scopo (m) o proposito (m)

aim (v) avere lo scopo di

air aria (f)

air freight trasporto (m) merci via aerea

air freight charges or rates spese trasporto merci via aerea

air letter lettera (f) aerea

air terminal terminal (m) della compagnia aerea

airfreight (v) trasportare merci via aerea

airline linea (f) aerea o compagnia (f) aerea

airmail (n) posta (f) aerea

airmail (v) spedire per posta aerea

airmail sticker etichetta (f) di posta aerea

airport aeroporto (m)

airport bus autobus (m) dell'aeroporto

airport tax tasse (fpl) aeroportuali

airport terminal terminal (m)

airtight packaging imballaggio (m) ermetico

all expenses paid tutte le spese pagate

all-in totale o globale

all-in price prezzo (m) tutto compreso

all-risks policy polizza (f) contro tutti i rischi

allocate stanziare

allow [agree] accettare o ammettere

allow [give] accordare o cedere

allow [permit] permettere

allow 10% for carriage calcolare 10% per il trasporto

allow for calcolare o dedurre

allowance for depreciation accantonamento (m) al fondo di ammortamento

alphabetical order ordine (m) alfabetico

alter modificare o cambiare

alteration modifica (f) o cambiamento (m)

alternative (adj) alternativo

alternative (n) alternativa (f)

amend correggere

amendment emendamento (m) o rettifica (f)

American (adj) americano

American (n) Americano, -ana

amortization ammortamento (m)

amortize ammortare o ammortizzare

amount [of money] ammontare (m) o importo (m)

amount owing importo (m) dovuto

amount paid importo (m) pagato

amount to ammontare a

analyse or analyze analizzare

analyse the market potential analizzare il potenziale del mercato

analysis analisi (f)

announce annunciare

announcement annuncio (m)

annual annuale o annuo

annual accounts rendiconti (mpl) annuali

annual general meeting (AGM) Assemblea (f) Generale degli Azionisti

annual report relazione (f) annuale al bilancio

annually annualmente

answer (n) risposta (f)

answer (v) rispondere

answer a letter rispondere a una lettera

answer the telephone rispondere al telefono

answering machine segreteria (f) telefonica

answering service servizio (m) segreteria telefonica

antedate retrodatare

apologize scusarsi

apology scusa (f)

appeal (n) *[against a decision]* ricorso (m) *o* appello (m)

appeal (n) *[attraction]* richiamo (m)

appeal (v) *[against a decision]* ricorrere in appello *o* appellare

appeal to (v) *[attract]* attirare

appear sembrare

appendix appendice (f)

applicant for a job candidato (m) a un posto di lavoro

application domanda (f) *o* istanza (f)

application for a job domanda (f) d'impiego

application form modulo (m) per domanda di assunzione

apply for *[ask for]* chiedere

apply for a job fare domanda d'impiego

apply in writing fare domanda scritta

apply to *[affect]* riguardare

appoint nominare

appointment *[job]* impiego (m) *o* posto (m)

appointment *[meeting]* appuntamento (m)

appointment *[to a job]* nomina (f)

appointments book agenda (f)

appointments vacant impieghi (mpl) disponibili

appreciate *[how good something is]* apprezzare

appreciate *[increase in value]* aumentare di valore

appreciation *[how good something is]* apprezzamento (m)

appreciation *[in value]* rivalutazione (f)

appropriate (v) *[funds]* destinare

approval benestare (m)

approval: on approval in prova *o* in esame

approve the terms of a contract approvare i termini di un contratto

approximate approssimativo

approximately approssimativamente

arbitrate in a dispute arbitrare una vertenza

arbitration arbitrato (m)

arbitration board *or* arbitration tribunal tribunale (m) arbitrale

arbitrator arbitro (m)

area *[of town]* zona (f) *o* quartiere (m)

area *[region]* area (f) *o* regione (f)

area *[subject]* campo (m)

area *[surface]* superficie (f)

area code codice (m) di zona

area manager direttore (m) di zona

argument discussione (f) *o* disputa (f)

arrange *[meeting]* stabilire *o* organizzare

arrange *[set out]* sistemare *o* disporre

arrangement *[compromise]* intesa (f) *o* accordo (m)

arrangement *[system]* sistemazione (f) *o* disposizione (m)

arrears arretrati (mpl)

arrival arrivo (m)

arrivals arrivi (mpl)

arrive arrivare

article *[clause]* clausola (f)

article *[item]* articolo (m) *o* prodotto (m)

articles of association atto (m) costitutivo di società o statuto (m) societario

articulated lorry or articulated vehicle camion/autocarro (m) articolato o veicolo articolato

as per advice come consigliato

as per invoice come da fattura

as per sample come da campione

asap (= as soon as possible) al più presto possibile o nel più breve termine

ask [someone to do something] chiedere (a qualcuno di fare qualcosa)

ask for [ask a price] chiedere (un prezzo)

ask for [something] chiedere o domandare

ask for a refund chiedere un rimborso

ask for further details or particulars chiedere ulteriori dettagli o particolari

assembly [meeting] assemblea (f)

assembly [putting together] assemblaggio (m) o montaggio (m)

assembly line catena (f) di montaggio

assess accertare o stabilire il valore

assess damages accertare i danni

assessment of damages accertamento (m) dei danni

asset bene (m) o cespite (m)

asset value valore (m) patrimoniale (di imprese)

assets and liabilities attività (fpl) e passività (fpl)

assign a right to someone attribuire un diritto a qualcuno

assignee assegnatario (m)

assignment [cession] cessione (f) o trasferimento (m)

assignment [work] incarico (m)

assignor cedente (m) o parte venditrice (f)

assist assistere

assistance aiuto (m) o assistenza (f)

assistant assistente (mf) o collaboratore (m)

assistant manager vice direttore

associate (adj) associato

associate (n) associato (m) o socio (m)

associate company società (f) collegata

association associazione (f)

assurance assicurazione (f)

assurance company compagnia (f) di assicurazione

assurance policy polizza (f) di assicurazione

assure someone's life assicurare la vita di qualcuno

attach attaccare o unire

attack attaccare o assalire

attend (meeting) assistere a

attend to occuparsi di

attention attenzione (f)

attorney procuratore (m)

attract attrarre

attractive salary stipendio (m) interessante

auction (n) asta (f)

auction (v) vendere all'asta

auction rooms sala (f) di vendita all'asta

audit (n) revisione (f) contabile

audit (v) verificare

audit the accounts verificare i conti

auditing revisione contabile (f) o certificazione (f)

auditor revisore (m) ufficiale dei conti

authenticate autenticare o legalizzare

authority autorità (f)

authorization autorizzazione (f)

authorize [give permission] autorizzare

authorize payment autorizzare un pagamento

authorized autorizzato

availability disponibilità (f)

available disponibile

available capital capitale (m) disponibile

average (adj) medio
average (n) media (f)
average (n) *[insurance]* avaria (f)
average (v) calcolare una media
average price prezzo (m) medio
avoid evitare
await instructions attendere istruzioni
award (n) giudizio (m) arbitrale
award (v) assegnare
award a contract to someone aggiudicare un contratto a qualcuno

Bb

back (n) dorso (m) *o* retro (m)
back orders ordinazioni (fpl) inevase
back payment pagamento (m) degli arretrati
back tax imposta (f) arretrata
backdate retrodatare
backer sostenitore (m) *o* avallante (m)
backhander bustarella (f)
backing appoggio (m) *o* aiuto (m)
backlog lavoro (m) arretrato
backup (adj) *[computer]* di salvaguardia
backup copy copia (f) di riserva
backwardation deporto (m)
bad buy cattivo acquisto (m)
bad debt credito (m) inesigibile
bag borsa (f)
bail someone out ottenere la liberazione (su cauzione) di qualcuno
balance (n) bilancio (m) *o* bilancia (f)
balance (v) bilanciare

balance (v) *[a budget]* pareggiare un budget
balance brought down *or* **brought forward** saldo (m) da riportare
balance carried down *or* **carried forward** saldo (m) riportato
balance due to us saldo (m) dovuto
balance of payments bilancia (f) dei pagamenti
balance of trade bilancia (f) commerciale
balance sheet bilancio (m) d'esercizio
ban (n) interdizione (f)
ban (v) interdire *o* vietare
bank (n) banca (f)
bank (v) depositare in banca *o* avere un conto in banca
bank account conto (m) bancario
bank balance saldo (m) in banca
bank base rate tasso (m) ufficiale di sconto
bank bill *[GB]* effetto (m) bancario
bank bill *[US]* banconota (f)
bank book libretto (m) di versamento
bank borrowings prestiti (mpl) bancari
bank charges spese (fpl) bancarie
bank credit credito (m) bancario
bank deposits depositi (mpl) bancari
bank draft assegno (m) circolare
bank holiday giorno (m) di chiusura degli sportelli bancari *o* festa (f) nazionale
bank loan prestito (m) bancario
bank manager direttore (m) di banca
bank statement estratto (m) conto bancario
bank transfer bonifico (m)
bankable paper effetti (mpl) bancabili *o* strumenti (mpl) scontabili
banker banchiere (m) *o* funzionario (m) di banca
banker's draft assegno (m) circolare

banker's order ordine (m) bancario
banking attività (f) bancaria
banking hours orario (m) di banca
banknote banconota (f)
bankrupt (adj) fallito
bankrupt (n) fallito (m)
bankrupt (v) fare fallire
bankruptcy fallimento (m)
bar chart diagramma (m) a barre
bar code codice (m) a barre
bargain (n) *[cheaper than usual]* affare (m) o occasione (f)
bargain (n) *[deal]* affare (m)
bargain (n) *[stock exchange]* vendita (f) di realizzo
bargain (v) contrattare o tirare sul prezzo
bargain offer offerta (f) d'occasione
bargain price prezzo (m) d'occasione
bargaining contrattazione (f)
bargaining position situazione (f) contrattuale
bargaining power potere (m) contrattuale
barrier barriera (f)
barter (n) baratto (m) o scambio (m)
barter (v) barattare
bartering scambio (m) di merci e prodotti
base (n) *[initial position]* base (f)
base (n) *[place]* base (f)
base (v) *[in a place]* essere di base a o avere la propria sede in
base (v) *[start to calculate from]* basarsi
base year anno (m) di base
basic (adj) *[most important]* di base o fondamentale
basic (adj) *[simple]* di base o basilare
basic discount sconto (m) di base
basic tax tassa (f) di base
basis base (f) o fondamento (m)
batch (n) *[of orders]* gruppo (m)
batch (n) *[of products]* partita (f) di merci

batch (v) mettere insieme
batch number numero (m) di partita
batch processing elaborazione (f) di massa
bear (n) *[Stock Exchange]* ribassista (m)
bear (v) *[carry]* portare
bear (v) *[interest]* fruttare
bear (v) *[pay for]* sostenere
bear market mercato (m) al ribasso
bearer portatore (m) o portatrice (f)
bearer bond obbligazione (f) al portatore
begin cominciare o iniziare
beginning inizio (m)
behalf: on behalf of a nome di o per conto di
belong to appartenere a
below-the-line expenditure spese (f) straordinarie
benchmark punto (m) di riferimento
beneficiary beneficiario (m)
benefit (n) beneficio (m) o utilità (f)
benefit from (v) trarre vantaggio da
berth (n) ormeggio (m)
berth (v) ormeggiare
best (adj) migliore
best (n) il meglio
best-selling car automobile (f) di grande successo
bid (n) *[at an auction]* offerta (f)
bid (n) *[offer to buy]* offerta (f)
bid (n) *[offer to do work]* offerta (f) d'appalto
bidder offerente (m)
bidding offerta (f)
bilateral bilaterale
bill (n) *[US]* banconota (f)
bill (n) *[in a restaurant]* conto (m)
bill (n) *[in Parliament]* progetto (m) di legge
bill (n) *[list of charges]* fattura (f) o bolletta (f)
bill (n) *[written promise to pay]* effetto (m) o cambiale (f)
bill (v) fatturare

bill of exchange cambiale (f)
bill of lading polizza (f) di carico
bill of sale fattura (f) *o* atto (m) di vendita
billing fatturazione (f)
billion *[UK]* bilione (m)
billion *[US]* miliardo (m)
bills for collection effetti (mpl) all'incasso
bills payable effetti (mpl) passivi *o* cambiali (fpl) da pagare
bills receivable effetti (mpl) attivi *o* cambiali (fpl) da incassare
binding vincolante
black economy economia (f) nera
black list (n) lista (f) nera
blacklist (v) inserire in una lista (f) di proscrizione
black market mercato (m) nero
blame (n) biasimo (m) *o* colpa (f)
blame (v) biasimare
blank (adj) in bianco *o* vuoto
blank (n) spazio (m) *o* vuoto (m)
blank cheque assegno (m) in bianco
blister pack pacco (m) con confezione 'blister' (in plastica trasparente con personalizzazione)
block (n) *[building]* palazzo (m)
block (n) *[of shares]* pacchetto (m) (azionistico)
block (v) bloccare
block booking noleggio (m) in blocco
blocked currency valuta (f) bloccata
blue chip titolo (m) di prim'ordine
blue-chip investments investimenti (mpl) in titoli di prim'ordine
board (n) *[group of people]* Consiglio (m) di Amministrazione
board (v) imbarcarsi
board meeting riunione (f) del consiglio di amministrazione
board of directors Consiglio (m) di Amministrazione
board: on board a bordo
boarding card *or* boarding pass carta (f) d'imbarco

boardroom sala (f) riunioni
bona fide in buona fede
bond *[borrowing by government]* obbligazione (f)
bonded warehouse magazzino (m) doganale
bonus gratifica (f) *o* premio (m)
bonus issue emissione (f) gratuita di azioni *o* aumento (m) gratuito di capitale
book (n) libro (m)
book (v) prenotare
book sales vendite (fpl) registrate
book value valore (m) contabile
booking registrazione (f) *o* prenotazione (f)
booking clerk impiegato (m) alla biglietteria
booking office ufficio (m) prenotazioni
bookkeeper contabile (mf) *o* ragioniere (m)
bookkeeping contabilità (f)
boom (n) sviluppo (m) favorevole dell'economia *o* boom (m)
boom (v) prosperare
boom industry industria (f) che si è sviluppata rapidamente
booming fiorente
boost (n) spinta (f)
boost (v) lanciare
border frontiera (f)
borrow prendere a prestito *o* mutuare
borrower mutuatario (m)
borrowing mutuo (m)
borrowing power potere (m) per ricorrere al prestito
boss (informal) capo (m)
bottleneck strozzatura (f) (nel processo aziendale)
bottom fondo (m)
bottom line nodo (m) della questione
bought ledger mastro (m) dei conti dei creditori
bought ledger clerk responsabile (m) del mastro dei conti dei creditori
bounce *[cheque]* respingere

box number   casella (f) postale

boxed set   presentazione (f) in cofanetto

boycott (n)   boicottaggio (m)

boycott (v)   boicottare

bracket (n) *[tax]*   fascia (f)

bracket together   raggruppare

branch   settore (m)

branch manager   direttore (m) di filiale

branch office   filiale (f)

brand   marchio (m) *o* marca (f)

brand image   immagine (f) del prodotto

brand loyalty   fedeltà (f) alla marca

brand name   marca (f) *o* nome del prodotto

brand new   nuovo di zecca

breach of contract   inadempimento (m) del contratto

breach of warranty   violazione (f) di garanzia

break (n)   pausa (f)

break (v) *[contract]*   rompere

break an agreement   infrangere un accordo

break down (v) *[itemize]* dettagliare

break down (v) *[machine]* rompersi

break down (v) *[talks]*   arenarsi *[di trattative]*

break even (v)   giungere al punto di pareggio

break off negotiations   sospendere le trattative

break the law   violare la legge

breakages   rotture (fpl) *o* danni (mpl)

breakdown (n) *[items]*   ripartizione (f)

breakdown (n) *[machine]*   guasto (m)

breakdown (n) *[talks]*   rottura (f)

breakeven point   punto (m) di pareggio fra costi e ricavi

bribe (n)   tangente (f) *o* bustarella (f)

bribe (v)   corrompere (con denaro *o* doni)

brief (v)   dare istruzioni

briefcase   borsa (f) *o* cartella (f)

bring   portare

bring a civil action   intentare causa civile

bring in   apportare *o* rendere

bring out   lanciare

British   britannico *o* inglese

brochure   fascicolo (m)

broke (informal)   al verde

broker   broker (m)

brokerage *or* **broker's commission**   commissione (f) di mediazione

brown paper   carta (f) da pacco

bubble pack   confezione (f) a bolla di plastica trasparente

budget (n) *[government]*   bilancio (m) dello Stato

budget (n) *[personal, company]*   bilancio (m) preventivo *o* budget (m)

budget (v)   budgettare

budget account *[in bank]*   contabilità (f) di bilancio

budgetary   budgetario *o* relativo al budget

budgetary control   controllo (m) budgetario

budgetary policy   politica (f) di budget

budgeting   preparazione (f) del budget

building society   istituto (m) di credito fondiario

built-in   incorporato *o* inserito

bulk   volume (m) *o* grande quantità (f)

bulk buying   acquisto (m) in massa

bulk shipments   spedizione (f) in massa

bulky   voluminoso

bull *[stock exchange]*   speculatore al rialzo

bull market   mercato (m) al rialzo

bulletin   bollettino (m)

bullion   oro (m) in verghe

bureau de change   ufficio (m) cambio

bus   autobus (m)

business *[commerce]*   affari (mpl)

business *[company]* impresa (f)
business *[discussion]* affare (m)
business address indirizzo (m)
d'ufficio
business call telefonata (f) d'affari
business card biglietto (m) da
visita
business centre centro (m)
d'affari
business class classe (f) business
business equipment
apparecchiatura (f) d'ufficio
business hours ore (f) d'ufficio
business letter lettera (f) d'affari
business lunch pranzo (m)
d'affari
business premises locali (mpl)
d'azienda *o* locali commerciali
business strategy strategia (f)
commerciale
business transaction transazione
(f) commerciale
business trip viaggio (m) d'affari
business: on business per affari
businessman *or* businesswoman
uomo (m) d'affari *o* donna (f)
d'affari
busy occupato
buy (v) comperare
buy back riacquistare
buy for cash comperare in contanti
buy forward comperare a termine
buyer *[for a store]* responsabile
(m) di un ufficio acquisti
buyer *[person]* compratore (m)
buyer's market mercato (m) al
ribasso
buying acquisto (m)
buying department ufficio (m)
acquisti
by-product prodotto (m) derivato

Cc

cable address indirizzo (m)
cablografico
calculate calcolare
calculation calcolo (m)
calculator calcolatore (m)
calendar month mese (m) solare
calendar year anno (m) solare
call (n) *[for money]* richiesta (f) di
pagamento
call (n) *[phone]* chiamata (f)
call (n) *[stock exchange]* opzione
(f) d'acquisto
call (n) *[visit]* visita (f)
call (v) *[ask to do something]*
invitare
call (v) *[meeting]* convocare
call (v) *[phone]* chiamare
call off a deal disdire un affare
call rate tasso (m) su prestiti a
breve
callable bond obbligazione (f)
redimibile
campaign campagna (f)
cancel cancellare *o* annullare
cancel a cheque annullare un
assegno
cancel a contract annullare un
contratto
cancellation cancellazione (f) *o*
disdetta (f)
cancellation clause clausola (f) di
rescissione
cancellation of an appointment
revoca (f) di una nomina
candidate candidato (m)
canvass procacciare
canvasser piazzista (m) *o*
propagandista (m)
canvassing propaganda (f)
canvassing techniques tecniche
(f) di propaganda
capable of capace di

capacity [ability] abilità (f) o capacità (f)

capacity [production] capacità (f) produttiva

capacity [space] capacità (f)

capacity utilization utilizzo (m) della capacità produttiva

capital capitale (m) o capitali (mpl)

capital account conto (m) capitale

capital assets immobilizzazioni (fpl)

capital equipment immobilizzi (mpl) tecnici

capital expenditure spese (fpl) conto capitali

capital gains plusvalenza (f)

capital gains tax imposta (f) sulle plusvalenze

capital goods beni (mpl) strumentali

capital loss perdita (f) di capitale

capital-intensive industry industria (f) a forte assorbimento di capitali

capitalization capitalizzazione (f)

capitalization of reserves capitalizzazione delle riserve

capitalize capitalizzare

capitalize on trarre vantaggio da

captive market mercato (m) controllato da un solo fornitore

capture impadronirsi

carbon copy copia (f) carbone

carbon paper carta (f) carbone

carbonless autocopiante

card [business card] biglietto (m)

card [material] cartoncino (m)

card [membership] tessera (f)

card [postcard] cartolina (f) postale

card index (n) schedario (m)

card phone telefono (m) a schede

card-index (v) schedare

card-index file fascicolo (m) dello schedario

card-indexing schedatura (f)

cardboard cartone (m)

cardboard box scatola (f) di cartone

care of (c/o) presso

cargo carico (m)

cargo ship nave (f) da carico

carnet [document] carnet (m)

carriage trasporto (m)

carriage forward porto (m) assegnato

carriage free franco di porto

carriage paid porto (m) pagato

carrier [company] trasportatore (m) o impresa (f) di trasporti

carrier [vehicle] camion (m)

carry [approve in a vote] far approvare

carry [have in stock] avere

carry [produce] produrre

carry [transport] portare o trasportare

carry forward riportare a nuovo

carry on a business svolgere esercizio d'impresa

carry over a balance riportare un pareggio

cartel cartello (m)

carton [box] cartone (m) o imballo (m) di cartone

carton [material] cartone (m)

case (n) [box] cassa (f)

case (n) [suitcase] valigia (f)

case (v) [put in boxes] imballare

cash (adv) in contanti

cash (n) [money] denaro (m) contante

cash a cheque incassare un assegno

cash account conto (m) di cassa

cash advance anticipo (m) in contanti

cash and carry supermercato (m) all'ingrosso

cash balance saldo (m) di cassa

cash book libro (m) cassa

cash card tessera (f) prelievo contanti

cash deal transazione (f) sul disponibile

cash deposit deposito (m) in contanti

cash desk sportello (m) di cassa

cash discount sconto (m) cassa o sconto per pagamento in contanti

cash dispenser cassa (f) automatica prelievi
cash float fondo (m) di cassa
cash flow flusso (m) di cassa
cash flow forecast previsioni (fpl) del flusso di cassa
cash flow statement rendiconto (m) del flusso di cassa
cash in hand fondo (m) di cassa
cash offer offerta (f) reale *o* offerta per contanti
cash on delivery (c.o.d.) pagamento (m) alla consegna
cash payment pagamento (m) in contanti
cash price prezzo (m) per contanti *o* condizioni (fpl) per pagamento in contanti
cash purchase acquisto (m) per contanti
cash register registratore (f) di cassa
cash reserves riserva (f) di cassa
cash sale vendita (f) per contanti
cash terms condizioni (fpl) per pagamento in contanti
cash till contenitore (m) di contanti
cash transaction transazione (f) sul disponibile
cash voucher pezza (f) giustificativa di cassa
cashable incassabile
cashier cassiere (m) *o* cassiera (f)
cashier's check *[US]* assegno (m) di cassa (spiccato dalla banca su se stessa in favore di terzi)
casting vote voto (m) decisivo
casual work lavoro (m) saltuario
casual worker lavoratore (m) saltuario
catalogue catalogo (m)
catalogue price prezzo (m) di catalogo
category categoria (f)
cater for provvedere di generi alimentari
caveat emptor 'l'acquirente presti la dovuta attenzione'
ceiling limite (m) massimo
ceiling price prezzo (m) massimo

cellular phone telefono (m) cellulare
central centrale
central bank banca (f) centrale
central purchasing acquisto (m) centralizzato
centralization centralizzazione (f)
centralize centralizzare
centre centro (m)
CEO (= chief executive officer) Direttore Generale (m)
certificate certificato (m)
certificate of approval certificato (m) di accettazione
certificate of deposit certificato (m) di deposito
certificate of guarantee certificato (m) di garanzia
certificate of origin certificato (m) d'origine
certificate of registration certificato (m) d'iscrizione
certificated certificato
certificated bankrupt debitore (m) autorizzato al concordato preventivo
certified accountant revisore (m) ufficiale dei conti *o* (in US) ragioniere (m) iscritto all'albo
certified cheque assegno (m) a copertura garantita
certified copy copia (f) autentica
certify certificare *o* autenticare
cession cessione (f)
chain *[of stores]* catena (f)
chain store negozio (m) che fa parte di una catena
chairman *[of committee]* presidente (m)
chairman *[of company]* presidente (m)
chairman and managing director presidente e amministratore delegato
Chamber of Commerce Camera (f) di Commercio
change (n) *[cash]* spiccioli (mpl)
change (n) *[difference]* cambiamento (m)
change (v) *[money]* cambiare
change hands essere venduto

change machine macchina (f) che cambia denaro in spiccioli

channel (n) canale (m)

channel (v) canalizzare

channels of distribution canali (mpl) di distribuzione

charge (n) *[in court]* accusa (f)

charge (n) *[money]* carico (m)

charge (n) *[on account]* addebito (m)

charge (v) *[money]* far pagare

charge a purchase addebitare un acquisto

charge account conto (m) personale

charge card carta (f) di credito

chargeable caricabile

charges forward pagamento (m) a carico del destinatario

charter (n) noleggio (m)

charter (v) noleggiare

charter an aircraft noleggiare un aeroplano

charter flight volo (m) charter

charter plane aeroplano (m) a noleggio

charterer noleggiatore (m) (di navi, aerei)

chartering noleggio (m)

chase *[an order]* dare la caccia a

chase *[follow]* inseguire

cheap economico o a basso prezzo

cheap labour manodopera (m) a basso prezzo

cheap money denaro (m) a buon mercato

cheap rate tariffa (f) ridotta

check (n) *[examination]* controllo (m)

check (n) *[stop]* arresto (m)

check (v) *[examine]* esaminare o controllare

check (v) *[stop]* arrestare

check in *[at airport]* presentarsi al check in

check in *[at hotel]* firmare il registro

check out *[of hotel]* lasciare libera la camera dell'albergo

check sample campione (m) (statistico) di controllo

check-in *[at airport]* controllo (m) passeggeri

check-in counter check in (m)

check-in time ora (f) di accettazione

checkout *[in supermarket]* cassa (f)

cheque assegno (m)

cheque (guarantee) card carta (f) assegni

cheque account conto (m) assegni

cheque book libretto (m) assegni

cheque number numero (m) dell'assegno

cheque stub matrice (f) dell'assegno

cheque to bearer assegno (m) al portatore

chief (adj) principale

chief clerk capo (m) ufficio

chief executive (officer) direttore (m) generale

choice (adj) di prima qualità

choice (n) *[choosing]* scelta (f)

choice (n) *[items to choose from]* scelta (f)

choice (n) *[thing chosen]* scelta (f)

choose scegliere

Christmas bonus gratifica (f) natalizia o tredicesima (f)

chronic cronico

chronological order ordine (m) cronologico

c.i.f. (= cost, insurance and freight) costo (m), assicurazione (f) e nolo (m)

circular (n) lettera (f) circolare

circular letter lettera (f) circolare

circular letter of credit lettera (f) di credito circolare

circulation *[money]* circolazione (f)

circulation *[newspaper]* tiratura (f)

civil law diritto (m) civile

claim (n) domanda (f) d'indennizzo o reclamo (m)

claim (v) [insurance] rivendicare o presentare una domanda d'indennizzo
claim (v) [right] rivendicare
claim (v) [suggest] affermare
claimant ricorrente o chi fa ricorso
claims department ufficio (m) indennità
claims manager responsabile (m) dei reclami
class classe (f) o categoria (f)
classification classificazione (f)
classified ads annunci (mpl) economici (su giornale) o inserzioni (fpl)
classified advertisements annunci economici
classified directory elenco (m) classificato
classify classificare
clause clausola (f)
clawback ricuperare mediante tassazione
clear (adj) [complete] libero
clear (adj) [easy to understand] chiaro
clear (v) [stock] liquidare
clear a cheque compensare un assegno
clear a debt estinguere un debito
clear profit utile (m) netto
clearance certificate certificato (m) di sdoganamento
clearance of a cheque compensazione (f) di un assegno
clearing [paying] saldo (m) di un debito
clearing bank banca (f) di compensazione
clerical impiegatizio o d'ufficio
clerical error errore (m) di trascrizione
clerical staff personale (m) impiegatizio
clerical work lavoro (m) d'ufficio
clerk impiegato (m)
client cliente (mf)
clientele clientela (f)
climb salire o ascendere
clinch concludere definitivamente

clipping service servizio (m) stralci giornalistici
close (n) [end] chiusura (f)
close (v) [after work] chiudere o finire
close a bank account chiudere un conto bancario
close a meeting togliere la seduta
close an account chiudere un conto
close down chiudere o sospendere un'attività
close to vicino a
closed chiuso
closed market mercato (m) chiuso
closing (adj) di chiusura finale
closing (n) chiusura (f)
closing balance bilancio (m) di chiusura
closing bid ultima offerta (f) (di licitazione)
closing date termine (m) ultimo o data di chiusura
closing price prezzo (m) di chiusura
closing stock giacenze (fpl) finali alla chiusura dell'esercizio
closing time ora (f) di chiusura
closing-down sale svendita (f) per chiusura d'esercizio
closure chiusura (f) o termine (m)
c/o (= care of) presso
co-creditor creditore (m) in solido
co-director condirettore (m)
co-insurance coassicurazione (f)
co-operate cooperare
co-operation cooperazione (m) o collaborazione (f)
co-operative (adj) cooperativo o cooperativa
co-operative (n) cooperativa (f)
co-opt someone cooptare qualcuno
co-owner comproprietario (m)
co-ownership comproprietà (f)
COD or c.o.d. (= cash on delivery) pagamento (m) alla consegna
code codice (m)
code of practice codice (m) di etica professionale

coding codifica (f) o codificazione (f)

coin moneta (f) (metallica)

cold call visita (f) a freddo

cold start partenza (f) fredda

cold storage conservazione (f) in ambiente frigorifero

cold store magazzino (m) frigorifero

collaborate collaborare

collaboration collaborazione (f)

collapse (n) crollo (m)

collapse (v) crollare o cadere

collateral (adj) collaterale

collateral (n) garanzia (f) collaterale

collect (v) *[fetch]* cogliere o raccogliere

collect (v) *[money]* recuperare

collect a debt recuperare un debito

collect call *[US]* telefonata (f) a carico del ricevente

collection *[of goods]* ritiro (m)

collection *[of money]* recupero (m)

collection *[postal]* levata (f)

collection charges or collection rates spese (fpl) d'incasso

collective collettivo

collective ownership proprietà (f) collettiva

collective wage agreement contratto (m) salariale collettivo

collector raccoglitore (m)

commerce commercio (m)

commercial (adj) commerciale

commercial (n) *[TV]* pubblicità (f) o spot (m)

commercial attaché addetto (m) commerciale

commercial college scuola (m) superiore di commercio

commercial course corso (m) a indirizzo commerciale

commercial directory annuario (m) commerciale

commercial district distretto (m) commerciale

commercial failure insuccesso (m) commerciale

commercial law diritto (m) commerciale

commercial traveller commesso (m) viaggiatore

commercial undertaking iniziativa (f) commerciale

commercialization commercializzazione (f)

commercialize commercializzare

commission *[committee]* comitato (m)

commission *[money]* commissione (f) o percentuale (f)

commission agent agente (m) commissionario

commission rep rappresentante (m) commissionario

commit *[crime]* commettere

commit funds to a project affidare fondi ad un progetto

commitments impegni (mpl)

commodity merce (f) o bene (m)

commodity exchange Borsa (f) Merci

commodity futures contratti (mpl) a termine su materie prime

commodity market mercato (m) delle materie prime

common *[frequent]* comune o usuale

common *[to more than one]* comune

common carrier vettore (m)

common ownership proprietà (f) comune

common pricing prezzi (mpl) correnti

communicate comunicare

communication *[general]* comunicazione (f)

communication *[message]* comunicazione (f)

communications comunicazioni (fpl)

community comunità (f)

commute *[exchange]* scambiare

commute *[travel]* fare il pendolare

commuter pendolare (m)

companies' register Registro (m) delle SPA

company compagnia (f) o società (di capitali)
company director amministratore (m) di società
company law diritto (m) societario
company secretary segretario (m) del consiglio d'amministrazione
comparability comparabilità (f)
comparable paragonabile
compare confrontare o paragonare
compare with essere paragonabile
comparison confronto (m)
compensate compensare
compensation compenso (m) o ricompensa (f)
compensation for damage risarcimento (m) di danni
compete with someone or with a company competere con qualcuno o con un'azienda
competing (adj) in concorrenza
competing firms aziende (f) in concorrenza
competing products prodotti (mpl) che si fanno concorrenza
competition concorrenza (f) o competizione (f)
competitive competitivo
competitive price prezzo (m) allineato
competitive pricing determinazione (f) del prezzo di concorrenza
competitive products prodotti (mpl) competitivi
competitively priced con prezzo competitivo
competitiveness competitività (f)
competitor concorrente (m)
complain (about) protestare o reclamare
complaint protesta (f) o reclamo (m)
complaints department ufficio (m) reclami
complementary complementare
complete (adj) completo
complete (v) finire o portare a termine
completion completamento (m)

completion date data (f) di ultimazione
completion of a contract adempimento (m) di un contratto
compliance adempimento (m)
complimentary in omaggio
complimentary ticket biglietto (m) omaggio
compliments slip cartoncino (m) della società
comply with conformarsi a o osservare
composition [with creditors] accomodamento (m)
compound interest interesse (m) composto
comprehensive comprensivo
comprehensive insurance assicurazione (f) globale
compromise (n) compromesso (m)
compromise (v) venire a un compromesso
compulsory obbligatorio
compulsory liquidation liquidazione (f) coatta
compulsory purchase espropriazione (f) per pubblica utilità
computer computer (m)
computer bureau ufficio (m) computer
computer department ufficio (m) computer
computer error errore (m) di computer
computer file archivio (m) (di un computer)
computer language linguaggio (m) di computer
computer listing registrazione (f) sul computer
computer printer stampante (f) lineare
computer printout tabulato (m)
computer program programma (m) di computer
computer programmer programmatore (m) di computer
computer programming programmazione (f) di computer

computer services servizi (mpl) di elaborazione elettronica

computer system sistema (m) elettronico di elaborazione

computer terminal terminale (m) di computer

computer time tempo (m) di elaborazione

computer-readable leggibile dal computer

computer-readable codes codici (mpl) leggibili dal computer

computerize computerizzare

computerized elaborato a mezzo computer

concealment of assets occultamento (m) di beni

concern (n) [business] azienda (f) o ditta (f)

concern (n) [worry] preoccupazione (f)

concern (v) [deal with] interessarsi di

concession [reduction] agevolazione (f)

concession [right] concessione (f)

concessionaire concessionario (m)

conciliation conciliazione (f)

conclude [agreement] concludere

condition [state] condizione (f)

condition [terms] condizione (f)

condition: on condition that a condizione che

conditional soggetto a condizioni

conditions of employment condizioni (fpl) di assunzione

conditions of sale condizioni (fpl) di vendita

conduct negotiations condurre una trattativa

conference [large] conferenza (f) o congresso (m)

conference [small] riunione (f)

conference phone telefono (m) per conferenze

conference room sala (f) riunioni

confidence fiducia (f)

confidential riservato

confidential report rapporto (m) riservato

confidentiality riservatezza (f)

confirm confermare

confirm a booking confermare una prenotazione

confirm someone in a job confermare l'assunzione di una persona

confirmation conferma (f)

conflict of interest conflitto (m) di interessi

conglomerate conglomerato (m)

connect collegare

connecting flight volo (m) di coincidenza

connection coincidenza (f)

consider considerare

consign consegnare

consignee consegnatario (m)

consignment [sending] spedizione (f)

consignment [things sent, received] invio (m)

consignment note lettera (f) di vettura

consignor mittente (m)

consist of consistere in

consolidate consolidare

consolidate [shipments] consolidare spedizioni

consolidated consolidato

consolidated shipment spedizione (f) consolidata

consolidation consolidamento (m)

consortium consorzio (m)

constant costante

consult consultarsi

consultancy consulenza (f)

consultancy firm ditta (f) di consulenza

consultant consulente (m)

consulting engineer consulente (m) tecnico

consumables generi (mpl) di consumo

consumer consumatore (m)

consumer credit credito (m) al consumatore

consumer durables beni (mpl) di consumo durevoli
consumer goods beni (mpl) di consumo
consumer panel gruppo (m) selezionato di consumatori
consumer price index indice (m) dei prezzi al consumo
consumer protection protezione (f) del consumatore
consumer research ricerca (f) di mercato sui bisogni dei consumatori
consumer spending spese (fpl) di consumo
consumption consumo (m)
contact (n) *[general]* contatto (m)
contact (n) *[person]* contatto (m)
contact (v) mettersi in contatto con
contain contenere
container *[box, tin]* contenitore (m)
container *[for shipping]* container (m)
container port scalo (m) per container
container ship nave (f) per trasporto di container
container terminal terminal (m) per container
containerization *[putting into containers]* containerizzazione (f)
containerization *[shipping in containers]* trasporto (m) in container
containerize *[put into containers]* containerizzare
containerize *[ship in containers]* spedire merce in container
contents contenuto (m)
contested takeover acquisizione (f) di controllo contestata
contingency contingenza (f)
contingency fund fondo (m) di previdenza
contingency plan piano (m) di contingenza
continual continuo
continually continuamente
continuation continuazione (f)

continue continuare
continuous continuo
continuous feed alimentazione (f) continua
continuous stationery moduli (mpl) a striscia continua
contra account conto (m) di contropartita
contra an entry stornare una registrazione
contra entry registrazione (f) di storno
contract (n) contratto (m)
contract (v) contrarre
contract law diritto (m) contrattuale
contract note fissato (m) bollato
contract of employment contratto (m) di lavoro
contract work lavoro (m) a contratto
contracting party parte (f) contraente
contractor imprenditore (m)
contractual contrattuale
contractual liability responsabilità (f) contrattuale
contractually contrattualmente
contrary contrario
contrast (n) contrasto (m)
contribute contribuire
contribution contributo (m)
contribution of capital apporto (m) di capitali
contributor sottoscrittore (m)
control (n) *[check]* controllo (m) *o* verifica (f)
control (n) *[power]* controllo (m) *o* potere (m)
control (v) controllare
control a business detenere il controllo azionario
control key tasto (m) di comando
control systems sistema (m) di controllo
controlled economy economia (f) controllata
controller *[US]* revisore (m) dei conti

controller [who checks] controllore (m)

controlling (adj) controllante

convene convocare

convenient comodo

conversion conversione (f)

conversion of funds conversione (f) di fondi

conversion price or conversion rate tasso (m) di conversione

convert convertire

convertibility convertibilità (f)

convertible currency valuta (f) convertibile

convertible loan stock obbligazioni (fpl) convertibili

conveyance trasmissione (f)

conveyancer notaio (m) o legale (m) che si occupa dei trapassi di proprietà

conveyancing esame (m) dei documenti e stesura degli atti necessari per il trasferimento di proprietà

cooling off period (after purchase) periodo (m) che permette un ripensamento (da parte dell'acquirente)

cooperative society società (f) cooperativa

copartner consocio (m)

copartnership associazione (f) in compartecipazione

cope essere all'altezza

copier copiatrice (f)

copy (n) [a document] copia (f)

copy (n) [book, newspaper] copia (f) o esemplare (m)

copy (n) [of document] copia (f)

copy (v) copiare o riprodurre

copying machine copiatrice (f)

corner (n) [angle] angolo (m)

corner (n) [monopoly] accaparramento (m) o monopolio (m)

corner shop negozio (m) d'angolo

corner the market accaparrarsi il mercato (m)

corporate image immagine (f) aziendale

corporate name ragione (f) sociale

corporate plan programma (m) aziendale

corporate planning programmazione (f) aziendale

corporate profits utili (mpl) societari

corporation corporazione (f)

corporation tax imposta (f) sulla società

correct (adj) corretto

correct (v) correggere

correction correzione (f)

correspond with someone essere in corrispondenza con qualcuno

correspond with something equivalere a qualcosa

correspondence corrispondenza (f)

correspondent [journalist] inviato (m)

correspondent [who writes letters] corrispondente (mf)

cost (n) costo (m)

cost (v) costare

cost accountant analista (m) dei costi

cost accounting contabilità (f) basata sui conti

cost analysis analisi (f) dei costi

cost centre centro (m) di costi

cost factor fattore (m) costo

cost of living costo (m) della vita o carovita (m)

cost of sales costo (m) delle vendite

cost plus costo (m) più una percentuale

cost price prezzo (m) sotto costo

cost, insurance and freight (c.i.f.) costo (m), assicurazione (f) e nolo (m)

cost-benefit analysis analisi (f) preventiva della convenienza dei costi

cost-cutting riduzione (f) dei costi

cost-effective redditizio

cost-effectiveness redditività (f) dei costi

cost-of-living allowance indennità (f) di contingenza

cost-of-living bonus contingenza (f)

cost-of-living increase aumento (m) del costo della vita

cost-of-living index indice (m) del costo della vita

cost-push inflation inflazione (f) da costi

costing valutazione (f) dei costi

costly costoso

costs spese (fpl)

counsel avvocato (mf)

count (v) [add] contare

count (v) [include] includere

counter banco (m)

counter staff personale (m) al banco

counter-claim (n) controrichiesta (f)

counter-claim (v) presentare una controrichiesta

counter-offer controfferta (f)

counterbid controfferta (f)

counterfeit (adj) contraffatto o falso

counterfeit (v) contraffare

counterfoil matrice (f)

countermand fermare

countersign contrassegno (m)

country [not town] campagna (f)

country [state] paese (m) o nazione (f)

country of origin paese (m) d'origine

coupon buono (m)

coupon ad materiale pubblicitario con buono

courier [guide] guida (f) (turistica)

courier [messenger] messaggero (m) o corriere (m)

court corte (f) di Giustizia

court case causa (f) legale

covenant (n) convenzione (f)

covenant (v) convenire

cover (n) [insurance] copertura (f) assicurativa

cover (n) [top] copertura (f)

cover (v) [expenses] coprire o pagare

cover (v) [put on top] coprire

cover a risk assicurarsi contro un rischio

cover charge prezzo (m) del coperto

cover costs coprire i costi

cover note polizza (f) provvisoria

covering letter lettera (f) di accompagnamento

covering note polizza (f) provvisoria

crane gru (f)

crash (n) [accident] incidente (m)

crash (n) [financial] crollo (m)

crash (v) [fail] crollare

crash (v) [hit] scontrarsi con

crate (n) cassa (f)

crate (v) imballare (merce) in casse

credit (n) credito (m)

credit (v) accreditare (un conto)

credit account conto (m) creditori

credit agency agenzia (f) per reperimento di referenze

credit balance differenza (f) a credito

credit bank istituto (m) di credito

credit card carta (f) di credito

credit card sale vendita (f) con carta di credito

credit ceiling massimale (m) di credito o tetto (m) salariale

credit column colonna (f) dell'avere

credit control controllo (m) del credito

credit entry registrazione (f) contabile a credito

credit facilities agevolazioni (fpl) creditizie

credit freeze blocco (m) del credito

credit limit limite (m) di credito

credit note nota (f) di accredito

credit policy politica (f) creditizia

credit rating grado (m) di solvibilità
credit side avere (m) *o* lato (m) dell'attivo
credit-worthy solvibile
credit: on credit a credito
creditor creditore (m)
cross a cheque sbarrare un assegno
cross off depennare
cross out cancellare
cross rate cambio (m) incrociato
crossed cheque assegno (m) sbarrato
cubic cubico
cubic measure misure (fpl) cubiche
cum con
cum coupon con coupon (m)
cum dividend con dividendo (m)
cumulative cumulativo
cumulative interest interesse (m) composto
cumulative preference shares azioni (fpl) privilegiate cumulative
currency moneta (f) legale
currency conversion conversione (f) della valuta
currency note banconota (f)
currency reserves riserve (fpl) valutarie
current corrente
current account conto (m) corrente
current assets attività (fpl) liquide
current cost accounting contabilità (f) a costi correnti
current liabilities passività (fpl) correnti
current price prezzo (m) corrente
current rate of exchange tasso (m) di cambio corrente
current yield rendimento (m) immediato
curriculum vitae (CV) curriculum (m) vitae
curve curva (f)
custom clientela (f)

custom-built *or* **custom-made** fatto appositamente
customer cliente (mf)
customer appeal richiamo (m) per i clienti
customer loyalty fedeltà (f) dei clienti
customer satisfaction soddisfazione (f) dei clienti
customer service department ufficio (m) assistenza ai clienti
customs dogana (f)
Customs and Excise Ufficio Dazio e Dogana
customs barrier barriera (f) doganale
customs broker agente (m) doganale
customs clearance svincolo (m) doganale
customs declaration dichiarazione (f) doganale
customs declaration form modulo (m) di dichiarazione doganale
customs duty dazio (m) doganale
customs entry point punto (m) per la dichiarazine doganale d'entrata
customs examination controllo (m) doganale
customs formalities formalità (fpl) doganali
customs officer doganiere (m)
customs official ufficiale (m) di dogana
customs receipt avviso (m) di ricevimento doganale
customs seal sigillo (m) doganale
customs tariff tariffa (f) doganale
customs union unione (f) doganale
cut (n) taglio (m)
cut (v) tagliare
cut down on expenses ridurre le spese
cut price (n) prezzo (m) ridotto
cut-price (adj) a prezzo ridotto
cut-price goods merce (f) a prezzo ridotto

cut-price petrol benzina (f) a prezzo ridotto
cut-price store negozio con merce a prezzi ridotti
cut-throat competition concorrenza (f) spietata
CV (= curriculum vitae) Curriculum (m) Vitae
cycle ciclo (m)
cyclical ciclico
cyclical factors elementi (mpl) ciclici

Dd

daily quotidiano
daisy-wheel printer stampante (f) con testina a margherita
damage (n) danno (m)
damage (v) danneggiare
damage survey perizia (f) d'avaria
damage to property danno (m) alla proprietà
damaged danneggiato
damages risarcimento (m) dei danni
data dati (mpl)
data processing elaborazione (f) dei dati
data retrieval ricerca (f) automatica dell'informazione
database base (f) di dati
date (n) data (f)
date (v) datare
date of receipt data (f) di ricevimento
date stamp datario (m)
dated datato
day [24 hours] giorno (m)
day [working day] giorno (m)
day shift turno (m) di giorno

day-to-day giorno per giorno
dead (adj) [person] morto
dead account conto (m) chiuso
dead loss perdita (f) secca
deadline termine (m) ultimo
deadlock (n) punto (m) morto
deadlock (v) essere a un punto morto
deadweight peso (m) morto
deadweight cargo carico (m) lordo
deadweight tonnage portata (f) lorda
deal (n) operazione (f) o affare (m)
deal in (v) commerciare o negoziare
deal with an order dare corso ad un'ordinazione
deal with someone trattare con qualcuno
dealer commerciante (m)
dealing [commerce] commercio (m)
dealing [stock exchange] transazioni (fpl) o operazioni (fpl)
dear caro
debenture obbligazione (f) (di società private)
debenture holder obbligazionista (m)
debit (n) addebito (m)
debit an account addebitare un conto
debit balance saldo (m) debitore
debit column colonna (f) del dare
debit entry registrazione (f) a debito
debit note nota (f) di addebito
debits and credits dare e avere
debt debito (m)
debt collection recupero (m) di crediti
debt collection agency agenzia (f) per il recupero dei crediti
debt collector esattore (m) dei crediti
debtor debitore (m)
debtor side colonna (f) del dare
debts due credito (m) esigibile
decentralization decentramento (m)

decentralize decentrare
decide decidere
decide on a course of action decidere una linea di condotta
deciding decisivo
deciding factor elemento (m) decisivo
decimal (n) decimale (m)
decimal point virgola (f) decimale
decision decisione (f)
decision maker persona (f) che prende decisioni
decision making processo (m) decisionale
decision-making processes processo (m) di decisione
deck piano (m)
deck cargo carico (m) di coperta
declaration dichiarazione (f)
declaration of bankruptcy dichiarazione (f) di fallimento
declaration of income dichiarazione (f) dei redditi
declare dichiarare
declare goods to customs dichiarare le merci alla dogana
declare someone bankrupt dichiarare qualcuno fallito
declared dichiarato
declared value valore (m) dichiarato
decline (n) declino (m)
decline (v) *[fall]* rifiutare
decontrol abolire i controlli (mpl)
decrease (n) diminuzione (f)
decrease (v) diminuire
decrease in price diminuzione (f) dei prezzi
decrease in value diminuzione (f) del valore
decreasing (adj) decrescente
deduct dedurre
deductible detraibile
deduction detrazione (f)
deed atto (m)
deed of assignment atto (m) di cessione
deed of covenant atto (m) di donazione

deed of partnership atto (m) costitutivo
deed of transfer atto (m) di trasferimento
default (n) inadempienza (f)
default (v) essere contumace
default on payments inadempienza (f) nel pagamento
defaulter inadempiente (m)
defect difetto (m)
defective *[faulty]* difettoso
defective *[not valid]* privo di validità *o* viziato
defence *[legal]* difesa (f)
defence *[protection]* difesa (f)
defence counsel avvocato (m) difensore
defend difendere
defend a lawsuit difendere una causa
defendant accusato (m)
defer differire
defer payment differire un pagamento
deferment rinvio (m)
deferment of payment rinvio (m) di pagamento
deferred differito
deferred creditor creditore (m) differito
deferred payment pagamento (m) differito
deficit deficit (m) *o* disavanzo (m)
deficit financing finanziamento (m) del disavanzo (m)
deflation deflazione (f)
deflationary deflazionistico
defray *[costs]* pagare
defray someone's expenses sostenere le spese di qualcuno
del credere star del credere
del credere agent agente (m) del credere
delay (n) ritardo (m)
delay (v) ritardare
delegate (n) delegato (m)
delegate (v) delegare
delegation *[action]* delega (f) *o* delegazione (f)

delegation *[people]* delegazione (f)

delete eliminare

deliver consegnare

delivered price prezzo (m) franco

delivery *[bill of exchange]* cessione (f) di una cambiale

delivery *[goods]* consegna (f) di merce

delivery date data (f) di consegna

delivery note bolla (f) di spedizione

delivery order ordine (m) di consegna

delivery time data (f) di consegna

delivery van furgone (m) per le consegne

deliveryman uomo (m) delle consegne *o* fattorino (m)

demand (n) *[for payment]* domanda (f) *o* richiesta (f)

demand (n) *[need]* domanda (f)

demand (v) domandare

demand deposit deposito (m) a vista

demonstrate dimostrare

demonstration dimostrazione (f)

demonstration model campione (m) per dimostrazione

demonstrator dimostratore (m)

demurrage ritardo (m)

department *[in government]* ministero (m)

department *[in office]* reparto (m) *o* sezione (f)

department *[in shop]* reparto (m)

department store grande magazzino (m)

departmental dipartimentale

departmental manager capo (m) servizio

departure *[going away]* partenza (f)

departure *[new venture]* nuovo orientamento (m)

departure lounge salone (m) delle partenze

departures partenze (fpl)

depend on contare su

depending on a condizione che

deposit (n) *[in bank]* deposito (m)

deposit (n) *[paid in advance]* acconto (m)

deposit (v) versare denaro

deposit account conto (m) di deposito

deposit slip distinta (f) di versamento

depositor depositante (m)

depository *[place]* deposito (m)

depot magazzino (m)

depreciate *[amortize]* ammortizzare

depreciate *[lose value]* svalutare

depreciation *[amortizing]* ammortamento (m)

depreciation *[loss of value]* svalutazione (f)

depreciation rate quota (f) d'ammortamento

depression depressione (f)

deputize for someone rappresentare qualcuno

deputy delegato (m) *o* sostituto (m)

deputy manager vice direttore (m)

deputy managing director vice amministratore (m) delegato

deregulation deregolamentazione (f) *o* abolizione (f) della regolamentazione

describe descrivere

description descrizione (f)

design (n) design (m) *o* progettazione (f)

design (v) progettare

design department dipartimento *o* ufficio design

desk scrivania (f)

desk diary agenda (f) da tavolo

desk-top publishing (DTP) desktop publishing (m)

destination destinazione (f)

detail (n) dettaglio (m)

detail (v) dettagliare

detailed dettagliato

detailed account resoconto (m) dettagliato

determine determinare

devaluation svalutazione (f)

devalue svalutare
develop *[build]* costruire o sviluppare
develop *[plan]* sviluppare
developing country paese (m) in via di sviluppo
development sviluppo (m) o progresso (m)
device congegno (m)
diagram diagramma (m)
dial (v) a number formare o comporre un numero telefonico
dial direct teleselezione (f)
dialling chiamata (f) (telefonica)
dialling code prefisso (m) telefonico
dialling tone segnale (m) di linea libera
diary diario
dictate dettare
dictating machine dittafono (m)
dictation dettatura (f)
differ dissentire
difference differenza (f)
differences in price differenze (fpl) di prezzo
different diverso
differential (adj) differenziale
differential tariffs tariffe (fpl) differenziali
digit cifra (f) o numero (m)
dilution of equity diluizione (f) della partecipazione azionaria
direct (adj) diretto
direct (adv) direttamente
direct (v) dirigere o guidare
direct cost costo (m) diretto
direct debit addebito (m) diretto
direct mail vendita (f) diretta tramite corrispondenza
direct mailing pubblicità (f) a mezzo posta
direct selling vendita (f) diretta
direct tax imposta (f) diretta
direct taxation tassazione (f) diretta
direct-mail advertising pubblicità (f) a mezzo posta
direction direzione (f) o istruzione (f)

directions for use istruzioni (fpl) per l'uso
directive direttiva (f)
director amministratore (m)
directory annuario (m)
disburse pagare
disbursement esborso (m) o pagamento (m)
discharge (n) *[of debt]* pagamento (m) di un debito
discharge (v) *[employee]* licenziare
discharge a debt estinguere un debito
disclaimer smentita (f)
disclose rivelare o divulgare
disclose a piece of information divulgare un'informazione
disclosure rivelazione (f) o divulgazione (f)
disclosure of confidential information divulgazione (f) di un'informazione riservata
discontinue interrrompere
discount (n) sconto (m)
discount (v) vendere sotto costo
discount house *[bank]* banca (f) di sconto
discount house *[shop]* negozio (m) di vendita a prezzi ridotti
discount price prezzo (m) scontato
discount rate tasso (m) di sconto
discount store magazzino (m) a prezzi scontati
discountable scontabile
discounted cash flow (DCF) sconto (m) del valore attuale
discounter scontista (m)
discrepancy discrepanza (f)
discuss discutere
discussion discussione (f)
dishonour non onorare
dishonour a bill non onorare un effetto
disk disco (m)
disk drive unità (f) a dischi magnetici
diskette dischetto (m)
dismiss an employee licenziare un dipendente

dismissal licenziamento (m)
dispatch (n) *[sending]* spedizione (f)
dispatch (v) *[send]* spedire
dispatch department servizio (m) spedizioni
dispatch note bolla (f) di spedizione
display (n) esposizione (f) *o* mostra (f)
display (v) esporre
display case vetrinetta (f)
display material materiale (m) da esposizione
display pack confezione (f) per esposizione
display stand banco (m) di esposizione
display unit video-unità
disposable da non restituire *o* da gettare
disposal vendita (f)
dispose of excess stock eliminare le scorte in eccesso
dissolve risolvere *o* dissolvere
dissolve a partnership sciogliere una società di persone
distress merchandise merci (fpl) vendute sottocosto
distress sale vendita (f) di merce sottocosto
distributable profit utili (mpl) distribuibili
distribute *[goods]* distribuire
distribute *[share]* distribuire
distribution distribuzione (f)
distribution channels canali (mpl) di distribuzione
distribution costs costi (mpl) di distribuzione
distribution manager direttore (m) delle distribuzioni
distribution network rete (f) di distribuzione
distributor distributore (m)
distributorship concessione (f) di vendita
diversification diversificazione (f)
diversify diversificare
dividend dividendo (m)

dividend cover rapporto (m) fra utile e dividendo
dividend warrant cedola (f) di dividendo
dividend yield reddito (m) da dividendi
division *[part of a company]* reparto (m)
division *[part of a group]* divisione (f)
dock (n) bacino (m)
dock (v) *[remove money]* decurtare
dock (v) *[ship]* entrare in porto *o* attraccare
docket elenco (m) delle cause
doctor's certificate certificato (m) medico
document documento (m)
documentary documentario (m)
documentary evidence documentazione (f)
documentary proof prova (f) documentata
documentation documentazione (f)
documents documenti (mpl)
dollar dollaro (m)
dollar area area (f) del dollaro
dollar balance bilancia (f) commerciale in dollari
dollar crisis crisi (f) del dollaro
domestic domestico
domestic market mercato (m) interno
domestic production produzione (f) nazionale
domestic sales vendite (fpl) interne
domestic trade commercio (m) interno
domicile domicilio (m)
door porta (f)
door-to-door a domicilio (m)
door-to-door salesman venditore (m) a domicilio
door-to-door selling vendita (f) porta a porta
dossier dossier (m) *o* pratica (f)

dot-matrix printer stampante (f) a matrice d'aghi
double (adj) doppio
double (v) raddoppiare
double taxation doppia tassazione (f)
double taxation agreement sgravio (m) per doppia tassazione
double-book riservare una camera a due clienti
double-booking prenotazione (f) di una camera a due clienti
down discendente o giù
down payment versamento (m) d'acconto
down time tempo (m) improduttivo
down-market mercato (m) in ribasso
downside factor fattore (m) negativo
downtown (adv) in centro
downtown (n) centro (m) (di città)
downturn regresso (m)
downward discendente o giù
dozen dozzina (f)
draft (n) [money] tratta (f)
draft (n) [rough plan] bozza (f)
draft (v) abbozzare o redigere
draft a contract preparare lo schema di un contratto
draft a letter stendere la minuta (f) di una lettera
draft plan bozza (f) di un piano
draft project bozza (f) di un progetto
draw [a cheque] emettere un assegno
draw [money] prelevare
draw up redigere
draw up a contract stipulare un contratto
drawee trattario (m)
drawer traente (m)
drawing account conto (m) corrente
drive (n) [campaign] campagna (f)
drive (n) [energy] grinta (f)
drive (n) [part of machine] trasmissione (f)
drive (v) [a car] condurre o guidare

driver conducente (m)
drop (n) caduta (f) o ribasso (m)
drop (v) cadere o calare
drop in sales ribasso (m) delle vendite
due [awaited] atteso
due [owing] dovuto
dues [orders] ordinazioni (fpl) inevase
duly [in time] come previsto
duly [legally] regolarmente o dovutamente
dummy fittizio o falso
dummy pack confezione (f) finta
dump bin scaffale (m) per esposizione (in negozi)
dump goods on a market svendere merci sul mercato
dumping vendita (f) sottocosto
duplicate (n) duplicato (m)
duplicate (v) duplicare
duplicate an invoice fare il duplicato di una fattura
duplicate receipt or duplicate of a receipt ricevuta (f) in duplicato
duplication duplicazione (f)
durable goods beni (mpl) durevoli
duty [tax] dazio (m)
duty-free esente da dazio
duty-free shop 'duty free shop' o negozio (m) esente da tasse
duty-paid goods merce (f) con dazio pagato

Ee

e. & o.e. (errors and omissions excepted) Salvo errori e omissioni (S. E. & O)
early prossimo

earmark funds for a project
accantonare fondi (mpl) per un
progetto
earn *[interest]* fruttare
earn *[money]* guadagnare
earning capacity capacità (f) di
guadagno
earnings *[profit]* utile (m) *o*
profitto (m)
earnings *[salary]* guadagni (mpl)
**earnings per share *or* earnings
yield** utile (m) per azione
easy facile
easy terms condizioni (fpl)
moderate
economic *[general]* economico
economic *[profitable]* vantaggioso
economic cycle ciclo (m)
economico
economic development sviluppo
(m) economico
economic growth crescita (f)
economica
economic indicators indicatori
(mpl) economici
economic model modello (m)
economico
economic planning
programmazione (f) economica
economic trends congiuntura (f)
economical economico
economics *[profitability]*
redditività (f)
economics *[study]* economia (f) *o*
scienze (fpl) economiche
economies of scale economia (f)
di massa
economist economista (mf)
economize economizzare
economy *[saving]* economia (f)
economy *[system]* economia (f)
economy class classe (f) turistica
**ecu *or* ECU (= European currency
unit)** ecu (m) (Unità di Conto
Europea)
effect (n) effetto (m)
effect (v) effettuare
effective effettivo
effective date data (f) di entrata in
vigore

effective demand domanda (f)
effettiva
effective yield rendimento (m)
effettivo
effectiveness efficacia (f)
efficiency efficienza (f)
efficient efficiente
effort sforzo (m)
elasticity elasticità (f)
elect eleggere
election elezione (f)
electronic mail posta (f) elettronica
electronic point of sale (EPOS)
punto (m) di vendita elettronico
elevator *[goods]* montacarichi (m)
elevator *[grain]* silo (m)
email (= electronic mail) posta (f)
elettronica
embargo (n) embargo (m)
embargo (v) mettere l'embargo su
embark imbarcare *o* imbarcarsi
embark on imbarcarsi in
embarkation imbarco (m)
embarkation card carta (f)
d'imbarco
embezzle appropriarsi
indebitamente
embezzlement appropriazione (f)
indebita
embezzler colpevole (m) di
appropriazione indebita
emergency emergenza (f)
emergency reserves riserve (fpl)
d'emergenza
employ impiegare *o* assumere
employed *[in job]* impiegato
employed *[money]* investito
employed *[used]* impiegato
employee dipendente (m)
employer datore (m) di lavoro
employment impiego (m)
employment agency agenzia (f) di
lavoro
employment bureau agenzia (f) di
lavoro
empty (adj) vuoto
empty (v) vuotare
**EMS (= European Monetary
System)** SME (Sistema Monetario
Europeo)

encash incassare

encashment incasso (m)

enclose allegare

enclosure allegato (m)

end (n) fine (f) *o* termine (m)

end (v) finire *o* concludere

end of season sale svendite (fpl) di fine stagione

end product prodotto (m) finito

end user utente (m) finale

endorse a cheque girare un assegno

endorsee giratario (m)

endorsement *[action]* girata (f)

endorsement *[on insurance]* restrizione (f)

endorser girante (m)

energy *[electricity]* energia (f)

energy *[human]* energia (f) *o* dinamismo (m)

energy-saving (adj) che risparmia energia

enforce applicare

enforcement imposizione (f)

engaged *[telephone]* occupato

engaged tone segnale (m) di linea occupata

enquire (= inquire) chiedere informazioni

enquiry (= inquiry) richiesta (f) di informazioni

enter *[go in]* entrare

enter *[write in]* registrare

enter into *[discussion]* prendere parte in

entering annotazione (f)

enterprise impresa (f)

entitle conferire il diritto

entitlement diritto (m)

entrepot port porto (m) di transito

entrepreneur imprenditore (m)

entrepreneurial imprenditoriale

entrust affidare

entry *[going in]* entrata (f)

entry *[writing]* scrittura (f) contabile

entry visa visto (m) d'ingresso

epos *or* EPOS (= electronic point of sale) punto (m) di vendita elettronico

equal (adj) uguale

equal (v) uguagliare

equalization equalizzazione (f)

equip equipaggiare

equipment apparecchiatura (f)

equities azioni (fpl) ordinarie

equity passivo (m) patrimoniale

equity capital capitale (m) effettivo

erode erodere

error errore (m)

error rate percentuale (f) d'errore

errors and omissions excepted (e. & o.e.) salvo errori e omissioni (S.E & O)

escalate intensificare

escape clause clausola (f) di salvaguardia

escrow account conto (m) a garanzia

essential indispensabile

establish stabilire *o* istituire

establishment *[business]* azienda (f) commerciale

establishment *[staff]* personale (m)

estimate (n) *[calculation]* valutazione (f)

estimate (n) *[quote]* preventivo (m)

estimate (v) stimare *o* valutare

estimated valutato

estimated figure cifra (f) preventivata

estimated sales vendite (fpl) presunte

estimation opinione (f)

EU (= European Union) UE (Unione (f) Europea)

euro euro (m)

Eurocheque euroassegno (m)

Eurocurrency euromoneta (f)

Eurodollar eurodollaro (m)

Euromarket euromercato (m)

European europeo

European Investment Bank (EIB) Banca (f) Europea per gli Investimenti (BEI)

European Monetary System (EMS) Sistema (m) Monetario Europeo (SME)

European Union (EU) Unione (f) Europea (UE)

evade evadere

evade tax sottrarsi al pagamento delle tasse

evaluate valutare

evaluate costs valutare i costi

evaluation valutazione (f)

evasion evasione (f) d'imposta

ex coupon ex cedola (f)

ex dividend ex dividendo (m)

ex-directory che non compare nell'elenco telefonico

exact (adj) esatto

exact (v) esigere

exactly esattamente

examination *[inspection]* esame (f)

examination *[test]* esame (f)

examine esaminare

exceed sorpassare *o* superare

excellent eccellente

except eccetto *o* tranne

exceptional eccezionale *o* straordinario

exceptional items voci (fpl) straordinarie

excess eccesso

excess baggage bagaglio (m) in eccesso

excess capacity capacità (f) produttiva in eccesso

excess profits sovrapprofitti (mpl)

excessive eccessivo

excessive costs costi (mpl) eccessivi

exchange (n) *[currency]* cambio (m)

exchange (v) *[currency]* cambiare

exchange (v) *[one thing for another]* scambiare con

exchange control controlli (mpl) valutari

exchange rate tasso (m) di cambio

exchangeable scambiabile

Exchequer Ministero del Tesoro

excise (v) *[cut out]* tagliare

excise duty imposta (f) indiretta

Excise officer daziere (m)

exclude escludere

excluding escluso

exclusion esclusione (f)

exclusion clause clausola (f) di esclusione

exclusive agreement accordo (m) in esclusiva

exclusive of escluso

exclusive of tax tassa (f) esclusa

exclusivity esclusività (f)

execute eseguire

execution esecuzione (f)

executive (adj) esecutivo

executive (n) dirigente (m)

executive director direttore (m) esecutivo

exempt (adj) esente

exempt (v) esentare

exempt from tax esente da tassa

exemption esenzione (f)

exemption from tax esenzione (f) da tassa

exercise (n) esercizio (m)

exercise (v) esercitare

exercise an option esercitare un'opzione

exercise of an option esercizio (m) di un'opzione

exhibit (v) esibire

exhibition esposizione (f) *o* mostra (f)

exhibition hall sala (f) esposizioni

exhibitor espositore (m) *o* standista (m)

expand ampliare

expansion allargamento (m)

expenditure spese (fpl)

expense spesa (f) *o* conto (m)

expense account conto (m) spese

expenses spese (fpl)

expensive costoso

experienced esperto

expertise 'expertise' (f) *o* perizia (f)

expiration termine (m)

expire terminare *o* scadere

expiry fine (f) *o* scadenza (f)

expiry date data (f) di scadenza

explain spiegare
explanation spiegazione (f)
exploit sfruttare
explore esplorare
export (n) esportazione (f)
export (v) esportare
export department reparto (m) esportazioni
export duty dazio (m) d'esportazione
export licence *or* **export permit** licenza (f) d'esportazione
export manager direttore (m) del reparto esportazioni
export trade commercio (m) d'esportazione
exporter esportatore (m)
exporting (adj) esportatore
exports esportazioni (fpl)
exposure rischio (m) finanziario
express (adj) *[fast]* espresso
express (adj) *[stated clearly]* espresso
express (v) *[send fast]* spedire per espresso
express (v) *[state]* esprimere
express delivery spedizione (f) per espresso
express letter lettera (f) espresso
extend *[grant]* accordare
extend *[make longer]* prolungare
extended credit credito (m) prorogato
extension *[making longer]* prolungamento (m)
extension *[telephone]* interno (m)
external *[foreign]* estero *o* straniero
external *[outside a company]* esterno
external account conto (m) estero (fuori l'area di sterlina)
external audit revisione (f) esterna
external auditor revisore (m) esterno
external trade commercio (m) estero
extra extra
extra charges spese (fpl) extra
extraordinary straordinario

extraordinary items voci (fpl) straordinarie
extras spese (fpl) supplementari

Ff

FAO (= for the attention of) all'attenzione di
face value valore (m) nominale
facilities servizi (mpl) *o* mezzi (mpl)
facility *[building]* edificio (m)
facility *[credit]* agevolazione (f)
facility *[ease]* agevolazione (f)
factor (n) *[influence]* fattore (m)
factor (n) *[person, company]* agente (m) di factoring *o* società di factoring
factor (v) fare del factoring
factoring factoring (m)
factoring charges costi (mpl) di factoring
factors of production fattori (mpl) di produzione
factory fabbrica (f)
factory inspector ispettore (m) aziendale
factory outlet punto (m) di vendita diretta della fabbrica
factory price prezzo (m) di fabbrica
fail *[go bust]* fallire
fail *[not to do something]* non riuscire *o* non fare
fail *[not to succeed]* fallire
failing that se non è possibile
failure insuccesso (m)
fair (adj) giusto *o* equo
fair dealing trattamento (f) equo
fair price prezzi (mpl) equi
fair trade commercio (m) libero

fair trading commercio (m) libero
fair wear and tear normale usura (f) e degrado (m)
fake (n) imitazione (f)
fake (v) falsificare
faked documents documenti (mpl) falsi
fall (n) caduta (f) *o* crollo (m)
fall (v) *[go lower]* cadere
fall (v) *[on a date]* scadere
fall behind *[be in a worse position]* rimanere indietro
fall behind *[be late]* essere in ritardo (nel fare una cosa)
fall due essere dovuto
fall off scendere *o* diminuire
fall through fallire *o* non arrivare a compimento
falling in ribasso
false falso
false pretences millantato credito (m)
false weight peso (m) contraffatto
falsification falsificazione (f)
falsify falsificare
family company ditta (f) a conduzione familiare
fare tariffa (f)
farm out work appaltare del lavoro
fast (adj) veloce
fast (adv) velocemente *o* rapidamente
fast-selling items articoli (mpl) che vendono rapidamente
fault *[blame]* colpa (f)
fault *[mechanical]* difetto (m)
faulty equipment apparecchiatura (f) difettosa
favourable favorevole
favourable balance of trade bilancia (f) commerciale attiva
fax (n) fax (m)
fax (v) inviare per fax
feasibility fattibilità (f)
feasibility report studio (m) della fattibilità
fee *[admission]* quota (f) d'iscrizione
fee *[for services]* emolumento (m) *o* compenso (m)

feedback controreazione (f)
ferry traghetto (m)
fiddle (n) imbroglio (m) *o* truffa (f)
fiddle (v) imbrogliare
field campo (m) *o* area (f)
field sales manager direttore (m) vendite esterne
field work attività (f) esterna di ricerca e di studio
FIFO (= first in first out) primo ad entrare primo ad uscire
figure cifra (f)
figures cifre (fpl) *o* numeri (mpl)
file (n) *[computer]* file (m) *o* archivio (m)
file (n) *[documents]* fascicolo (m)
file (v) *[request]* inoltrare
file a patent application inoltrare una domanda di brevetto
file documents depositare documenti
filing *[action]* schedatura (f)
filing cabinet schedario (m)
filing card scheda (f)
fill a gap colmare una lacuna (f)
final finale
final demand domanda (f) finale
final discharge quietanza (f) finale
final dividend dividendo (m) finale
finalize completare
finance (n) finanza (f) *o* attività (f) finanziaria
finance (v) finanziare
finance an operation finanziare un'operazione
finance company società (f) finanziaria
finance director direttore (m) delle finanze
finances finanze (fpl)
financial finanziario *o* economico
financial assets disponibilità (fpl) finanziarie
financial crisis crisi (f) finanziaria
financial institution Istituto (m) finanziario
financial position posizione (f) finanziaria
financial resources risorse (fpl) finanziarie

financial risk rischio (m) finanziario

financial settlement regolamento (m) finanziario

financial year esercizio (m) finanziario

financially finanziariamente

financing finanziamento (m)

fine (adv) [very good] molto bene

fine (adv) [very small] fine

fine (n) multa (f)

fine (v) multare

fine tuning perfetta sintonia (f)

finished finito

finished goods prodotti (mpl) finiti

fire (n) fuoco (m) o incendio (m)

fire damage danno (m) causato da un incendio

fire insurance assicurazione (f) contro gli incendi

fire regulations norme (fpl) antincendio

fire risk rischio (m) d'incendio

fire-damaged goods merce (f) danneggiata da incendio

firm (adj) stabile o solido

firm (n) ditta (f) o azienda (f) o impresa (f)

firm (v) consolidarsi

firm price prezzo (m) stabile

first primo

first in first out (FIFO) primo ad entrare primo ad uscire

first option prima opzione (f)

first quarter primo trimestre (m)

first-class prima classe

fiscal fiscale

fiscal measures provvedimenti (mpl) fiscali

fittings accessori (mpl)

fix [arrange] fissare

fix [mend] riparare

fix a meeting for 3 p.m. fissare una riunione per le 3 del pomeriggio

fixed fisso o fissato

fixed assets immobilizzi (mpl)

fixed costs costi (mpl) fissi

fixed deposit deposito (m) vincolato

fixed exchange rate tasso (m) fisso di cambio

fixed income reddito (m) fisso

fixed interest interesse (m) fisso

fixed scale of charges tabella (f) fissa dei prezzi

fixed-interest investments investimenti (mpl) ad interessi fissi

fixed-price agreement contratto (m) a prezzo fisso

fixing fissaggio (m)

flat (adj) [dull] piatto

flat (adj) [fixed] fisso

flat (n) appartamento (m)

flat rate importo (m) fisso

flexibility flessibilità (f)

flexible flessibile

flexible prices prezzi (mpl) flessibili

flexible pricing policy politica (f) dei prezzi flessibile

flight [of money] fuga (f) (di denaro)

flight [of plane] volo (m)

flight information informazioni (fpl) di volo

flight of capital capitale (m) in fuga

flip chart blocco (m) di fogli per lavagna

float (n) [money] anticipo (m)

float (n) [of company] lancio (m) di una società

float (v) [a currency] far fluttuare

float a company lanciare una società

floating fluttuante

floating exchange rates tasso fluttuante di cambio

floating of a company lancio (m) di una società

flood (n) inondazione (f)

flood (v) inondare

floor [level] piano (m)

floor [surface] pavimento (m)

floor manager capo (m) reparto

floor plan planimetria (f)

floor space superficie (f) di pavimento

flop (n) insuccesso (m)

flop (v) fare fiasco

flotation lancio (m) di una società

flourish prosperare

flourishing fiorente

flourishing trade attività (f) commerciale fiorente

flow (n) flusso (m)

flow (v) fluire

flow chart schema (m) del ciclo

flow diagram diagramma (m) del ciclo di lavorazione

fluctuate fluttuare *o* oscillare

fluctuating fluttuante

fluctuation fluttuazione (f)

FOB *or* **f.o.b. (free on board)** franco a bordo

follow seguire *o* fare seguito

follow up aggiornamento (m) *o* sollecito (m)

follow-up letter lettera (f) di sollecito

for sale in vendita

forbid proibire

force majeure causa (f) di forza maggiore

force prices down provocare la diminuzione dei prezzi

force prices up far salire i prezzi

forced forzato

forced sale vendita (f) coatta

forecast (n) previsione (f)

forecast (v) prevedere

forecasting attività (f) previsionale

foreign straniero *o* estero

foreign currency divise (fpl) *o* moneta (f) straniera

foreign exchange *[changing money]* mercato (m) dei cambi

foreign exchange *[currency]* divise (fpl) *o* valuta (f) estera

foreign exchange broker agente (m) in cambi

foreign exchange dealer operatore (m) in cambi

foreign exchange market mercato (m) dei cambi

foreign investments investimenti (mpl) esteri

foreign money order ordine (m) di pagamento di valuta estera

foreign trade commercio (m) estero

forfeit (n) multa (f) *o* penalità (f)

forfeit (v) perdere (un diritto)

forfeit a deposit perdere un deposito

forfeiture perdita (f) (di un diritto)

forge falsificare

forgery *[action]* contraffazione (f)

forgery *[copy]* falso (m)

fork-lift truck carrello (m) elevatore (a forche)

form (n) modulo (m)

form (v) formare *o* comporre

form of words formulazione (f)

formal formale

formality formalità (f)

forward spedire

forward buying acquisto (m) a termine

forward contract contratto (m) a termine

forward market mercato (m) a termine

forward rate corso (m) per operazioni a termine

forward sales vendite (fpl) a termine

forwarding spedizione (f) *o* inoltro (m)

forwarding address indirizzo (m) d'inoltro

forwarding agent spedizioniere (m) (per via terra)

forwarding instructions istruzioni (fpl) per la spedizione

fourth quarter quarto trimestre (m)

fragile fragile

franchise (n) concessione (f)

franchise (v) concedere il diritto di esclusiva

franchisee concessionario (m)

franchiser concedente (m)

franchising concessione (f) di vendita

franco senza spese (fpl) *o* franco

frank (v) affrancare

franking machine macchina (f) affrancatrice

fraud frode (f)

fraudulent fraudolento *o* disonesto
fraudulent transaction operazione (f) disonesta
fraudulently disonestamente
free (adj) *[no payment]* gratis
free (adj) *[no restrictions]* libero
free (adj) *[not busy]* libero
free (adj) *[not occupied]* libero
free (adv) *[no payment]* gratis *o* gratuitamente
free (v) liberare
free delivery consegna (f) gratuita
free gift omaggio (m) *o* dono (m)
free market economy economia (f) di mercato libero
free of charge gratuito *o* franco di spese
free of duty franco dogana (f)
free of tax esente da tasse
free on board (f.o.b.) franco a bordo
free on rail franco su rotaia
free port porto (m) franco
free sample campione (m) gratuito
free trade libero scambio (m)
free trade area zona (f) di libero scambio
free trade zone zona (f) di libero scambio
free trial prova (f) gratuita
free zone zona (f) franca
freelance (n) "freelance" *o* libero professionista (m)
freeze (n) blocco (m) (commerciale)
freeze (v) *[prices]* congelare
freeze credits congelare un credito
freeze wages and prices bloccare i salari e i prezzi
freight *[carriage]* trasporto (m) (via mare)
freight costs spese (fpl) di trasporto
freight depot scalo (m) merci
freight forward porto (m) assegnato
freight plane aereo (m) da carico
freight rates tariffe (fpl) di nolo
freight train treno (m) merci
freightage trasporto (m) di merci

freighter *[plane]* aereo (m) da carico
freighter *[ship]* nave (f) da carico
freightliner treno (m) merci
frequent frequente
frozen congelato *o* bloccato
frozen account conto (m) congelato
frozen assets cespiti (mpl) congelati
frozen credits crediti (mpl) congelati
fulfil an order evadere un'ordinazione
fulfilment adempimento (m)
full pieno *o* intero
full discharge of a debt pieno scarico (m) di un debito
full payment pagamento (m) a saldo *o* pagamento totale
full price prezzo (m) intero
full refund rimborso (m) totale
full-scale (adj) in scala (f) naturale
full-time orario (m) pieno
full-time employment impiego (m) a tempo pieno
fund (n) fondo (m) *o* fondi (mpl)
fund (v) finanziare
funding (financing) finanziamento (m)
funding *[of debt]* consolidamento (m)
further to in seguito a
future delivery futura consegna (f)
futures contratti (mpl) a termine e a premio

Gg

gain (n) *[getting bigger]* aumento (m)

gain (n) *[increase in value]* guadagno (m)

gain (v) *[become bigger]* aumentare

gain (v) *[get]* ottenere

gap divario (m)

gap in the market apertura (f) sul mercato

GDP (= gross domestic product) prodotto (m) interno lordo (PIL)

gear ingranaggio (m)

gearing rapporto (m) di indebitamento

general generale

general audit revisione (f) contabile periodica

general average avaria (f) generale

general manager direttore (m) generale

general meeting assemblea (f) generale

general office ufficio (m) pubblico

general post office Amministrazione Centrale delle Poste (UK)

general strike sciopero (m) generale

gentleman's agreement accordo (m) sulla parola (f)

genuine vero *o* autentico

genuine purchaser acquirente (m) genuino

get procurarsi

get along cavarsela

get back *[something lost]* avere indietro

get into debt indebitarsi

get rid of something liberarsi di qualcosa

get round *[a problem]* aggirare

get the sack essere licenziato

gift regalo (m)

gift coupon buono (m) premio

gift shop negozio (m) per articoli da regalo

gift voucher buono (m) premio

gilt-edged securities titoli (mpl) di prim'ordine

gilts titoli (mpl) di prim'ordine

giro account conto corrente di corrispondenza

giro account number numero (m) di conto corrente di corrispondenza

giro system (sistema di) giroconto (m)

give *[as gift]* regalare

give *[pass]* dare

give away regalare

glut (n) saturazione (f)

glut (v) saturare

GNP (= gross national product) prodotto (m) nazionale lordo (PNL)

go andare

go into business mettersi in affari

go-ahead (adj) intraprendente

go-slow sciopero (m) bianco

going andamento (m)

going rate tariffa (f) in vigore

gold card carta (f) di credito d'oro

good buono

good buy buon affare (m)

good management buona gestione (f)

good quality buona qualità (f)

good value (for money) conveniente

goods merce (f)

goods depot deposito (m) merci

goods in transit merce (f) in transito

goods train treno (m) merci

goodwill avviamento (m) commerciale

government (adj) governativo *o* del governo

government (n) governo (m)

government bonds titoli (mpl) di stato

government contractor fornitore (m) allo stato *o* statale

government stock titoli (mpl) di
stato
government-backed con
l'appoggio del governo
government-controlled a controllo
statale
government-regulated a controllo
statale
government-sponsored
sponsorizzato dal governo
graded advertising rates tariffe
(fpl) pubblicitarie differenziali
graded hotel albergo (m)
selezionato
graded tax imposta (f) progressiva
gradual graduale
graduate trainee laureato (m) che
fa tirocinio come dirigente
graduated graduato
graduated income tax imposta (f)
progressiva sul reddito
gram *or* **gramme** grammo (m)
grand total totale (m) generale
grant (n) concessione (f) *o* borsa
(f) di studio
grant (v) concedere *o* accordare
gratis gratis
grid griglia (f) *o* reticolo (m)
grid structure struttura a rete
gross (adj) lordo
gross (n) (= 144) grossa (f) (dodici
dozzine)
gross (v) avere un ricavo lordo *o*
incassare
gross domestic product (GDP)
prodotto (m) interno lordo (PIL)
gross earnings guadagno (m)
lordo
gross income reddito (m) lordo
gross margin margine (m) lordo
gross national product (GNP)
prodotto (m) nazionale lordo (PNL)
gross profit utile (m) lordo
gross salary stipendio (m) lordo
gross tonnage tonnellaggio (m)
lordo
gross weight peso (m) lordo
gross yield rendimento (m) lordo
group *[of businesses]* gruppo (m)
industriale

group *[of people]* gruppo (m)
growth crescita (f)
growth index indice (m) di crescita
growth rate percentuale (f) di
crescita
guarantee (n) garanzia (f)
guarantee (v) garantire
guarantee a debt garantire un
debito
guaranteed minimum wage
salario (m) minimo garantito
guarantor avallante (m)
guideline direttiva (f)
guild gilda (f) *o* corporazione (f)

Hh

haggle mercanteggiare
half (adj) mezzo
half (n) metà (f)
half a dozen *or* **a half-dozen**
mezza dozzina (f)
half-price sale saldo (m) a metà
prezzo
half-year semestre (m)
half-yearly accounts contabilità (f)
semestrale
half-yearly payment pagamento
(m) semestrale
half-yearly statement resoconto
(m) semestrale
hand in consegnare *o* restituire
hand luggage bagaglio (m) a
mano
hand over passaggio (m) delle
consegne
handle (v) *[deal with]* occuparsi di
handle (v) *[sell]* commerciare
handling maneggio (m) *o* gestione
(f)

handling charge spese (fpl) di confezione, spedizione
handwriting calligrafia (f)
handwritten scritto a mano
handy maneggevole *o* pratico
harbour porto (m)
harbour dues diritti (mpl) portuali
harbour facilities impianti (mpl) portuali
hard bargain affare (m) poco vantaggioso
hard bargaining trattative (fpl) difficili
hard copy copia (f) in chiaro
hard currency valuta (f) solida
hard disk hard disk (m)
hard selling campagna (di vendita, di pubblicità) aggressiva
harmonization armonizzazione (f)
haulage trasporto (m)
haulage contractor trasportatore (m)
haulage costs *or* haulage rates prezzo (m) del trasporto
head of department capo (m) reparto
head office sede (f)
headquarters (HQ) sede (f) centrale
heads of agreement capi (mpl) d'intesa
health salute (f) *o* sanità (f)
health insurance assicurazione (f) malattie
healthy profit buon guadagno (m)
heavy [important] grave
heavy [weight] pesante
heavy costs *or* heavy expenditure forti costi (mpl) *o* spese (fpl)
heavy equipment apparecchiatura (f) pesante
heavy goods vehicle (HGV) veicolo (m) per merci pesanti
heavy industry industria (f) pesante
heavy machinery macchinario (m) pesante
hectare ettaro (m)
hedge (n) barriera (f) *o* protezione (f)

hedging copertura (f)
HGV (= heavy goods vehicle) veicolo (m) per merci pesanti
hidden asset attività (fpl) occulte
hidden reserves riserve (fpl) occulte
high interest interesse (m) alto
high rent affitto (m) alto
high taxation tassazione (f) alta
high-quality di qualità superiore
high-quality goods prodotti (mpl) di alta qualità
highest bidder migliore offerente (m)
highly motivated sales staff personale (m) di vendita molto motivato
highly qualified altamente qualificato
highly-geared company azienda (f) con forte indebitamento
highly-paid altamente retribuito
highly-priced ad alto prezzo
hIre (n) noleggio (m)
hire a car noleggiare un'automobile
hire car automobile (f) a noleggio
hire purchase (HP) acquisto (m) rateale
hire staff assumere personale
hire-purchase company ditta (f) di vendita a rate
historic(al) cost costo (m) effettivo
historical figures cifre (fpl) effettive
hive off assegnare la produzione di qualcosa ad un'azienda consociata
hoard ammasso (m)
hoarding [for posters] tabellone (m)
hoarding [of goods] accaparramento (m)
hold (n) [ship] stiva (f)
hold (v) [contain] contenere
hold (v) [keep] tenere
hold a meeting *or* a discussion tenere una seduta
hold out for fare il braccio di ferro per
hold over posporre

hold the line please *or* **please hold**
resti in linea per favore
hold up (v) *[delay]* trattenere
hold-up (n) *[delay]* ritardo (m)
holder *[person]* titolare (m)
holder *[thing]* contenitore (m) *o*
sostegno (m)
holding company 'holding' (f) *o*
società (f) controllante
holiday pay retribuzione (f) ferie
home address indirizzo (m)
personale
home consumption consumo (m)
interno *o* nazionale
home market mercato (m)
nazionale
home sales vendite (fpl) nazionali
o vendite sul mercato interno
homeward freight carico (m) di
ritorno
homeward journey viaggio (m) di
ritorno
homeworker lavoratore (m) a
domicilio
honorarium onorario (m)
honour a bill onorare una cambiale
honour a signature onorare una
firma
horizontal communication
comunicazione (f) orizzontale
horizontal integration integrazione
(f) orizzontale
hotel hotel (m) *o* albergo (m)
hotel accommodation ricettività
(f) alberghi
hotel bill conto dell'albergo
hotel manager direttore (m)
d'albergo
hotel staff personale (m)
alberghiero
hour ora (f)
hourly orario
hourly rate retribuzione (f) a ore
hourly wage salario (m) orario
hourly-paid workers dipendenti
(mpl) pagati a ore
house *[company]* ditta (f) *o*
impresa (f)
house *[for family]* casa (f)

house insurance assicurazione (f)
sulla casa
house magazine rivista (f)
aziendale
house-to-house a domicilio *o* di
casa in casa
house-to-house selling vendita (f)
a domicilio
HP (= hire purchase) sistema (m)
di acquisti a rate
HQ (= headquarters) sede centrale
hurry up affrettarsi
hype (n) montatura (f) giornalistica
hype (v) fare un grosso lancio
pubblicitario di
hypermarket ipermercato (m)

illegal illegale
illegality illegalità (f)
illegally illegalmente
illicit illecito
**ILO (= International Labour
Organization)** Organizzazione
Internazionale del Lavoro (OIL)
**IMF (= International Monetary
Fund)** Fondo Monetario
Internazionale
imitation imitazione (f)
immediate immediato
immediately immediatamente
imperfect imperfetto
imperfection imperfezione (f)
implement (n) strumento (m)
implement (v) attuare *o* realizzare
implement an agreement rendere
effettivo un accordo
implementation attuazione (f)
import (n) importazione (f)
import (v) importare

import ban divieto (m) di importazione

import duty dazio (m) doganale

import levy prelievo (m) sulle importazioni

import licence or import permit licenza (f) di importazione

import quota contingente (m) di importazione

import restrictions restrizioni (fpl) alle importazioni

import surcharge soprattassa (f) di importazione

import-export (adj) importazioni-esportazioni

importance importanza (f)

important importante

importation importazione (f)

importer importatore (m)

importing (adj) importatore, importatrice

importing (n) importazione (f)

imports importazioni (fpl)

impose imporre

impulse impulso (m)

impulse buyer acquirente (mf) che compra per impulso

impulse purchase acquisto (m) fatto per impulso

in-house interno (alla ditta, allo stabilimento)

in-house training addestramento (m) interno (alla ditta)

incentive incentivo (m)

incentive bonus gratifica (f) di bilancio

incentive payments premio (m) d'operosità

incidental expenses spese (fpl) impreviste

include includere

inclusive incluso

inclusive charge spesa (f) compresa

inclusive of tax comprese tasse (fpl)

income reddito (m)

income tax imposta (f) sul reddito

incoming call telefonata (f) in arrivo

incoming mail posta (f) in arrivo

incompetent incapace

incorporate [a company] costituire

incorporation costituzione (f)

incorrect scorretto

incorrectly scorrettamente

increase (n) aumento (m)

increase (n) [higher salary] aumento (m)

increase (v) aumentare

increase (v) in price aumentare di prezzo

increasing crescente

increasing profits utile (m) in aumento

increment incremento (m)

incremental incrementativo

incremental cost costo (m) marginale

incremental scale scala (f) incrementale

incur incorrere (in)

incur [costs] sostencre spese

incur debts contrarre debiti

indebted indebitato

indebtedness indebitamento (m)

indemnification indennità (f) o indennizzo (m)

indemnify risarcire o indennizzare

indemnify someone for a loss risarcire qualcuno per una perdita

indemnity garanzia (f) o assicurazione (f)

independent indipendente

independent company azienda (f) autonoma

index (n) [alphabetical] indice (m)

index (n) [of prices] indice (m)

index (v) elencare

index card scheda (f)

index number indice (m) economico

index-linked indicizzato

indexation or index-linking indicizzazione (f)

indicator indicatore (m)

indirect indiretto

indirect labour costs costi (mpl) indiretti del lavoro

indirect tax imposte (fpl) indirette

indirect taxation tassazione (f) indiretta

induction inserimento (m) in un nuovo lavoro

induction course *or* **induction training** corso (m) introduttivo

industrial industriale

industrial accident infortunio (m) sul lavoro

industrial arbitration tribunal tribunale (m) di arbitrato industriale

industrial capacity capacità (f) industriale

industrial centre centro (m) industriale

industrial design disegno (m) industriale

industrial disputes vertenza (f) operaia

industrial espionage spionaggio (m) industriale

industrial estate zona (f) industriale

industrial expansion espansione (f) industriale

industrial processes processi (mpl) industriali

industrial relations relazioni (fpl) industriali

industrial tribunal tribunale (m) del lavoro

industrialist industriale (m)

industrialization industrializzazione (f)

industrialize industrializzare

industrialized societies paesi (mpl) industrializzati

industry *[companies]* industria (f)

industry *[general]* industria (f)

inefficiency inefficienza (f)

inefficient inefficiente

inflated currency moneta (f) inflazionata

inflated prices prezzi (mpl) inflazionati

inflation inflazione (f)

inflationary inflazionistico

influence (n) influenza (f)

influence (v) influenzare

inform informare

information informazione (f)

information bureau ufficio (m) informazioni

information officer impiegato (m) addetto alle informazioni

infrastructure infrastruttura (f)

infringe infrangere

infringe a patent usurpare un brevetto

infringement of customs regulations violazione (f) dei regolamenti doganali

infringement of patent usurpazione (f) di brevetto

initial (adj) iniziale

initial (v) siglare

initial capital capitale (m) d'apporto

initiate iniziare

initiate discussions iniziare un dibattito (m)

initiative iniziativa (f)

inland interno *o* del territorio nazionale

innovate innovare

innovation innovazione (f)

innovative innovativo

innovator innovatore (m)

input (v) information immettere informazioni nel computer

input tax IVA (Imposta sul Valore Aggiunto)

inquire chiedere informazioni

inquiry richiesta (f)

insider persona (f) che dispone di informazioni riservate

insider dealing compravendita (f) di azioni da parte degli stessi amministratori della Società

insolvency insolvenza (f)

insolvent insolvente

inspect esaminare

inspection ispezione (f)

instalment rata (f)

instant (adj) *[current]* corrente

instant (adj) *[immediate]* immediato *o* istantaneo

instant credit credito (m) immediato

institute (n) istituto (m)

institute (v) istituire
institution istituzione (f)
institutional istituzionale
institutional investors investitori
(mpl) istituzionali
instruction istruzione (f)
instrument *[device]* strumento (m)
instrument *[document]*
documento (m) *o* strumento (m)
insufficient funds *[US]* fondi (mpl)
insufficienti
insurable assicurabile
insurance assicurazione (f)
insurance agent agente (m) di
assicurazione
insurance broker mediatore (m)
assicurativo
insurance claim richiesta (f) di
indennizzo assicurativo
insurance company compagnia (f)
di assicurazione
insurance contract contratto (m)
di assicurazione
insurance cover copertura (f)
assicurativa
insurance policy polizza (f) di
assicurazione
insurance premium premio (m) di
assicurazione
insurance rates tariffe (fpl) di
assicurazione
insurance salesman venditore (m)
di assicurazioni
insure assicurare
insurer assicuratore (m)
intangible intangibile
intangible assets attività (fpl)
immateriali
interest (n) *[investment]*
partecipazione (f)
interest (n) *[paid on investment]*
interesse (m)
interest (v) interessare
interest charges addebiti (mpl)
per interessi
interest rate tasso (m) d'interesse
interest-bearing deposits depositi
(mpl) fruttiferi
interest-free credit credito (m)
esente da interessi

interface (n) interfaccia (f)
interface (v) fungere da interfaccia
interim dividend dividendo (m) in
acconto
interim payment pagamento (m)
provvisorio
interim report relazione (f)
provvisoria
intermediary intermediario (m)
internal *[inside a company]*
interno
internal *[inside a country]* interno
internal audit revisione (f) interna
internal auditor revisore (m)
interno
internal telephone telefono (m)
interno
international internazionale
international call telefonata (f)
internazionale
international direct dialling
teleselezione (f) internazionale
International Labour Organization
ILO) Organizzazione Internazionale
del Lavoro (OIL)
international law diritto (m)
internazionale
International Monetary Fund
(IMF) Fondo Monetario
Internazionale (FMI)
international trade commercio (m)
internazionale
interpret interpretare
interpreter interprete (mf)
intervention price prezzo (m)
d'intervento
interview (n) intervista (f)
interview (n) *[for a job]* intervista
(f) *o* colloquio (m)
interview (v) intervistare
interview (v) *[for a job]* avere un
colloquio con
interviewee intervistato (m)
interviewer intervistatore (m)
introduce introdurre *o* presentare
introduction *[bringing into use]*
introduzione (m)
introduction *[letter]* lettera (f) di
presentazione

introductory offer offerta (f) di propaganda

invalid inabile *o* privo di validità

invalidate invalidare

invalidation annullamento (m)

invalidity inabilità (f) *o* invalidità (f)

inventory (n) *[list of contents]* inventario (m)

inventory (n) *[stock]* inventario (m) *o* scorte (fpl) *o* stock (m)

inventory (v) inventariare *o* fare l'inventario

inventory control controllo (m) di magazzino

invest investire

investigate investigare

investigation analisi (f) *o* indagine (f)

investment investimento (m)

investment income reddito (m) da investimenti

investor investitore (m)

invisible assets beni (mpl) invisibili

invisible earnings proventi (mpl) da partite invisibili

invisible trade commercio (m) invisibile

invitation invito (m)

invite invitare

invoice (n) fattura (f)

invoice (v) fatturare

invoice number numero (m) di fattura

invoice value prezzo (m) di fattura

invoicing fatturazione (f)

invoicing department ufficio (m) addetto alla fatturazione

IOU (= I owe you) riconoscimento (m) scritto di un debito *o* pagherò (m)

irrecoverable debt debito (m) inesigibile

irredeemable bond obbligazione (f) irredimibile

irregular irregolare

irregularities irregolarità (fpl)

irrevocable irrevocabile

irrevocable acceptance effetto (m) accettato irrevocabilmente

irrevocable letter of credit lettera (f) di credito irrevocabile

issue (n) *[magazine]* numero (m)

issue (n) *[of shares]* rilascio (m) *o* emissione (f)

issue (v) *[shares]* emettere

issue a letter of credit aprire una lettera di credito

issue instructions diramare istruzioni

issuing bank banca (f) d'emissione

item *[information]* voce (f)

item *[on agenda]* argomento (m) *o* questione (f)

item *[thing for sale]* articolo (m)

itemize specificare *o* dettagliare

itemized account conto (m) dettagliato

itemized invoice fattura (f) dettagliata

itinerary itinerario (m)

Jj

job *[employment]* impiego (m) *o* lavoro (m)

job *[piece of work]* lavoro (m)

job analysis analisi (f) delle mansioni

job application domanda (f) di lavoro

job cuts riduzione (f) di posti lavorativi

job description descrizione (f) dei compiti

job satisfaction soddisfazione (f) sul lavoro

job security sicurezza (f) del posto di lavoro

job specification specificazione (f) delle mansioni

job title denominazione (f) della mansione

join unire

joint congiunto *o* unito

joint account conto (m) congiunto

joint discussions discussione (f) collettiva

joint management condirezione (f)

joint managing director condirettore (m)

joint owner comproprietario (m)

joint ownership comproprietà (f)

joint signatory firmatario (m) congiunto

joint venture 'joint venture' (f) *o* associazione (f) in partecipazione

jointly in comune

journal *[accounts book]* libro (m) giornale

journal *[magazine]* rivista (f) *o* periodico (m)

journey order ordine trasmesso dal dettagliante al fornitore tramite commesso viaggiatore

judge (n) giudice (m) *o* magistrato (m)

judge (v) giudicare

judgement *or* **judgment** verdetto (m) *o* decisione (f)

judgment debtor debitore (m) riconosciuto da tribunale

judicial processes procedimenti (mpl) legali

jump the queue passare in testa ad una coda

junior (adj) junior *o* giovane

junior clerk apprendista (m)

junior executive *or* **junior manager** dirigente (m) di grado inferiore

junior partner socio di minore importanza (più recente)

junk bonds obbligazioni (fpl) 'cartastraccia'

junk mail opuscoli (mpl) pubblicitari

jurisdiction giurisdizione (f)

Kk

keen competition concorrenza (f) accanita

keen demand forte richiesta (f)

keen prices prezzi (mpl) concorrenziali

keep a promise mantenere una promessa

keep back trattenere

keep up tenere su

keep up with the demand stare al passo con la richiesta

key (adj) *[important]* chiave

key *[on keyboard]* tasto (m)

key *[to door]* chiave (f)

key industry industria (f) chiave/di base

key personnel *or* **key staff** personale-chiave

key post posto (m) chiave

keyboard (n) tastiera (f)

keyboard (v) digitare

keyboarder operatore (m) su tastiera

keyboarding immissione (f) mediante tastiera

kilo *or* **kilogram** chilo (m) *o* chilogrammo (m)

knock down (v) *[price]* ridurre *o* abbassare

knock off *[reduce price]* abbassare *o* ridurre il prezzo di

knock off *[stop work]* cessare di lavorare

knock-on effect effetto (m) a catena

knockdown prices riduzione (f) di prezzi

krona *[currency used in Sweden]* corona (f) (svedese)

krone *[currency used in Denmark and Norway]* corona (danese, norvegese)

Ll

label (n) etichetta (f)
label (v) etichettare
labelling etichettatura (f)
labour lavoro (m)
labour costs costo (m) della manodopera
labour disputes vertenza (f) di lavoro
labour force forza (f) lavoro
lack of funds mancanza (f) di fondi
land (n) terra (f) *o* terreno (m)
land (v) *[of plane]* atterrare
land (v) *[passengers, cargo]* sbarcare
land goods at a port scaricare merce in un porto
landed costs costi (mpl) fondiari
landing card carta (f) di sbarco
landing charges spese (fpl) di scarico (da nave)
landlord locatore (m)
lapse (v) scadere
laser printer stampante (f) laser
last in first out (LIFO) ultimo a entrare, primo a uscire
last quarter ultimo trimestre (m)
late (adv) tardi *o* in ritardo
late-night opening aprire fino a notte tarda-
latest recentissimo
launch (n) lancio (m)
launch (v) lanciare
launching lancio (m)
launching costs costi (mpl) di lancio
launching date data (f) del lancio
launder (money) riciclare
law *[rule]* legge (f)
law *[study]* diritto (m)
law courts tribunale (m)
law of diminishing returns legge (f) del rendimento decrescente

law of supply and demand legge (f) dell'offerta e della domanda
lawful legittimo
lawful trade commercio (m) legittimo
lawsuit causa (f)
lawyer avvocato (m)
lay off workers licenziare personale (per mancanza di attività)
LBO (= leveraged buyout) finanziamento (m) per l'acquisto del pacchetto azionario contro garanzia delle attività finanziarie
L/C (= letter of credit) lettera (f) di credito
lead time intervallo (m) (fra ordinazione e consegna)
leaflet volantino (m)
leakage dispersione (f)
lease (n) affitto (m)
lease (v) *[of landlord]* affittare *o* dare in affitto
lease (v) *[of tenant]* affittare *o* tenere in affitto
lease back praticare il leasing (m) immobiliare
lease equipment affittare *[impianti]*
lease-back leasing (m) immobiliare
leasing 'leasing' (m)
leave (n) congedo (m)
leave (v) *[go away]* partire *o* lasciare
leave (v) *[resign]* abbandonare *o* lasciare
leave of absence aspettativa (f) *o* congedo (m) autorizzato
ledger libro (m) mastro
left *[not right]* sinistro
left luggage office ufficio (m) deposito bagagli
legal *[according to law]* legale
legal *[referring to law]* giuridico
legal advice consulenza (f) legale
legal adviser consulente (m) legale
legal costs *or* **legal charges** spese (fpl) legali
legal currency moneta (f) legale

legal department ufficio (m) legale
legal expenses spese (fpl) legali
legal proceedings vie (fpl) legali
legal status stato (m) giuridico
legal tender moneta (f) a corso legale
legislation legislazione (f)
lend prestare
lender prestatore (m)
lending prestito (m)
lending limit limite (m) del prestito
lessee affittuario (m)
lessor locatore (m)
let (n) affitto (m)
let (v) affittare
let an office affittare un negozio
letter lettera (f)
letter of application richiesta (f) di iscrizione
letter of appointment lettera (f) di assunzione
letter of complaint lettera (f) di reclamo
letter of credit (L/C) lettera (f) di credito
letter of intent lettera (f) di intenti
letter of reference lettera (f) di referenze
letters of administration nomina (f) di amministratore giudiziario
letters patent brevetto (m)
letting agency agenzia (f) immobiliare
level (n) livello (m)
level off *or* level out stabilizzarsi
leverage leva (f) finanziaria
leveraged buyout (LBO) finanziamento (m) per l'acquisto del pacchetto azionario contro garanzia delle attività societarie
levy (n) imposta (f)
levy (v) imporre (una tassa)
liabilities passività (fpl)
liability responsabilità (f) *o* obbligo (m)
liable for responsabile per
liable to passibile di
licence licenza (f)
license autorizzare

licensee concessionario (m)
licensing concessione (f) di licenze
lien privilegio (m)
life assurance assicurazione (f) sulla vita
life insurance assicurazione (f) sulla vita
life interest usufrutto (m) *o* rendita (f) vitalizia
LIFO (= last in first out) metodo (m) LIFO (ultimo a entrare, primo a uscire)
lift (n) ascensore (m)
lift (v) *[remove]* togliere
lift an embargo togliere l'embargo
limit (n) limite (m)
limit (v) limitare
limitation restrizione (f)
limited limitato
limited (liability) company (Ltd) società (f) di capitali a responsabilità limitata
limited liability responsabilità (f) limitata
limited market mercato (m) limitato
limited partnership società (f) in accomandita semplice
line (n) linea (f)
line management linea (f) gerarchica
line organization organizzazione (f) gerarchica
line printer stampante (f) lineare
liquid assets liquidità (fpl)
liquidate a company mettere in liquidazione una società
liquidate stock mettere in liquidazione scorte di magazzino
liquidation liquidazione (f)
liquidator liquidatore (m)
liquidity liquidità (f)
liquidity crisis crisi (f) di mancanza di liquidità
lira *[currency used in Turkey]* lira (f) (turca)
list (n) lista (f)
list (n) *[catalogue]* listino (m) *o* catalogo (m)
list (v) elencare

list price prezzo (m) di listino
litre litro (m)
Lloyd's register Registro (m) dei Lloyd (di classificazione delle navi)
load (n) carico (m)
load (v) caricare
load (v) *[computer program]* caricare
load a lorry *or* **a ship** caricare un camion *o* una nave
load factor coefficiente (m) di carico
load line linea (f) di carico
loading bay area (f) di carico
loading ramp rampa (f) di carico
loan (n) prestito (m) *o* mutuo (m)
loan (v) prestare *o* dare in prestito
loan capital capitale (m) mutuato
loan stock capitale (m) obbligazionario
local locale/del luogo
local call telefonata (f) urbana
local government ente (m) locale
local labour manodopera (m) locale
lock (n) serratura (f)
lock (v) chiudere a chiave
lock up a shop *or* **an office** chiudere a chiave un negozio *o* un ufficio
lock up capital investire capitali
lock-up premises immobile (m) con chiusura di sicurezza
log (v) registrare
log calls registrare chiamate
logo logogramma (m)
long lungo *o* per molto tempo
long credit credito (m) a lungo termine
long-dated bill effetto (m) a lunga scadenza
long-distance flight volo (m) a lunga percorrenza
long-haul flight volo (m) a lungo raggio
long-range a lunga scadenza
long-standing di vecchia data
long-standing agreement accordo (m) di lunga data
long-term a lungo termine

long-term debts debiti (mpl) a lungo termine
long-term forecast previsione (f) a lungo termine
long-term liabilities passività (fpl) a lungo termine
long-term loan mutuo (m) a lunga scadenza
long-term planning pianificazione (f) a lunga scadenza
loose sciolto
lorry camion (m)
lorry driver camionista (m)
lorry-load carico (di camion)
lose *[fall to a lower level]* cadere
lose an order perdere un'ordinazione
lose money perdere denaro
loss *[not a profit]* perdita (f)
loss *[of something]* perdita (f)
loss of an order perdita (f) di un'ordinazione
loss of customers perdita (f) di clientela
loss-leader articolo (m) di richiamo per la clientela
lot *[of items]* partita (f) (di merci)
low (adj) basso *o* scadente
low (n) basso livello (m)
low sales vendite (fpl) basse
low-grade di qualità inferiore
low-level di livello inferiore
low-quality di qualità inferiore
lower (adj) inferiore *o* più basso
lower (v) abbassare
lower prices abbassare i prezzi
lowering calo (m)
Ltd (= limited company) a responsabilità limitata
luggage bagaglio (m)
lump sum importo (m) forfettario
luxury goods articoli (mpl) di lusso

Mm

machine macchina (f)
macro-economics macroeconomia (f)
magazine rivista (f)
magazine insert fascicolo (m) supplementare (in una rivista)
magazine mailing invio (m) di riviste per posta
magnetic tape *or* **mag tape** nastro (m) magnetico
mail (n) *[letters sent or* **received]** posta (f)
mail (n) *[postal system]* posta (f)
mail (v) spedire per posta
mail shot campagna (f) promozionale a mezzo posta
mail-order ordinazioni (fpl) per corrispondenza
mail-order business *or* **mail-order firm** *or* **mail-order** società (f) di vendita per corrispondenza
mail-order catalogue catalogo (m) di vendita per corrispondenza
mailing invio (m) (per posta)
mailing list elenco (m) di indirizzi
mailing piece materiale (m) promozionale preparato specificatamente per l'invio (per posta)
mailing shot campagna (f) promozionale a mezzo posta
main principale
main building edificio (m) principale
main office sede (f) centrale *o* direzione (f) centrale
maintain *[keep at same level]* mantenere
maintain *[keep going]* tenere in efficienza
maintenance *[keeping in working order]* manutenzione (f)

maintenance *[keeping things going]* mantenimento (m)
maintenance of contacts mantenimento (m) di contatti
maintenance of supplies mantenimento (m) delle provvigioni
major maggiore *o* importante
major shareholder azionista (m) principale
majority maggioranza (f)
majority shareholder azionista (m) di maggioranza
make good *[a defect or loss]* indennizzare *o* risarcire
make money fare soldi
make out *[invoice]* compilare
make provision for provvedere a
make up for compensare
make-ready time periodo (m) di avviamento
maladministration cattiva amministrazione (f)
man (n) uomo (m)
man (v) fornire il personale (necessario)
man-hour ora (f) lavorativa
manage amministrare *o* gestire
manage property amministrare un patrimonio
manage to riuscire a
manageable trattabile *o* controllabile
management *[action]* gestione (f)
management *[managers]* direzione (f)
management accounts conti (mpl) gestione
management buyout (MBO) acquisto (m) di una società da parte dei suoi stessi dirigenti
management consultant consulente (m) di direzione aziendale
management course corso (m) in amministrazione
management team quadri (mpl) direttivi
management techniques tecniche (fpl) gestionali

management trainee apprendista (m) in direzione aziendale
management training addestramento (m) dei dirigenti
manager [of branch or shop] direttore (m), direttrice (f)
manager [of department] direttore (m), direttrice (f)
managerial direttivo o gestionale
managerial staff personale (m) dirigente
managing director (MD) amministratore delegato
mandate mandato (m)
manifest manifesto (m)
manned aperto
manning organico (m)
manning levels livello (m) di organico
manpower manodopera (f)
manpower forecasting previsione (f) della necessità di manodopera
manpower planning programmazione (f) delle assunzioni di manodopera
manpower requirements esigenza (f) di manodopera
manpower shortage carenza (f) di manodopera
manual (adj) manuale
manual (n) manuale (m)
manual work lavoro (m) manuale
manual worker manovale (m)
manufacture (n) lavorazione (f) o fabbricazione (f)
manufacture (v) produrre o fabbricare
manufactured goods manufatti (mpl)
manufacturer produttore (m) o fabbricante (m)
manufacturer's recommended price (MRP) prezzo (m) di fabbrica consigliato
manufacturing manifatturiero
manufacturing capacity capacità (f) di produzione
manufacturing costs costi (mpl) di produzione

manufacturing overheads spese (fpl) generali di produzione
margin [profit] margine (m)
margin of error margine (m) di errore
marginal marginale
marginal cost costo (m) marginale
marginal pricing determinazione (f) marginale del prezzo
marine marittimo
marine insurance assicurazione (f) marittima
marine underwriter assicuratore (m) marittimo
maritime marittimo o navale
maritime law diritto (m) della navigazione
maritime lawyer avvocato (m) che si occupa del diritto della navigazione
maritime trade commercio (m) marittimo
mark (n) impronta (f)
mark (v) notare
mark down abbassare il prezzo (di articoli)
mark up aumentare il prezzo (di articoli)
mark-down diminuzione (f) di prezzo
mark-up [action] aumento (m) di prezzo
mark-up [profit margin] margine (m) o utile lordo
marker pen evidenziatore (m)
market (n) [place] mercato (m)
market (n) [possible sales] mercato (m)
market (n) [where a product might sell] mercato (m)
market (v) vendere o commercializzare
market analysis analisi (f) di mercato
market analyst analista (m) di mercato
market capitalization capitalizzazione (f) di mercato
market economist economista (mf) di mercato

market forces forze (fpl) di mercato

market forecast previsioni (fpl) di mercato

market leader prodotto-guida (m) del mercato *o* azienda (f) primaria sul mercato

market opportunities possibilità (fpl) di mercato

market penetration penetrazione (f) di mercato

market price prezzo (m) di mercato

market rate prezzo (m) di mercato

market research ricerca (f) di mercato

market share quota (f) di mercato

market trends tendenza (f) di mercato

market value valore (m) di mercato

marketable commerciabile

marketing marketing (m)

marketing agreement accordo (m) di marketing

marketing department servizio (m) di marketing

marketing division reparto (m) marketing

marketing manager direttore di marketing

marketing strategy strategia (f) di marketing

marketing techniques tecniche (fpl) di marketing

marketplace *[in town]* (piazza (f) del) mercato (m)

marketplace *[place where something is sold]* mercato (m)

mass *[of people]* massa (f)

mass *[of things]* massa (f) *o* grande quantità (f)

mass market product prodotto (m) per il mercato di massa

mass marketing marketing (m) di massa

mass media mass-media (mpl) *o* mezzi (mpl) di comunicazione di massa

mass production produzione (f) in serie

mass-produce produrre in serie

mass-produce cars produrre automobili in serie

Master's degree in Business Administration (MBA) master (m) in gestione d'impresa

materials control controllo (m) dei materiali

materials handling movimentazione (f) dei materiali

maternity leave congedo (m) per maternità

matter (n) *[problem]* faccenda (f) *o* problema (f)

matter (n) *[to be discussed]* argomento (m) *o* questione (f)

matter (v) avere importanza

mature (v) scadere

mature economy economia (f) matura

maturity date data (f) di scadenza

maximization massimizzazione (f)

maximize massimizzare

maximum (adj) massimo

maximum (n) massimo (m)

maximum price prezzo (m) massimo

MBA (= Master in Business Administration) master (m) in gestione d'impresa

MBO (= management buyout) acquisto (m) di una società da parte dei suoi stessi dirigenti

MD (= managing director) direttore generale

mean (adj) medio

mean (n) media (f)

mean annual increase aumento (m) medio annuale

means *[money]* mezzi (mpl)

means *[ways]* mezzi (mpl) *o* strumenti (mpl)

means test accertamento (m) patrimoniale

measurement of profitability misura (f) della redditività

measurements misure (fpl)

media coverage diffusione (f) nei mass-media
median valore (m) mediano
mediate mediare
mediation mediazione (f)
mediator mediatore (m)
medium (adj) medio *o* di mezzo
medium (n) mezzo (m)
medium-sized di medie dimensioni
medium-term a medio termine
meet *[be satisfactory]* soddisfare
meet *[expenses]* far fronte *[a una spesa]*
meet *[someone]* incontrare
meet a deadline rispettare una scadenza
meet a demand andare incontro ad una richiesta
meet a target raggiungere un obiettivo
meeting riunione (f)
meeting place luogo (m) d'incontro
member *[of a group]* socio (m)
membership *[all members]* gli iscritti (mpl)
membership *[being a member]* iscrizione (f)
memo memorandum (m)
memorandum memorandum (m)
memory *[computer]* memoria (f)
merchandise (n) merce (f)
merchandize (v) commerciare
merchandize a product esercitare il commercio di un prodotto
merchandizer commerciante (m)
merchandizing attività (f) promozionale
merchant mercante (m)
merchant bank 'merchant bank' (f) *o* banca (f) mercantile
merchant navy marina (f) mercantile
merchant ship *or* merchant vessel nave (f) mercantile
merge incorporare
merger fusione (f)
merit merito (n)

merit award *or* merit bonus premio (m) di merito
message messaggio (m)
messenger fattorino (m)
micro-economics microeconomia (f)
microcomputer microelaboratore (m)
mid-month accounts contabilità (f) di metà mese
mid-week metà settimana (f)
middle management quadri (mpl) intermedi
middle-sized company società (f) di medie dimensioni
middleman intermediario (m)
million milione (m)
millionaire miliardario (m)
minimum (adj) minimo
minimum (n) minimo (m)
minimum dividend dividendo (m) minimo
minimum payment pagamento (m) minimo
minimum wage salario (m) minimo
minor shareholders azionista (m) di secondaria importanza
minority minoranza (f)
minority shareholder azionista (m) di minoranza
minus meno *o* negativo
minus factor fattore (m) negativo
minute (n) *[time]* minuto (m)
minute (v) verbalizzare *o* mettere a verbale
minutes (n) *[of meeting]* verbale (m) (di assemblea)
misappropriate appropriarsi indebitamente
misappropriation appropriazione (f) indebita
miscalculate fare male i propri calcoli
miscalculation calcolo (m) sbagliato
miscellaneous miscellaneo *o* vario
miscellaneous items articoli (mpl) diversi
mismanage dirigere male

mismanagement cattiva amministrazione (f)
miss *[not to hit]* mancare
miss *[not to meet]* mancare
miss *[train, plane]* perdere
miss a target mancare il bersaglio
miss an instalment non pagare una rata
mistake errore (m)
misunderstanding malinteso (m)
mixed *[different sorts]* misto
mixed *[neither good nor bad]* misto
mixed economy economia (f) di tipo misto
mobility mobilità (f)
mobilize mobilizzare
mobilize capital mobilizzare capitali
mock-up modello (m) in scala
mode modo (m)
mode of payment modalità (fpl) di pagamento
model (n) *[person]* indossatrice (f)
model (n) *[small copy]* modello (m)
model (n) *[style of product]* modello (m)
model (v) *[clothes]* presentare (un modello)
model agreement accordo-tipo (m)
modem modem (m)
moderate (adj) moderato
moderate (v) moderare
monetary monetario
monetary base base (f) monetaria
monetary unit unità (f) monetaria
money denaro (m)
money changer cambiavalute (m)
money markets mercati (mpl) monetari
money order vaglia (m) (mandato di pagamento)
money rates tassi (mpl) monetari
money supply disponibilità (f) di capitali
money up front soldi (mpl) in anticipo
money-making redditizio

money-making plan progetto (m) redditizio
moneylender finanziatore (m) *o* chi fa prestiti
monitor (n) *[screen]* monitor (m)
monitor (v) controllare
monopolization monopolizzazione (f)
monopolize monopolizzare
monopoly monopolio (m)
month mese (m)
month end fine (f) del mese
month-end accounts contabilità (f) di fine mese
monthly (adj) mensile
monthly (adv) mensilmente
monthly payments pagamenti (mpl) mensili
monthly statement resoconto (m) mensile
moonlight (v) lavorare al nero
moonlighter (n) lavoratore (m) al nero
moonlighting (n) lavoro (m) nero
moratorium moratoria (f)
mortgage (n) ipoteca (f)
mortgage (v) ipotecare
mortgage payments pagamenti (mpl) ipotecari
mortgagee creditore (m) ipotecario
mortgager *or* **mortgagor** debitore (m) ipotecario
most-favoured nation nazione (f) più favorita
motivated motivato
motivation motivazione (f)
motor insurance assicurazione (f) auto
mount up aumentare
mounting in aumento
move *[be sold]* vendersi
move *[house, office]* traslocare
move *[propose]* proporre
movement movimento (m)
movements of capital movimenti (m) di capitali
MRP (= manufacturer's recommended price) prezzo (m) consigliato di fabbrica

multicurrency operation
operazione (f) a denominazione
valutaria multipla
multilateral multilaterale
multilateral agreement accordo
(m) multilaterale
multilateral trade commercio (m)
multilaterale
multinational (n) multinazionale
(f)
multiple (adj) multiplo
multiple entry visa visto (m)
consolare multiplo
multiple ownership proprietà (f)
multipla
multiple store negozio (m)
appartenente ad una catena
multiplication moltiplicazione (f)
multiply moltiplicare
mutual (adj) mutuo o reciproco
mutual (insurance) company
società (f) mutua (di assicurazioni)

Nn

national nazionale
national advertising pubblicità (f)
su tutto il territorio nazionale
nationalization nazionalizzazione
(f)
nationalized industry industria (f)
statalizzata
nationwide di dimensioni nazionali
natural resources risorse (fpl)
naturali
natural wastage numero di
lavoratori (mpl) che abbandonano
l'attività per pensionamento
near letter-quality (NLQ) ad alta
definizione

necessary necessario
negative cash flow reddito (m)
societario negativo
neglected business attività (f)
trascurata
neglected shares azioni (fpl)
trascurate
negligence negligenza (f)
negligent negligente
negligible trascurabile
negotiable trattabile o negoziabile
negotiable instrument strumento
(m) negoziabile
negotiate negoziare o trattare
negotiation negoziato (m) o
trattativa (f)
negotiator negoziatore (m)
net (adj) netto
net (v) ricavare al netto
net assets or **net worth** valore (m)
patrimoniale netto
net earnings or **net income** utili
(mpl) netti
net income or **net salary** reddito
(m) netto
net loss perdita (f) netta
net margin margine (m) netto
net price prezzo (m) netto
net profit utile (m) netto
net receipts incassi (mpl) netti
net sales ricavi (mpl) netti
net weight peso (m) netto
net yield rendimento (m) netto
network (n) rete (f) o sistema (m)
network (v) *[computers]* collegare
in rete
news agency agenzia (f) di stampa
newspaper giornale (m)
niche nicchia (f)
night notte (f)
night rate tariffa (f) notturna
night shift turno (m) di notte
nil nulla (m) o zero (m)
nil return ricavo (m) nullo
NLQ (= near letter-quality) ad alta
definizione
no-claims bonus premio (m) agli
assicurati che non hanno denunciato
sinistri

no-strike agreement *or* **no-strike clause** accordo (m) *o* clausola (f) che stabilisce il divieto di sciopero

nominal capital capitale (m) nominale

nominal ledger mastro (m) nominale

nominal rent affitto (m) nominale

nominal value valore (m) nominale

nominee candidato (m)

nominee account conto (m) di prestanome

non profit-making senza scopo di lucro

non-delivery mancata consegna (f)

non-executive director direttore (m) senza poteri esecutivi

non-negotiable instrument strumento (m) non negoziabile

non-payment *[of a debt]* omesso pagamento (m) di un debito

non-recurring items articoli (mpl) non ricorrenti

non-refundable deposit deposito (m) non rimborsabile

non-returnable packing imballo (m) a perdere

non-stop senza scalo *o* ininterrotto

non-taxable income reddito (m) non imponibile

nonfeasance reato (m) di omissione

norm norma (f)

notary public notaio (m)

note (n) nota (f)

note (v) *[details]* notare

note of hand pagherò (m) cambiario

notice *[piece of information]* avviso (m)

notice *[that worker is leaving his job]* preavviso (m)

notice *[time allowed]* preavviso (m)

notice *[warning that a contract is going to end]* preavviso (m)

notification notificazione (f)

notify notificare

null nullo

number (n) *[figure]* numero (m)

number (v) numerare

numbered account conto (m) numerato

numeric *or* **numerical** numerico

numeric keypad tastierino (m) numerico

Oo

objective (adj) obiettivo *o* oggettivo

objective (n) obiettivo (m)

obligation *[debt]* debito (m)

obligation *[duty]* dovere (m) *o* impegno (m)

obsolescence invecchiamento (m)

obsolescent obsolescente

obsolete antiquato

obtain ottenere

obtainable conseguibile *o* ottenibile

occupancy occupazione (f)

occupancy rate percentuale (f) di occupazione

occupant occupante (m) *o* chi occupa

occupational occupazionale *o* professionale

occupational accident incidente (m) professionale

odd *[not a pair]* spaiato

odd *[not even]* dispari

odd numbers numeri (mpl) dispari

off *[away from work]* assente

off *[cancelled]* annullato

off *[reduced by]* con sconto di

off the record ufficiosamente

off-peak non di punta

off-season fuori stagione

off-the-job training corsi (mpl) di addestramento esterni (al posto di lavoro)
offer (n) offerta (f)
offer (v) *[to buy]* offrire *o* proporre
offer (v) *[to sell]* offrire (in vendita)
offer for sale offerta (f) di vendita
offer price prezzo (m) d'offerta
office ufficio (m)
office equipment attrezzatura (f) per ufficio
office furniture arredamento (m) per ufficio
office hours orario (m) d'ufficio
office security sistema (m) di sorveglianza dell'ufficio
office space area (f) uffici
office staff personale (m) d'ufficio
office stationery cancelleria (f) d'ufficio
offices to let affitansi uffici (mpl)
official (adj) ufficiale
official (n) funzionario (m)
official receiver liquidatore (m)
official return reddito (m) ufficiale
officialese linguaggio (m) burocratico
offload scaricare
offshore offshore *o* all'estero
oil *[cooking]* olio (m)
oil *[petroleum]* petrolio (m)
oil price prezzo (m) del petrolio
oil-exporting countries paesi (mpl) esportatori di petrolio
oil-producing countries paesi (mpl) produttori di petrolio
old vecchio
old-established di vecchia istituzione (f)
old-fashioned antiquato
ombudsman difensore (m) civico
omission omissione (f)
omit trascurare *o* omettere
on a short-term basis a breve termine
on account in acconto
on agreed terms secondo i termini convenuti
on an annual basis annualmente

on an average in media
on approval salvo vista e verifica
on behalf of per conto di
on board a bordo
on business per affari
on condition that a condizione che
on credit a credito
on favourable terms a condizioni (fpl) vantaggiose
on line *or* **online** in linea
on order (che è stato) ordinato
on request su richiesta
on sale in vendita
on the increase in aumento
on time puntuale
on-the-job training addestramento (m) sul lavoro
one-off unico
one-off item articolo (m) unico
one-sided parziale
one-sided agreement accordo (m) parziale
one-way fare biglietto (m) di andata
one-way trade commercio (m) a senso unico
OPEC (= Organization of Petroleum Exporting Countries) Organizzazione (f) dei paesi esportatori di petrolio
open (adj) *[not closed]* aperto
open (v) *[begin]* iniziare
open (v) *[start new business]* aprire
open a bank account aprire un conto bancario
open a line of credit aprire una linea di credito
open a meeting aprire una seduta
open account conto (m) aperto
open an account aprire un conto
open cheque assegno (m) non sbarrato
open credit credito (m) aperto
open market mercato (m) libero
open negotiations aprire trattative
open ticket biglietto (m) aperto (senza data di ritorno)
open to offers aperto ad offerte

open-ended agreement accordo (m) aperto

open-plan office ufficio (m) a pianta aperta

opening (adj) iniziale *o* d'apertura

opening (n) apertura (f)

opening balance bilancio (m) d'apertura

opening bid offerta (f) d'apertura

opening hours orario (m) d'apertura

opening price prezzo (m) d'apertura

opening stock rimanenze (fpl) iniziali

opening time orario (m) d'apertura

operate funzionare

operating (n) funzionamento (m)

operating budget budget (m) operativo

operating costs *or* operating expenses costi (mpl) d'esercizio *o* spese (fpl) d'esercizio

operating manual manuale (m) operativo

operating profit utile (m) d'esercizio

operating system sistema (m) operativo

operation operazione (f)

operational operativo

operational budget budget (m) di gestione

operational costs costi (mpl) di gestione

operative (adj) operativo

operative (n) operatore (m)

operator operatore (m)

opinion poll sondaggio (m) d'opinione

opportunity opportunità (f)

option to purchase opzione (f) per l'acquisto

optional facoltativo

optional extras spese (fpl) supplementari

order (n) *[certain way]* ordine (m)

order (n) *[for goods]* ordinazione (f)

order (n) *[instruction]* ordine (m)

order (n) *[money]* mandato (m) di pagamento *o* vaglia (m)

order (v) *[goods]* ordinare

order (v) *[put in order]* mettere in ordine

order book registro (m) delle ordinazioni

order fulfilment evasione (f) di un'ordinazione

order number numero (m) d'ordinazione

order picking selezione (f) delle ordinazioni

order processing elaborazione (f) delle ordinazioni

order: on order essere stato ordinato

ordinary ordinario

ordinary shares azioni (fpl) ordinarie

organization *[institution]* organizzazione (f)

organization *[way of arranging]* organizzazione (f)

organization and methods organizzazione (f) e metodo (m)

organization chart organigramma (m)

Organization of Petroleum Exporting Countries (OPEC) Organizzazione (f) dei paesi esportatori di petrolio

organizational organizzativo

organize organizzare

origin origine (f)

original (adj) originario

original (n) originale (m)

OS (= outsize) di taglia forte

out of control fuori controllo

out of date non attuale

out of pocket rimetterci

out of stock esaurito

out of work disoccupato

out-of-pocket expenses piccole spese (fpl)

outbid offrire un prezzo superiore

outgoing in uscita

outgoing mail posta (f) in partenza

outgoings spese (fpl)

outlay esborso (m)

outlet sbocco (m)
output (n) [computer] output (m) *o* dati (mpl) di emissione
output (n) [goods] produzione (f)
output (v) [computer] emettere
output tax IVA
outright assoluto
outside esteriore
outside director direttore esterno
outside line linea (f) esterna
outside office hours fuori orario d'ufficio
outsize (OS) di taglia forte
outstanding [exceptional] straordinario
outstanding [unpaid] non pagato
outstanding debts debiti (mpl) insoluti
outstanding orders ordinazioni (fpl) da evadere
overall totale
overall plan piano (m) globale
overbook prenotare più (stanze, posti ecc.) di quanti siano disponibili
overbooking prenotazione (f) di più (stanze, posti, ecc.) di quanti siano disponibili
overcapacity capacità (f) in eccedenza
overcharge (n) prezzo (m) eccessivo
overcharge (v) far pagare troppo
overdraft scoperto (di c/c)
overdraft facility facilitazioni (fpl) di scoperto
overdraw emettere allo scoperto
overdrawn account conto (m) scoperto
overdue scaduto
overestimate (v) sopravvalutare
overhead budget budget (m) generale
overhead costs *or* **expenses** spese (fpl) generali
overheads spese (fpl) generali
overmanning personale (m) in eccedenza
overpayment pagamento (m) in più

overproduce produrre in eccesso
overproduction produzione (f) in eccesso
overseas (adj) all'estero
overseas (n) l'estero (m) *o* i paesi stranieri
overseas markets mercati (mpl) esteri
overseas trade commercio (m) estero
overspend spendere oltre le proprie possibilità
overspend one's budget spendere oltre il proprio budget
overstock (v) saturare di prodotti
overstocks sovraccarico (m) di scorte
overtime lavoro (m) straordinario
overtime ban blocco (m) del lavoro straordinario
overtime pay compenso (m) per lavoro straordinario
overvalue sopravvalutare
overweight: to be overweight di peso eccedente
owe essere debitore
owing dovuto *o* a debito
owing to a causa di
own (v) possedere
own brand goods prodotti (mpl) con marchio proprio
own label goods prodotti (mpl) con etichetta propria
owner proprietario (m)
ownership proprietà (f)

Pp

p & p (= postage and packing) spese (fpl) postali e imballo

PA (= personal assistant) segretaria (f) personale

pack (n) pacco (m)

pack (v) imballare *o* impacchettare

pack goods into cartons imballare le merci

pack of envelopes pacchetto (m) di buste

package [of goods] pacco (m)

package [of services] contratto (m) globale

package deal pacchetto (m) rivendicativo

packaging [action] imballaggio (m)

packaging [material] materiale (m) d'imballaggio

packaging material materiale (m) d'imballaggio

packer impacchettatore (m)

packet pacchetto (m)

packet of cigarettes pacchetto (m) di sigarette

packing [action] imballaggio (m)

packing [material] materiali (mpl) di imballaggio

packing case cassa (f) da imballaggio

packing charges spese (f) d'imballo

packing list *or* packing slip distinta (f) d'imballaggio

paid [for work] pagato *o* remunerato

paid [invoice] pagato

pallet paletta (f)

palletize palettizzare *o* trasportare a mezzo di palette

panel pannello (m)

panic buying incetta (f) in previsione di aumento dei prezzi

paper bag sacchetto (m) di carta

paper feed alimentatore (m) di fogli

paper loss perdita (f) sulla carta

paper profit utili (mpl) ipotetici

paperclip graffetta (f)

papers incartamenti (mpl)

paperwork lavoro (m) d'ufficio

par pari

par value valore (m) nominale

parcel (n) pacco (m)

parcel (v) impacchettare

parcel post servizio (m) pacchi postali

parent company società (f) controllante

parity parità (f)

part (n) parte (f)

part exchange permuta (f) come pagamento parziale

part-owner comproprietario (m)

part-ownership comproprietà (f)

part-time orario (m) ridotto

part-time work *or* part-time employment lavoro (m) a orario ridotto

part-timer lavoratore (m) a orario ridotto

partial loss perdita (f) parziale

partial payment pagamento (m) parziale

particulars dettagli (mpl)

partner socio (m) *o* compagno/a

partnership società (f) di persone

party parte (f) *[legale]*

patent brevetto (m)

patent agent agente (m) di brevetti

patent an invention brevettare un'invenzione

patent applied for *or* patent pending brevetto (m) richiesto *o* in attesa di brevetto

patented brevettato

pay (n) [salary] paga (f) *o* retribuzione (f) *o* stipendio (m)

pay (v) [bill] pagare *o* saldare

pay (v) [worker] pagare *o* remunerare

pay a bill pagare un conto

pay a dividend pagare un dividendo

pay an invoice pagare una fattura
pay back rimborsare
pay by cheque pagare con un assegno
pay by credit card pagare con carta di credito
pay cash pagare in contanti
pay cheque assegno (m) dello stipendio
pay desk banco (m) dei pagamenti
pay in advance pagare anticipatamente
pay in instalments pagare a rate
pay interest pagare gli interessi
pay money down pagare in contanti
pay off *[debt]* estinguere (un debito)
pay off *[worker]* liquidare
pay out sborsare
pay phone telefono (m) a gettoni
pay rise aumento (m) salariale
pay up pagare
payable pagabile
payable at sixty days pagabile a sessanta giorni
payable in advance pagabile anticipatamente
payable on delivery pagabile alla consegna
payable on demand pagabile su richiesta
payback recupero (m) dell'investimento
payback clause clausola (f) di recupero dell'investimento
payback period periodo (m) di recupero
payee beneficiario (m)
payer chi paga
paying (adj) redditizio
paying (n) pagamento (m)
paying-in slip distinta (f) di versamento
payload carico (m) utile
payment pagamento (m)
payment by cheque pagamento (m) tramite assegno
payment by results pagamento (m) in base al lavoro effettuato

payment in cash pagamento (m) in contanti
payment in kind pagamento (m) in natura
payment on account pagamento (m) in acconto
PC (= personal computer) personal computer (m) *o* elaboratore (m) ad uso personale
P/E ratio (= price/earnings ratio) rapporto (m) corso/utili
peak (n) valore (m) massimo
peak (v) raggiungere un punto massimo *o* culminare
peak output livello (m) massimo di produzione
peak period periodo (m) di massima attività
peg prices bloccare i prezzi
penalize penalizzare
penalty penale (f) *o* multa (f)
penalty clause clausola (f) di penalità
pending pendente
penetrate a market realizzare la penetrazione di un mercato
pension pensione (f)
pension fund fondo (m) pensioni
pension scheme piano (m) pensioni
per per *o* per mezzo
per annum all'anno
per capita pro-capite
per cent per cento
per day al giorno
per head per persona
per hour all'ora
per week alla settimana
per year all'anno
percentage percentuale (f)
percentage discount sconto (m) percentuale
percentage increase aumento (m) percentuale
percentage point punto (m) percentuale
performance prestazione (f)
performance rating valutazione (f) della prestazione
period periodo (m)

period of notice periodo (m) di preavviso

period of validity periodo (m) di validità

periodic or **periodical (adj)** periodico

periodical (n) pubblicazione (f) periodica

peripherals periferiche (fpl)

perishable deperibile

perishable goods or **items** or **cargo** merci (fpl) o articoli (mpl) o derrate (fpl) deperibili

perishables merci (fpl) deperibili

permission autorizzazione (f)

permit (n) permesso (m)

permit (v) autorizzare (qualcuno a fare qualcosa)

personal personale

personal allowances detrazioni (fpl) personali

personal assets attivo (m) mobiliare

personal assistant (PA) segretaria (f) personale

personal computer (PC) personal computer (m) o elaboratore (m) ad uso personale

personal income reddito (m) personale

personalized personalizzato

personalized briefcase ventiquattrore (f) personalizzata

personalized cheques assegni (mpl) personalizzati

personnel personale (m)

personnel department ufficio (m) del personale

personnel management direzione (f) del personale

personnel manager capo (m) del personale

petty di scarsa importanza

petty cash piccola cassa (f)

petty cash box scatola (f) per la piccola cassa

petty expenses piccole spese (fpl)

phase in introdurre gradualmente

phase out eliminare gradualmente

phoenix syndrome sindrome (f) della fenice

phone (n) telefono (m)

phone (v) telefonare

phone back ritelefonare

phone call chiamata (f) telefonica

phone card carta (f) di credito telefonica

phone number numero (m) di telefono o numero telefonico

photocopier fotocopiatrice (f)

photocopy (n) fotocopia (f)

photocopy (v) fotocopiare

photocopying fotocopiatura (f)

photocopying bureau ufficio (m) dove si fanno fotocopie

picking list lista (f) di selezione

pie chart grafico (m) a settori

piece pezzo (m)

piece rate retribuzione (f) a cottimo

piecework lavoro (m) a cottimo

pilferage or **pilfering** furto (m) di scarsa entità

pilot (adj) pilota

pilot (n) *[person]* pilota (m)

pilot scheme progetto (m) pilota

pioneer (n) pioniere (m)

pioneer (v) fare da pioniere in

place (n) *[in a competition]* posto (m)

place (n) *[in a text]* segno (m)

place (n) *[job]* posto (m) o impiego (m)

place (n) *[situation]* posto (m) o luogo (m)

place (v) posare o mettere

place an order fare un'ordinazione

place of work posto (m) di lavoro

plaintiff querelante (m)

plan (n) *[drawing]* pianta (f)

plan (n) *[project]* piano (m) o progetto (m)

plan (v) progettare o organizzare

plan investments pianificare investimenti

plane aereo (m)

planner pianificatore (m)

planning pianificazione (f)

plant (n) *[factory]* fabbrica (f) *o* stabilimento (m)

plant (n) *[machinery]* impianti (mpl)

plant-hire firm ditta (f) di noleggio impianti

platform *[railway station]* binario (m)

PLC *or* plc (= Public Limited Company) Società di capitali a sottoscrizione pubblica (SpA)

plug (n) *[electric]* spina (f) elettrica

plug (v) *[block]* tappare

plug (v) *[publicize]* pubblicizzare

plus positivo

plus factor fattore (m) positivo

pocket (n) tasca (f)

pocket (v) incassare

pocket calculator *or* pocket diary calcolatrice (f) tascabile *o* agenda (f) tascabile

point punto (m)

point of sale (p.o.s. *or* POS) punto (m) di vendita

point of sale material (POS material) materiale (m) per punto di vendita

policy *[plan of action]* politica (f)

policy *[insurance]* polizza (f)

pool resources mettere insieme le risorse

poor quality qualità (f) scadente

poor service servizio (m) scadente

popular popolare

popular prices prezzi (mpl) popolari

port *[computer]* porta (f) *[di computer]*

port *[harbour]* porto (m)

port authority autorità (fpl) portuali

port charges *or* port dues diritti (mpl) di porto

port of call porto (m) di scalo

port of embarkation porto (m) d'imbarco

port of registry porto (m) d'armamento

portable portatile

portfolio *[file]* cartella (f) *o* portfolio (m)

portfolio *[of shares]* portafoglio (m)

portfolio management gestione (f) del portafoglio

p.o.s. *or* POS (= point of sale) punto (m) di vendita

POS material (point of sale material) materiale (m) per punto di vendita

position *[job]* impiego (m) *o* lavoro (m)

position *[state of affairs]* posizione (f) *o* situazione (f)

positive positivo

positive cash flow flusso (m) di cassa positivo

possess possedere

possibility possibilità (f)

possible possibile

post (n) *[job]* posto (m) di lavoro *o* impiego (m)

post (n) *[letters]* posta (f)

post (n) *[system]* posta (f) *o* servizio (m) postale

post (v) spedire per posta

post an entry registrare una voce (contabile)

post free franco posta

postage spesa (f) postale

postage and packing (p & p) spese postali e imballo

postage paid porto pagato

postal postale

postal charges *or* postal rates spese (fpl) postali

postal order vaglia (m) postale

postcode codice (m) d'avviamento postale

postdate postdatare

poste restante fermoposta (m)

postpaid affrancatura (f) pagata

postpone differire *o* rinviare

postponement dilazione (f) *o* rinvio (m)

potential (adj) potenziale

potential (n) potenziale (m)

potential customers clienti (mpl) eventuali

potential market mercato (m) potenziale

pound *[money]* sterlina (f)

pound *[weight: 0.45kg]* libbra (f) *[peso]*

pound sterling lira sterlina

power of attorney procura (f)

PR (= public relations) pubbliche relazioni

pre-empt acquistare con diritto di prelazione

pre-financing prefinanziamento (m)

prefer preferire

preference preferenza (f)

preference shares azioni (fpl) privilegiate

preferential preferenziale

preferential creditor creditore (m) privilegiato

preferential duty *or* **preferential tariff** dazio (m) preferenziale

preferred creditor creditore (m) privilegiato

premises locali (mpl)

premium *[extra charge]* maggiorazione (f)

premium *[insurance]* premio (m) di assicurazione

premium *[on lease]* importo (m) aggiuntivo

premium offer offerta (f) premio

premium quality qualità (f) extra

prepack *or* **prepackage** preconfezionare

prepaid pagato in anticipo

prepay pagare in anticipo

prepayment pagamento (m) anticipato

present (adj) *[being there]* presente

present (adj) *[now]* attuale

present (n) *[gift]* regalo (m)

present (v) *[give]* regalare *o* offrire

present (v) *[show a document]* presentare

present a bill for acceptance presentare un effetto (m) per l'accettazione

present a bill for payment presentare un effetto (m) per il pagamento

present value valore (m) attuale

presentation *[exhibition]* presentazione (f)

presentation *[showing a document]* presentazione (f)

press stampa (f)

press conference conferenza (f) stampa

press release comunicato (m) stampa

prestige prestigio (m)

prestige product prodotto (m) di prestigio

pretax profit utile (m) al lordo delle imposte

prevent prevenire

prevention prevenzione (f)

preventive preventivo

previous precedente

price (n) prezzo (m)

price (v) stabilire il prezzo

price ceiling tetto (m) dei prezzi

price control contollo (m) dei prezzi

price controls controlli (mpl) dei prezzi

price differential disparità (f) dei prezzi

price ex quay prezzi (mpl) franco banchina

price ex warehouse prezzi (mpl) franco magazzino

price ex works prezzo (m) franco stabilimento

price label cartellino (m) del prezzo

price list listino (m) prezzi

price range gamma (f) dei prezzi

price reductions diminuzione (f) dei prezzi

price stability stabilità (f) dei prezzi

price tag cartellino (m) del prezzo

price ticket cartellino (m) del prezzo

price war guerra (f) dei prezzi

price-cutting war guerra (f) della diminuzione dei prezzi

price-sensitive product prodotto (m) sensibile ai cambiamenti di prezzo

price/earnings ratio (P/E ratio) rapporto (m) corso/utili

pricing determinazione (f) del prezzo

pricing policy politica (f) della determinazione dei prezzi

primary primario

primary industry industria (f) primaria

prime primo o di prima qualità

prime cost costi (mpl) diretti

prime rate tasso (m) di base

principal (adj) principale

principal (n) [money] capitale (m)

principal (n) [person] capo (m) o direttore (m), direttrice (f)

principle principio (m)

print out stampare

printer [company] tipografia (f)

printer [machine] stampante (f)

printout stampato (m)

prior precedente

private privato

private enterprise iniziativa (f) privata

private limited company società (f) a responsabilità limitata (Srl)

private ownership proprietà (f) privata

private property proprietà (f) privata

private sector settore (m) privato

privatization privatizzazione (f)

privatize privatizzare

pro forma (invoice) (fattura) proforma

pro rata prorata o proporzionale

probation prova (f)

probationary probatorio

problem problema (m)

problem area area (f) problematica

problem solver persona (f) che risolve problemi

problem solving risoluzione (f) di problemi

procedure procedura (f)

proceed procedere

process (n) processo (m)

process (v) [deal with] trattare

process (v) [raw materials] lavorare o trattare

process figures elaborare cifre

processing of information or of statistics elaborazione (f) delle informazioni o delle statistiche

produce (n) [food] prodotti (mpl) agricoli

produce (v) [bring out] produrre o presentare

produce (v) [interest] fruttare o rendere

produce (v) [make] produrre o fabbricare

producer produttore (m)

product prodotto (m)

product advertising pubblicità (f) di un prodotto

product cycle vita (f) ciclica di un prodotto

product design progettazione (f) del prodotto

product development sviluppo (m) del prodotto

product engineer responsabile (m) di un prodotto

product line linea (f) di prodotti

product mix gamma (f) di prodotti

production [making] produzione (f)

production [showing] presentazione (f)

production costs costi (mpl) di produzione

production department ufficio (m) produzioni

production line catena (f) di montaggio

production manager direttore (m) di produzione

production standards standard (m) di produzione

production targets obiettivi (mpl) di produzione

production unit complesso (m) produttivo

productive produttivo
productive discussions
discussione (f) produttiva
productivity produttività (f)
productivity agreement accordo
(m) sulla produttività
productivity bonus premio (m) di
produttività
professional (adj) *[expert]*
professionale
professional (n) *[expert]*
professionista (m) *o* esperto (m)
professional qualifications
qualifiche (fpl) professionali
profit profitto (m) *o* utile (m)
profit after tax utile (m) al netto
delle imposte
profit and loss account conto (m)
profitti e perdite
profit before tax utile (m) al lordo
delle imposte
profit centre centro (m) di profitto
profit margin marginc (m) di utile
profit-making a scopo di lucro
profit-oriented company società
(f) orientata al profitto
profit-sharing compartecipazione
(f) agli utili
profitability *[making a profit]*
redditività (f)
profitability *[ratio of profit to cost]*
coefficiente (m) di redditività
profitable remunerativo *o* proficuo
o redditizio
program a computer programmare
un computer
programme *or* program
programma (m)
programming language
linguaggio (m) di programmazione
progress (n) progresso (m)
progress (v) avanzare *o* fare
progressi
progress chaser addetto (m) al
controllo dell'avanzamento
progress payments pagamento
(m) progressivo

progress report relazione (f)
sull'avanzamento
progressive taxation imposte (fpl)
progressive
prohibitive proibitivo
project *[plan]* progetto (m)
project analysis analisi (f) del
progetto
project manager direttore (m) del
progetto
projected progettato
projected sales vendite (fpl)
previste
promise (n) promessa (f)
promise (v) promettere
promissory note pagherò (m)
promote *[advertise]* promuovere
promote *[give better job]*
promuovere
promote a corporate image
promuovere un'immagine aziendale
promote a new product
pubblicizzare un nuovo prodotto
promotion *[publicity]* promozione
(f)
promotion *[to better job]*
promozione (f)
promotion budget budget (m) per
le spese di promozione
promotion of a product
promozione (f) di un prodotto
promotional promozionale
promotional budget stanziamento
(m) promozionale
prompt sollecito
prompt payment pagamento (m) in
contanti
prompt service servizio (m)
sollecito
proof prova (f)
proportion proporzione (f)
proportional proporzionale
proposal *[insurance]* proposta (f)
(di assicurazione)
proposal *[suggestion]* proposta (f)
propose *[a motion]* proporre
propose to *[do something]*
intendere

proprietary company *[US]* società (f) controllante
proprietor proprietario (m)
proprietress proprietaria (f)
prosecute perseguire (legalmente)
prosecution *[legal action]* procedimento (m) giudiziario
prosecution *[party in legal action]* parte (f) querelante
prosecution counsel avvocato (m) della parte querelante
prospective probabile
prospective buyer possibile acquirente (m)
prospects prospettive (fpl)
prospectus prospetto (m)
protective protettivo
protective tariff tariffa (f) protezionistica
protest (n) *[against something]* protesta (f)
protest (n) *[official document]* protesto (m) (per mancato pagamento)
protest (v) *[against something]* protestare contro qualcosa
protest a bill protestare una cambiale
protest strike sciopero (m) di protesta
provide provvedere
provide for provvedere a
provided that *or* providing a patto che
provision *[condition]* condizione (f) *o* clausola (f)
provision *[money put aside]* accantonamento (m) *o* riserva (f)
provisional provvisorio
provisional budget budget (m) provvisorio
provisional forecast of sales previsione (f) delle vendite provvisoria
proviso clausola (f) condizionale
proxy *[deed]* procura (f) *o* delega (f)
proxy *[person]* mandatario (m)
proxy vote voto (m) per delega

public (adj) pubblico
public finance finanza (f) pubblica
public funds fondi (mpl) pubblici
public holiday festa (f) nazionale
public image immagine (f) pubblica
Public Limited Company (Plc) società (f) di capitali a sottoscrizione pubblica
public opinion opinione (f) pubblica
public relations (PR) pubbliche relazioni (fpl)
public relations department ufficio (m) delle pubbliche relazioni
public relations man addetto (m) alle pubbliche relazioni
public relations officer dirigente (m) delle pubbliche relazioni
public sector settore (m) pubblico
public transport trasporti (mpl) pubblici
publicity pubblicità (f)
publicity budget budget (m) pubblicitario
publicity campaign campagna (f) pubblicitaria
publicity department ufficio (m) della pubblicità
publicity expenditure spese (f) pubblicitarie
publicity manager direttore (m) della pubblicità
publicize pubblicizzare
purchase (n) acquisto (m)
purchase (v) acquistare *o* comperare
purchase ledger libro (m) mastro degli acquisti
purchase order ordine (m) d'acquisto
purchase price prezzo (m) d'acquisto
purchase tax imposta (f) generale sugli acquisti
purchaser compratore (m)
purchasing acquisto (m)
purchasing department ufficio (m) acquisti

purchasing manager direttore (m) dell'ufficio acquisti
purchasing power potere (m) d'acquisto
put (v) *[place]* mettere
put back *[later]* posticipare
put in writing mettere per iscritto
put money down dare soldi come anticipo

quote (v) *[a reference number]* quotare
quote (v) *[estimate costs]* indicare un prezzo *o* quotare
quoted company società (f) quotata in Borsa
quoted shares azioni (fpl) quotate

Qq

qty (= quantity) quantità (f) (q)
qualified *[skilled]* abile *o* qualificato
qualified *[with reservations]* con riserve *o* condizionato
qualify as qualificarsi
quality qualità (f)
quality control controllo (m) di qualità
quality controller controllore (m) della qualità
quality label marchio (m) di qualità
quantity quantità (f)
quantity discount sconto (m) sul quantitativo
quarter *[25%]* quarto (m)
quarter *[three months]* trimestre
quarter day primo giorno (m) del trimestre
quarterly (adj) trimestrale
quarterly (adv) trimestralmente
quay molo (m)
quorum numero (m) minimo legale
quota quota (f)
quotation *[estimate of cost]* quotazione (f)
quote (n) *[estimate of cost]* quotazione (f)

Rr

R&D (= research and development) RS (ricerca e sviluppo)
racketeer organizzatore (m) di attività illegali
racketeering attività (f) illegale
rail ferrovia (f)
rail transport trasporto (m) ferroviario
railroad *[US]* ferrovia (f)
railway *[GB]* ferrovia (f)
railway station stazione (f) ferroviaria
raise (v) *[a question]* sollevare
raise (v) *[increase]* aumentare
raise (v) *[obtain money]* raccogliere fondi
raise an invoice emettere una fattura
rally (n) ripresa (f)
rally (v) rafforzarsi
random accidentale *o* casuale
random check sondaggio (m)
random error errore (m) casuale
random sample campione (m) casuale
random sampling campionatura (f) casuale
range (n) *[series of items]* gamma (f)

range (n) [variation] variazioni (fpl) o scala (f)

range (v) variare o estendersi

rate (n) [amount] tasso (m)

rate (n) [price] quota (f) o tariffa (f) o tasso (m)

rate of exchange tasso (m) di cambio

rate of inflation tasso (m) d'inflazione

rate of production tasso (m) di produzione

rate of return indice (m) di rendimento

ratification ratifica (f)

ratify ratificare

rating quotazione (f)

ratio rapporto (m)

rationalization razionalizzazione (f)

rationalize razionalizzare

raw materials materie (fpl) prime

re-elect rieleggere

re-election rielezione (f)

re-employ riassumere

re-employment riassunzione (f)

re-export (n) riesportazione (f)

re-export (v) riesportare

reach [arrive] raggiungere

reach [come to] arrivare a

reach a decision arrivare ad una decisione

reach an agreement giungere ad un accordo

readjust riadattare

readjustment riassestamento (m)

ready pronto

ready cash pronta cassa (f)

real reale

real estate proprietà (f) immobiliare

real income or real wages reddito (m) effettivo

real-time system sistema (m) in tempo reale

realizable assets attivo (m) esigibile o cespiti (mpl) realizzabili

realization of assets realizzazione (f) di cespiti

realize [sell for money] realizzare

realize [understand] capire o rendersi conto di

realize a project or a plan realizzare un progetto o un piano

realize property or assets realizzare beni o cespiti

reapplication nuova domanda (f)

reappoint ricollocare

reappointment ricollocamento (m)

reassess fare una nuova stima

reassessment nuovo accertamento (m)

rebate [money back] rimborso (m)

rebate [price reduction] riduzione (f) o sconto (m)

receipt [paper] ricevuta (f)

receipt [receiving] ricevimento (m)

receipt book registro (m) delle ricevute

receipts entrate (fpl)

receivable da ricevere

receivables effetti (mpl) attivi

receive ricevere

receiver [liquidator] liquidatore (m)

receiving ricevente

reception portineria (f)

reception clerk portiere (f)

reception desk portineria (f) o banco (m) d'albergo

receptionist receptionist (m)

recession recessione (f)

reciprocal mutuo o reciproco

reciprocal agreement accordo (m) bilaterale

reciprocal trade commercio (m) bilaterale

reciprocity scambio (m)

recognition riconoscimento (m)

recognize a union riconoscere un sindacato

recommend [say something is good] raccomandare

recommend [suggest action] consigliare

recommendation raccomandazione (f)

reconcile riconciliare

reconciliation riconciliazione (f)

reconciliation of accounts riconciliazione (f) dei conti

record (n) *[better than before]* primato (m)

record (n) *[for personnel]* archivi (mpl)

record (n) *[of what has happened]* rapporto (m)

record (v) registrare

record sales *or* record losses *or* record profits vendite (fpl) record *o* perdite (fpl) record *o* utili (mpl) record

record-breaking da primato

recorded delivery raccomandata (f) con ricevuta di ritorno

records documentazione (f) *o* archivio (m)

recoup one's losses rifarsi delle perdite

recover *[get better]* riprendersi

recover *[get something back]* ricuperare

recoverable recuperabile

recovery *[getting better]* ripresa (f)

recovery *[getting something back]* ricupero (m)

rectification rettifica (f)

rectify correggere

recurrent ricorrente

recycle riciclare

recycled paper carta (f) riciclata

red tape lungaggine (f) burocratica

redeem estinguere

redeem a bond rimborsare un'obbligazione

redeem a debt estinguere un debito

redeem a pledge riscattare un pegno

redeemable redimibile

redemption *[of a loan]* riscatto (m) (di un prestito)

redemption date data (f) di rimborso

redevelop adibire ad altro uso

redevelopment progetto (m) edilizio di ricostruzione

redistribute ridistribuire

reduce ridurre

reduce a price ridurre un prezzo

reduce expenditure ridurre le spese

reduced rate tasso (m) ridotto

reduction ribasso (m)

redundancy cassa (f) integrazione

redundant in cassa integrazione

refer *[pass to someone]* sottoporre

refer *[to item]* riferirsi *o* fare riferimento a

reference *[dealing with]* riferimento (m)

reference *[person who reports]* persona che è chiamata a dare referenza

reference *[report on person]* referenze (fpl) *o* attestato (m)

reference number numero (m) di riferimento

refinancing of a loan rifinanziamento (m) di un prestito

refresher course corso (m) d'aggiornamento

refund (n) rimborso (m)

refund (v) rimborsare

refundable rimborsabile

refundable deposit caparra (f) rimborsabile

refunding of a loan conversione (f) di un prestito

refusal rifiuto (m)

refuse (v) rifiutare

regarding riguardante

regardless of senza tener conto di

regional regionale

register (n) *[large book]* registro (m) *o* libro (m) contabile

register (n) *[official list]* registro (m)

register (v) *[at hotel]* firmare il registro

register (v) *[in official list]* iscriversi

register (v) *[letter]* fare una lettera raccomandata

register a company iscrivere una società

register a property iscrivere al catasto una proprietà immobiliare

register a trademark depositare un marchio di fabbrica

register of directors registro (m) degli amministratori

register of shareholders registro (m) degli azionisti o registro (m) delle azioni

registered (adj) registrato

registered letter raccomandata (f)

registered office sede (f) legale

registered trademark marchio (m) di fabbrica depositato

registrar ufficiale (m) di stato civile

Registrar of Companies Conservatore (m) del Registro delle Società

registration registrazione (f)

registration fee tassa (f) di registrazione

registration form modulo (m) d'iscrizione

registration number numero (m) di matricola

registry registrazione (f)

registry office anagrafe (f)

regular *[always at same time]* consueto o fisso

regular *[ordinary]* regolare o normale

regular customer cliente (mf) abituale

regular income reddito (m) fisso

regular size formato (m) normale

regular staff personale (m) di ruolo

regulate *[adjust]* regolare

regulate *[by law]* regolarizzare

regulation regolamento (m)

regulations regolamenti (mpl) o disposizioni (fpl)

reimbursement rimborso (m)

reimbursement of expenses rimborso (m) delle spese

reimport (n) reimportazione (f)

reimport (v) reimportare

reimportation reimportazione (f)

reinsurance riassicurazione (f)

reinsure riassicurare

reinsurer riassicuratore (m)

reinvest reinvestire

reinvestment reinvestimento (m)

reject (n) scarto (m)

reject (v) rifiutare o respingere

rejection rifiuto (m)

relating to relativo a

relations relazioni (fpl)

release (n) rilascio (m)

release (v) *[free]* liberare

release (v) *[make public]* rilasciare

release (v) *[put on the market]* mettere in vendita

release dues liquidare gli ordini arretrati

relevant relativo

reliability attendibilità (f)

reliable attendibile

remain *[be left]* restare

remain *[stay]* restare

remind rammentare

reminder sollecito (m)

remit (n) competenza (f)

remit (v) rimettere

remit by cheque inviare rimessa a mezzo assegno

remittance rimessa (f)

remote control telecomando (m)

removal *[sacking someone]* destituzione (f)

removal *[to new house]* trasloco (m)

remove rimuovere

remunerate retribuire

remuneration retribuzione (f)

render an account presentare un conto

renew rinnovare

renew a bill of exchange *or* **renew a lease** rinnovare una cambiale o rinnovare un contratto d'affitto

renew a subscription rinnovare un abbonamento

renewal rinnovo (m)

renewal notice avviso (m) di rinnovo

renewal of a lease *or* **of a subscription** *or* **of a bill** rinnovo (m) di un contratto d'affitto o un abbonamento o una cambiale

renewal premium premio (m) di rinnovo

rent (n) affitto (m)

rent (v) *[pay money for]* prendere in affitto

rent collector esattore (m) di affitti

rent control blocco (m) degli affitti

rent tribunal sindacato (m) degli inquilini

rent-free esente da canone d'affitto

rental affitto (m)

rental income reddito (m) da affittanze

renunciation rinuncia (f)

reorder (n) nuova ordinazione (f)

reorder (v) riordinare

reorder level livello (m) di riordinazione

reorganization riorganizzazione (f)

reorganize riorganizzare

rep (= representative) rappresentante (m)

repair (n) riparazione (f)

repair (v) aggiustare *o* riparare

repay ripagare

repayable rimborsabile

repayment rimborso (m)

repeat replica (f)

repeat an order ripetere un'ordinazione

repeat order ordinazione (f) rinnovata

replace sostituire

replacement *[item]* sostituzione (f)

replacement *[person]* sostituto (m) *o* rimpiazzo (m)

replacement value valore (m) di sostituzione

reply (n) risposta (f)

reply (v) rispondere

reply coupon coupon (m) con risposta pagata

report (n) rapporto (m)

report (v) riferire

report (v) *[go to a place]* presentarsi

report a loss dichiarare una perdita

report for an interview presentarsi per un colloquio di lavoro

report on the progress of the work *or* of the negotiations relazionare sull'andamento di un lavoro *o* dei negoziati

report to someone dover rispondere a qualcuno

repossess recuperare

represent rappresentare

representative (adj) rappresentativo

representative *[company]* ufficio (m) di rappresentanza

representative *[person]* rappresentante (m) di commercio

repudiate ripudiare

repudiate an agreement rifiutare un accordo

request (n) richiesta (f)

request (v) richiedere *o* domandare

request: on request su richiesta

require *[demand]* richiedere

require *[need]* aver bisogno di

requirements richieste (fpl)

resale rivendita (f)

resale price prezzo (m) di rivendita

rescind rescindere

research (n) ricerca (f)

research (v) documentarsi su *o* fare ricerche

research and development (R & D) ricerca (f) e sviluppo (m) (RS)

research programme programma (m) di ricerca

research worker ricercatore (m), ricercatrice (f)

researcher ricercatore (m), ricercatrice (f)

reservation prenotazione (f)

reserve (n) *[money]* fondo (m)

reserve (n) *[supplies]* riserva (f)

reserve (v) riservare

reserve a room *or* a table *or* a seat riservare una camera *o* un tavolo *o* un posto

reserve currency valuta (f) di riserva

reserve price prezzo (m) minimo

reserves riserve (fpl)
residence residenza (f)
residence permit permesso (m) di soggiorno
resident (adj) residente
resident (n) residente (m) *o* abitante (m)
resign dimettersi
resignation dimissioni (fpl)
resolution risoluzione (f)
resolve decidere
resources risorse (fpl)
respect (v) rispettare
response reazione (f)
responsibilities responsabilità (fpl)
responsibility responsabilità (f)
responsible (for) responsabile di
responsible to someone che deve rispondere a qualcuno
restock rifornire
restocking rifornimento (m)
restraint restrizione (f)
restraint of trade limitazione (f) agli scambi commerciali
restrict limitare
restrict credit limitare il credito
restriction restrizione (f)
restrictive restrittivo
restrictive practices pratiche (fpl) restrittive
restructure ristrutturare
restructuring ristrutturazione (f)
restructuring of a loan rifinanziamento (m) (di un prestito)
restructuring of the company riorganizzazione (f) di una società
result [general] risultato (m)
result from derivare
result in avere come risultato
results [company's profit or loss] risultati (mpl)
resume riprendere
resume negotiations riprendere le trattative
retail (n) vendita (f) al dettaglio
retail (v) [goods] vendere al dettaglio
retail (v) [sell for a price] vendersi a

retail dealer dettagliante (m)
retail goods merce per la vendita al dettaglio
retail outlets punto (m) di vendita al dettaglio
retail price prezzo (m) al dettaglio
retail price index Indice (m) dei prezzi al dettaglio
retailer dettagliante (m)
retailing vendita (f) al dettaglio
retire [from one's job] andare in pensione
retirement pensionamento (m)
retirement age età (f) della pensione
retiring uscente
retrain riaddestrare
retraining riaddestramento (m)
retrenchment riduzione (f) delle spese
retrieval reperimento (m)
retrieval system sistema (m) di recupero delle informazioni
retrieve reperire
retroactive retroattivo
retroactive pay rise aumento (m) di paga retroattivo
return (n) [declaration] dichiarazione (f)
return (n) [going back] ritorno (m)
return (n) [profit] profitto (m) *o* guadagno (m)
return (n) [sending back] restituzione (f)
return (v) [declare] dichiarare
return (v) [send back] respingere *o* mandare indietro
return a letter to sender rimandare una lettera al mittente
return address indirizzo (m) del mittente
return on investment (ROI) reddito (m) sugli investimenti
returnable restituibile
returned empties vuoti (mpl) a rendere
returns [profits] incassi (mpl)
returns [unsold goods] merce (f) non venduta
revaluation rivalutazione (f)

revalue rivalutare

revenue reddito (m)

revenue accounts conto (m) delle entrate

revenue from advertising ricavo (m) dalla pubblicità

reversal inversione (f)

reverse (adj) inverso

reverse (v) invertire

reverse charge call telefonata (f) a carico del ricevente

reverse takeover acquisizione (f) di controllo inversa

reverse the charges addebitare una telefonata al ricevente

revise riesaminare

revoke revocare

revolving credit credito (m) rinnovabile automaticamente

revolving credit credito (m) rinnovabile automaticamente

rider clausola (f) addizionale

right (adj) *[not left]* destro

right (adj) *[not wrong]* corretto

right (n) *[legal title]* diritto (m)

right of veto diritto (m) di veto

right of way diritto (m) di precedenza

right-hand man uomo (m) di fiducia

rightful giusto

rightful claimant pretendente (m) di diritto

rightful owner proprietario (m) legittimo

rights issue emissione (f) di diritti

rise (n) *[increase]* aumento (m)

rise (n) *[salary]* aumento (m)

rise (v) aumentare

risk (n) rischio (m)

risk (v) *[money]* rischiare

risk capital capitale (m) di rischio

risk premium premio (m) di rischio

risk-free investment investimento (m) privo di rischio

risky rischioso

rival company società (f) rivale

road strada (f)

road haulage trasporto (m) su strada (di merci)

road haulier trasportatore (m) su strada

road tax tassa (f) di circolazione

road transport trasporto (m) su strada

rock-bottom prices prezzo (m) ridottissimo

ROI (= return on investment) reddito (m) sugli investimenti

roll on/roll off ferry roll on/roll off *o* traghetto (m) per automezzi

rolling plan piano (m) continuo

room *[general]* stanza (f)

room *[hotel]* camera (f)

room *[space]* spazio (m)

room reservations prenotazioni (fpl) di camera

room service servizio (m) in camera

rough approssimativo

rough calculation calcolo (m) approssimativo

rough draft bozza (f)

rough estimate valutazione (f) approssimativa

round down arrotondare diminuendo

round up arrotondare aumentando

routine (adj) abituale

routine (n) routine (f) *o* ordinaria amministrazione (f)

routine call telefonata (f) di routine

routine work lavoro (m) di routine

royalty diritto (m) di concessione

rubber check *[US]* assegno (m) a vuoto

rule (n) norma (f)

rule (v) *[be in force]* essere in vigore

rule (v) *[give decision]* decretare

ruling (adj) corrente

ruling (n) decreto (m)

run (n) *[regular route]* percorso (m)

run (n) *[work routine]* serie (f) *o* sequela (f)

run (v) *[be in force]* essere valido *o* entrare in vigore

run (v) *[buses, trains]* fare servizio

run (v) *[manage]* dirigere
run (v) *[work machine]* far
funzionare
run a risk correre un rischio
run into debt contrarre debiti
run out of esaurire
running (n) *[of machine]* marcia
(f) *o* funzionamento (m)
**running costs *or* running
expenses** spese (fpl) d'esercizio *o*
costi (mpl) di gestione di un'azienda
running total totale (m) corrente
rush (n) ressa (f)
rush (v) affrettarsi
rush hour ora (f) di punta
rush job lavoro (m) urgente
rush order ordinazione (f) urgente

Ss

sack someone licenziare qualcuno
safe (adj) sicuro *o* prudente
safe (n) cassaforte (f)
safe deposit deposito (m) in
cassetta di sicurezza
safe investment investimento (m)
sicuro
safeguard salvaguardia (f)
safety sicurezza (f)
safety measures misure (fpl) di
sicurezza
safety precautions misure (fpl) di
sicurezza
safety regulations norme (fpl) di
sicurezza
salaried stipendiato
salary stipendio (m)
salary cheque assegno (m) dello
stipendio
salary review revisione (f) dello
stipendio

sale (n) *[at a low price]* saldo (m)
sale (n) *[selling]* vendita (f)
sale by auction vendita (f) all'asta
sale *or* return venduto con
possibilità di resa
saleability vendibilità (f)
saleable vendibile
sales vendite (fpl) *o* fatturato (m)
sales analysis analisi (f) delle
vendite
sales book libro (m) vendite
sales budget previsione (f) di
vendita
sales campaign campagna (f) di
vendite
sales chart grafico (m) delle
vendite
sales clerk addetto (m) alle
vendite
sales conference raduno (m) dei
venditori
sales curve curva (f) delle vendite
sales department ufficio (m)
vendite
sales executive dirigente (m) delle
vendite
sales figures volume (m) d'affari
sales force forza (f) vendita *o*
personale (m) addetto alle vendite
sales forecast previsione (f) di
vendita
sales ledger partitario (m) delle
vendite
sales ledger clerk impiegato (m)
addetto al partitario delle vendite
sales literature materiale (m)
illustrativo delle vendite
sales manager direttore (m)
commerciale
sales people venditori (mpl)
sales pitch imbonimento (m)
sales promotion promozione (f)
delle vendite
sales receipt ricevuta (f) (di
vendita)
sales representative
rappresentante (m)
sales revenue fatturato (m)
sales target obiettivo (m) di
vendita

sales tax imposta (f) sul volume di affari

sales team personale (m) addetto alle vendite

sales volume volume (m) delle vendite

salesman *[in shop]* commesso (m)

salesman *[representative]* rappresentante (m) (di commercio)

salvage (n) *[action]* recupero (m)

salvage (n) *[things saved]* materiale (m) di recupero

salvage (v) salvare o recuperare

salvage vessel nave (f) di salvataggio

sample (n) *[group]* campione (m)

sample (n) *[part]* campione (m) o saggio (m)

sample (v) *[ask questions]* fare un sondaggio

sample (v) *[test]* campionare

sampling *[statistics]* campionamento (m)

sampling *[testing]* campionamento (m)

satisfaction soddisfazione (f)

satisfy *[customer]* soddisfare

satisfy a demand soddisfare una richiesta

saturate saturare

saturate the market rendere saturo il mercato

saturation saturazione (f)

save (v) *[money]* risparmiare

save (v) *[not waste]* risparmiare o economizzare

save (v) *[on computer]* salvare su disco

save on economizzare

save up mettere da parte denaro

savings risparmi (mpl)

savings account conto (m) di risparmio

scale *[system]* scala (f)

scale down ridurre proporzionalmente

scale of charges tariffa (f)

scale up aumentare proporzionalmente

scarcity value valore alto dettato dalla scarsità di fornitura

scheduled flight volo (m) di linea

scheduling elencazione (f)

screen candidates selezionare candidati

scrip documento (m) provvisorio

scrip issue emissione (f) di certificati azionari provvisori

seal (n) sigillo (m)

seal (v) *[attach a seal]* sigillare

seal (v) *[envelope]* chiudere o incollare

sealed envelope busta (f) chiusa

sealed tenders offerta (f) in busta chiusa

season *[time for something]* stagione (f) o periodo (m)

season *[time of year]* stagione (f)

season ticket tessera (f) (di abbonamento ferroviario)

seasonal stagionale o periodico

seasonal adjustments adattamento (m) stagionale

seasonal demand richiesta (f) stagionale

seasonal variations variazioni (fpl) stagionali

seasonally adjusted figures cifre (fpl) destagionalizzate

second (adj) secondo

second (v) *[member of staff]* trasferire o distaccare

second quarter secondo trimestre (m)

second-class seconda classe (sui mezzi di trasporto) o seconda categoria (di merci)

secondary industry industria (f) secondaria

secondhand usato o di seconda mano

seconds prodotti (mpl) di seconda qualità

secret (adj) segreto

secret (n) segreto (m)

secretarial college scuola (f) per segretarie d'azienda

secretary segretaria/o (fm)

secretary *[company official]* segretario (m) del consiglio di amministrazione

secretary *[government minister]* ministro (m)

sector settore (m)

secure funds procurarsi fondi

secure investment investimento (m) garantito

secure job lavoro (m) stabile

secured creditor creditore (m) privilegiato

secured debts debiti (mpl) privilegiati

secured loan mutuo (m) garantito

securities titoli (mpl)

security *[being safe]* sicurezza (f)

security *[guarantee]* garanzia (f)

security guard guardia (f) giurata

security of employment sicurezza (f) dell'impiego

security of tenure sicurezza (f) di possesso

see-safe vendita (f) con possibilità di resa

seize sequestrare

seizure sequestro (m)

selection selezione (f)

selection procedure procedura (f) di selezione

self-employed che lavora in proprio

self-financing (adj) che può autofinanziarsi

self-financing (n) autofinanziamento (m)

self-regulation autoregolazione (f)

self-regulatory autoregolatore

sell vendere

sell forward vendere a termine

sell off svendere

sell out *[all stock]* vendere tutto

sell out *[sell one's business]* vendere (un impresa)

sell-by date data (f) di scadenza

seller venditore (m)

seller's market mercato (m) favorevole ai venditori

selling (n) vendita (f)

selling price prezzo (m) di vendita

semi-finished products prodotti (mpl) semilavorati

semi-skilled workers lavoratori (mpl) parzialmente qualificati

send inviare

send a package by airmail spedire un pacco per via aerea

send a package by surface mail spedire un pacco per posta ordinaria

send a shipment by sea mandare un carico per mare

send an invoice by post spedire una fattura (per posta)

sender mittente (m)

senior anziano *o* piu vecchio

senior manager *or* **senior executive** dirigente (m) in capo *o* direttore (m)

senior partner socio (m) anziano

separate (adj) separato

separate (v) separare

sequester *or* **sequestrate** sequestrare

sequestration sequestro (m)

sequestrator sequestratario (m)

serial number numero (m) di serie

serve servire

serve a customer servire un cliente

service (n) *[business which helps]* società (f) di servizi

service (n) *[dealing with customers]* servizio (m)

service (n) *[of machine]* revisione (f) *o* manutenzione (f)

service (n) *[regular working]* servizio (m)

service (n) *[working for a company]* servizio (m)

service (v) *[a machine]* revisionare

service a debt pagare un debito

service centre centro (m) assistenza

service charge percentuale (f) per il servizio

service department ufficio (m) assistenza

service manual manuale (m) di manutenzione

set (adj) fisso

set (n) serie (f)

set (v) fissare
set against contrapporre
set price prezzo (m) stabilito
set targets fissare obiettivi
set up a company costituire una società (f)
set up in business mettersi in affari
setback battuta (f) d'arresto
settle [an invoice] liquidare o pagare una fattura
settle [arrange things] sistemare
settle a claim definire una domanda d'indennizzo
settle an account saldare un conto
settlement [agreement] accordo (m)
settlement [payment] pagamento (m)
setup [company] organizzazione (f)
setup [organization] organizzazione (f)
share (n) [in a company] azione (f)
share (v) [divide among] spartire o dividere
share (v) [use with someone] dividere
share an office spartire un ufficio
share capital capitale (m) sociale
share certificate certificato (m) azionario
share issue emissione (f) azionaria
shareholder azionista (m)
shareholding partecipazione (f) azionaria
sharp practice pratica (f) spregiudicata
sheet of paper foglio (m) di carta
shelf scaffale (m)
shelf filler persona addetta al rifornimento degli scaffali
shelf life of a product periodo (m) medio di permanenza di un prodotto
shell company società (f) esistente solo di nome
shelter riparo (m)
shelve accantonare o differire

shelving [postponing] accantonamento (m)
shelving [shelves] scaffalatura (f)
shift (n) [change] cambiamento (m)
shift (n) [team of workers] turno (m) (di lavoro)
shift key tasto (m) delle maiuscole
shift work lavoro (m) con turni
ship (n) nave (f)
ship (v) trasportare o spedire
ship broker agente (m) marittimo
shipment trasporto (m) marittimo
shipper spedizioniere (m) marittimo
shipping spedizione (f) marittima
shipping agent spedizioniere (m) marittimo
shipping charges or shipping costs costi (mpl) per la spedizione marittima
shipping clerk impiegato (m) di spedizioniere
shipping company società (f) di navigazione
shipping instructions istruzioni (fpl) per la spedizione
shipping line linea (f) di navigazione
shipping note bolla (f) di spedizione
shop negozio (m)
shop around confrontare i prezzi
shop assistant commesso/a (mf) di negozio
shop window vetrina (f)
shop-soiled articolo (m) sciupato per prolungata esposizione
shopkeeper negoziante (m)
shoplifter taccheggiatore (m)
shoplifting taccheggiare
shopper acquirente (mf) o cliente (mf)
shopping [action] spesa (f)
shopping [goods bought] acquisti (mpl)
shopping arcade galleria (f) (con negozi) o centro (m) commerciale
shopping centre centro (m) commerciale

shopping mall galleria (f) (con negozi) *o* centro (m) commerciale

shopping precinct zona (f) commerciale

short credit credito (m) a breve termine

short of a meno di

short-dated bills effetti (mpl) a breve termine

short-term (adj) a breve *o* a breve termine

short-term contract contratto (m) a breve termine

short-term credit credito (m) a breve

short-term debts indebitamento (m) a breve

short-term loan mutuo (m) a breve scadenza

shortage scarsità (f)

shortfall ammanco (m)

shortlist (n) lista (f) ristretta (di candidati)

shortlist (v) iscrivere qualcuno in una rosa di candidati

show (n) *[exhibition]* mostra (f)

show (v) mostrare

show a profit indicare un profitto

showcase bacheca (f)

showroom sala (f) di esposizione

shrink-wrapped imballato con metodo termocontrattile

shrink-wrapping imballaggio (m) termocontrattile

shrinkage restringimento (m) *o* deprezzamento (m)

shut (adj) chiuso

shut (v) chiudere

side lato (m)

sideline attività (f) secondaria

sight vista (f)

sight draft tratta (f) a vista

sign (n) insegna (f)

sign (v) firmare

sign a cheque firmare un assegno

sign a contract firmare un contratto

signatory firmatario (m)

signature firma (f)

simple interest interesse (m) semplice

single singolo

Single European Market Mercato Europeo Unico

sister company società (f) sorella

sister ship nave (f) gemella

sit-down protest protesta (f) con occupazione

sit-down strike sciopero (m) con occupazione

site luogo (m)

site engineer ingegnere (m) edile

sitting tenant affittuario (m) occupante

situated situato

situation *[place]* posizione (f) *o* collocazione (f)

situation *[state of affairs]* situazione (f)

situations vacant offerte (fpl) d'impiego

size dimensione (f)

skeleton staff personale (m) ridotto al minimo

skill abilità (f) tecnica

skilled specializzato

skilled labour *or* **skilled workers** manodopera (f) qualificata

slack lento *o* stagnante

slash prices *or* **credit terms** tagliare i prezzi *o* le condizioni di credito

sleeping partner socio (m) accomandante

slip (n) *[mistake]* errore (m)

slip (n) *[piece of paper]* foglietto (m)

slow lento

slow down rallentare

slow payer pagatore (m) tardivo

slowdown rallentamento (m)

slump (n) *[depression]* crollo (m) *o* crisi (f) economica

slump (n) *[rapid fall]* brusca caduta (f)

slump (v) crollare *o* subire una forte flessione

slump in sales discesa (f) delle vendite

small piccolo
small ads piccoli annunci (mpl)
small businesses piccole imprese (fpl)
small businessman piccolo affarista/uomo d'affari
small change moneta (f) spicciola
small-scale in scala (f) ridotta
small-scale enterprise iniziativa (f) su scala ridotta
soar salire alle stelle
social sociale
social costs costi (mpl) sociali
social security previdenza (f) sociale
society [club] associazione (f) o circolo (m)
society [general] società (f)
socio-economic groups gruppi (mpl) socioeconomici
soft currency valuta (f) debole
soft loan prestito (m) agevolato
soft sell tecnica (f) di vendita basata sulla persuasione
software software (m)
sole solo o unico
sole agency rappresentanza (f) esclusiva
sole agent rappresentante (m) esclusivo
sole owner unico proprietario (m)
sole trader commerciante (m) in proprio
solicit orders sollecitare un'ordinazione
solicitor procuratore (m) legale
solution soluzione (f)
solve a problem risolvere un problema
solvency solvibilità (f)
solvent (adj) solvente
source of income fonte (f) di reddito
spare part pezzo (m) di ricambio
spare time tempo (m) libero
special speciale
special drawing rights (SDRs) diritti (mpl) speciali di prelievo (DSP)
special offer offerta (f) speciale

specialist specialista (m)
specialization specializzazione (f)
specialize essere specializzato
specification specifica (f)
specify specificare
speech of thanks discorso (m) di ringraziamento
spend [money] spendere
spend [time] passare il tempo a
spending money denaro (m) per le piccole spese
spending power potere (m) d'acquisto
spinoff sottoprodotto (m)
spoil rovinare o viziare
sponsor (n) sponsor (m) o garante (m)
sponsor (v) garantire o sponsorizzare o patrocinare
sponsorship sponsorizzazione (f) o avallo (m)
spot [place] posto (m) o luogo (m)
spot cash pagamento (m) in contanti
spot price prezzo (m) per merce pronta
spot purchase transazione (f) a pronti
spread a risk ripartire un rischio
spreadsheet [computer] foglio (m) di calcolo elettronico
stability stabilità (f)
stabilization stabilizzazione (f)
stabilize stabilizzare
stable fermo o stabile
stable currency moneta (f) stabile
stable economy economia (f) solida
stable exchange rate tasso (m) di cambio stabile
stable prices prezzi (mpl) stabili
staff (n) personale (m)
staff (v) fornire di personale
staff appointment nomina (f) del personale
staff meeting assemblea (f) del personale
stage (n) stadio (m)
stage (v) [organize] organizzare
stage a recovery riprendersi

staged payments pagamenti (mpl) scaglionati

stagger scaglionare

stagnant stagnante

stagnation ristagno (m)

stamp (n) [device] timbro (m)

stamp (n) [post] francobollo (m)

stamp (v) [letter] affrancare o mettere francobolli

stamp (v) [mark] timbrare

stamp duty imposta (f) di bollo

stand (n) [at exhibition] stand (m)

stand down ritirare la propria candidatura

stand security for avallare

stand surety for someone garantire per qualcuno

standard (adj) standard

standard (n) norma (f)

standard letter lettera (f) standard

standard rate (of tax) aliquota (f) d'imposta base

standardization standardizzazione (f)

standardize standardizzare

standby arrangements accordo (m) creditizio di sostegno

standby credit credito (m) di appoggio

standby ticket biglietto (m) aereo privo di prenotazione

standing legittimazione (f)

standing order ordine (m) permanente

staple (n) punto (m) metallico

staple (v) cucire con punti metallici o graffare

staple industry industria (f) di base

staple papers together graffare insieme fogli

staple product prodotti (mpl) essenziali

stapler cucitrice (f) o graffatrice (f)

start (n) avvio (m)

start (v) iniziare o cominciare

start-up avviamento (m)

start-up costs spese (fpl) di avviamento

starting (adj) iniziale

starting date data (f) d'inizio

starting point punto (m) di partenza

starting salary stipendio (m) iniziale

state (n) [condition] condizione (f) o stato (m)

state (n) [country] stato (m) o nazione (f)

state (v) dichiarare o precisare

state-of-the-art all'avanguardia

statement rendiconto (m)

statement of account estratto (m) conto

statement of expenses rendiconto (m) delle spese

station [train] stazione (f)

statistical statistico

statistical analysis analisi (f) statistica

statistician esperto (m) di statistica

statistics statistica (f)

status condizione (f) sociale

status inquiry informazioni (fpl) commerciali

status symbol simbolo (m) di successo

statute of limitations prescrizione (f)

statutory statutario

statutory holiday giorno (m) festivo legale

stay (n) [time] permanenza (f)

stay (v) fermarsi

stay of execution sospensiva (f)

steadiness saldezza (f)

sterling lira (f) sterlina

stevedore stivatore (m) o scaricatore (m) (di porto)

stiff competition concorrenza (f) dura

stimulate the economy stimolare l'economia

stimulus stimolo (m)

stipulat e stipulare

stipulation stipula (f)

stock (adj) *[normal]* standard *o* usuale

stock (n) *[goods]* stock (m) *o* scorte (fpl)

stock (v) *[goods]* rifornire *o* tenere

stock code codice (m) di magazzino

stock control controllo (m) delle scorte

stock controller persona (f) addetta al controllo delle scorte

stock exchange Borsa (f) *o* Borsa Valori

stock level livello (m) delle scorte

stock list inventario (m)

stock market mercato (m) azionario

stock market valuation valutazione (f) del mercato azionario

stock of raw materials riserva (f) di materia prima

stock size misura (f) *o* taglia (f) standard

stock turnover rotazione (f) delle scorte

stock up immagazzinare

stock valuation valutazione (f) delle scorte

stockbroker agente (m) di cambio

stockbroking mediazione (f) di cambio

stockist rivenditore (m)

stocklist inventario (m)

stockpile (n) scorta (f) (di materie prime)

stockpile (v) costruire riserve *o* stoccare

stockroom magazzino (m)

stocktaking inventario (m)

stocktaking sale saldi (mpl) per inventario

stop (n) stop (m) *o* fine (f) *o* arresto (m)

stop (v) *[doing something]* cessare *o* finire

stop a cheque bloccare un assegno

stop an account bloccare un conto

stop payments sospendere i pagamenti

stoppage *[act of stopping]* sospensione (f)

stoppage of payments sospensione (f) dei pagamenti

storage (n) *[computer]* memoria (f)

storage (n) *[cost]* spese (fpl) di immagazzinamento

storage (n) *[in warehouse]* magazzinaggio (m) *o* deposito (m)

storage capacity capienza (f) di magazzino

storage facilities impianti (m) di magazzinaggio

storage unit impianto (m) di magazzinaggio

store (n) *[items kept]* riserva (f)

store (n) *[large shop]* negozio (m) *o* grande magazzino (m)

store (n) *[place where goods are kept]* deposito (m) *o* magazzino (m)

store (v) *[keep for future]* mettere in serbo

store (v) *[keep in warehouse]* immagazzinare

storeroom magazzino (m)

storm damage danni (mpl) causati da un temporale

straight line depreciation ammortamento (m) a quote costanti

strategic strategico

strategic planning pianificazione (f) strategica

strategy strategia (f)

street directory guida (f) stradale

strike (n) sciopero (m)

strike (v) scioperare

striker scioperante (m)

strong forte

strong currency divisa (f) forte

structural strutturale

structural adjustment correzione (f) strutturale

structural unemployment disoccupazione (f) strutturale

structure (n) struttura (f)

structure (v) *[arrange]* strutturare
study (n) studio (m)
study (v) studiare
sub judice in contenzioso
subcontract (n) subappalto (m)
subcontract (v) dare in subappalto
subcontractor subappaltatore (m)
subject to soggetto a
sublease (n) subaffitto (m)
sublease (v) subaffittare
sublessee subaffittuario (m)
sublessor subaffittante (m)
sublet subaffittare
subsidiary (adj) sussidiario
subsidiary (n) filiale (f)
subsidiary company affiliata (f)
subsidize sovvenzionare
subsidy sussidio (m) *o*
sovvenzione (f)
subtotal totale (m) parziale
subvention sovvenzione (f)
succeed *[do as planned]* riuscire
succeed *[do well]* riuscire *o* avere
successo
succeed *[follow someone]*
succedere
success successo (m)
successful di successo
successful bidder miglior
offerente (m)
sue citare *o* intentare causa
suffer damage subire un danno
sufficient sufficiente
sum *[of money]* somma (f)
sum *[total]* totale (m)
summons citazione (f) in giudizio
sundries articoli (mpl) vari
sundry items partite (fpl) varie
superior (adj) *[better quality]*
superiore
superior (n) *[person]* superiore
(m)
supermarket supermercato (m)
superstore grande supermercato
(m) *o* ipermercato (m)
supervise sorvegliare
supervision supervisione (f) *o*
vigilanza (f)
supervisor supervisore (m)

supervisory ispettivo *o* di
supervisione
supplementary supplementare
supplier fornitore (m)
supply (n) *[action]* fornitura (f)
supply (n) *[stock of goods]*
provvista (f)
supply (v) fornire *o*
approvvigionare
supply and demand offerta (f) e
domanda (f)
supply price prezzo (m) d'offerta
supply side economics economia
(f) dell'offerta
support price prezzo (m) di
sostegno
surcharge sovrapprezzo (m)
surety (n) *[person]* garante (m)
surety (n) *[security]* garanzia (f)
surface mail posta (f) ordinaria
surface transport trasporto (m) di
superficie
surplus surplus (m) *o* sovrappiù
(m)
surrender (n) *[insurance policy]*
riscatto (m)
surrender (v) *[insurance]*
riscattare
surrender a policy riscattare una
polizza
surrender value valore (m) di
riscatto
survey (n) *[examination]* indagine
(f) *o* studio (m)
survey (n) *[general report]* quadro
(m) generale
survey (v) *[inspect]* esaminare *o*
ispezionare
surveyor perito (m)
suspend sospendere
suspension sospensione (f)
suspension of deliveries
cessazione (f) delle consegne
suspension of payments
sospensione (f) dei pagamenti
swap (n) scambio (m)
swap (v) scambiare
swatch ritaglio (m) (di campioni)
switch (v) *[change]* cambiare

switch over to passare a
switchboard centralino (m)
swop (= swap) scambiare
sympathy strike sciopero (m) di
solidarietà
synergy sinergia (f)
system sistema (m)
systems analysis analisi (f) dei
sistemi
systems analyst analista (m) dei
sistemi

Tt

tabulate tabulare
tabulation tabulazione (f)
tabulator tabulatore (m)
tachograph tachigrafo (m)
tacit agreement tacito accordo (m)
tacit approval tacito consenso (m)
take (n) [money received] incasso
(m)
take (v) [need] volere *o* richiedere
take (v) [receive money]
guadagnare
take a call prendere una telefonata
take a risk correre un rischio
take action agire
take legal action intentare azione
legale
take legal advice ricorrere a
consulenza legale
take note prendere nota
take off [deduct] dedurre *o* fare
uno sconto di
take off [plane] decollare
take off [rise fast] decollare
take on freight prendere un carico
(m) a bordo
take on more staff assumere altro
personale

take out a policy sottoscrivere una
polizza
take over [from someone else]
succedere
take place avere luogo
take someone to court portare
qualcuno in tribunale
take stock fare l'inventario
take the initiative prendere
l'iniziativa
take the soft option scegliere la
strada più facile
take time off work prendersi giorni
di ferie
take up an option esercitare il
diritto d'opzione
takeover acquisizione (f) di
controllo
takeover bid offerta (f) pubblica
d'acquisto
takeover target obiettivo (m) di
rilevamento
takings incassi (mpl)
tangible tangibile
tangible assets beni (mpl) reali
tanker petroliera (f)
tare tara (f)
target (n) obiettivo (m)
target (v) stabilire come obiettivo
target market mercato (m)
prescelto
tariff [price] tariffa (f)
tariff barriers barriere (fpl)
tariffarie
tax (n) tassa (f) *o* imposta (f)
tax (v) tassare *o* gravare d'imposta
tax adjustments adeguamento (m)
fiscale
tax allowance riduzione (f)
d'imposta
tax assessment accertamento (m)
fiscale
tax avoidance evasione (f) fiscale
tax code codice (m) fiscale
tax collection riscossione (f) delle
imposte
tax collector esattore (m) delle
imposte
tax concession concessione (f)
fiscale

tax consultant consulente (m) fiscale

tax credit credito (m) d'imposta

tax deducted at source imposta (f) trattenuta alla fonte

tax deductions *[taken from salary to pay tax]* detrazioni (fpl) d'imposta

tax evasion evasione (f) fiscale

tax exemption esenzione (f) fiscale

tax form modulo (m) delle tasse

tax haven rifugio (m) fiscale

tax inspector ispettore (m) delle tasse

tax loophole sotterfugio (m) fiscale

tax offence infrazione (f) fiscale

tax paid imposta (f) pagata

tax rate aliquota (f) d'imposta

tax reductions riduzioni (fpl) d'imposta

tax relief agevolazione (f) fiscale

tax return *or* **tax declaration** denuncia (f) dei redditi

tax shelter scappatoia (f) fiscale

tax system sistema (m) tributario

tax year anno (m) fiscale

tax-deductible detraibile dal reddito imponibile

tax-exempt esentasse

tax-free esente da tasse

taxable tassabile

taxable income reddito (m) imponibile

taxation tassazione (f)

taxpayer contribuente (m)

telephone (n) telefono (m)

telephone (v) telefonare

telephone book elenco (m) telefonico

telephone call chiamata (f) telefonica

telephone directory elenco (m) telefonico

telephone exchange centralino (m) telefonico

telephone line linea (f) telefonica

telephone number numero (m) telefonico *o* numero di telefono

telephone subscriber abbonato (m) al telefono

telephone switchboard centralino (m) telefonico

telephonist telefonista (mf)

telesales vendite (fpl) per telefono

telex (n) telescrivente (f) *o* telex (m)

teller sportellista (m)

temp (n) segretaria (f) temporanea

temp agency agenzia (f) che fornisce personale temporaneo

temporary employment lavoro (m) a contratto a termine

temporary staff personale (m) avventizio

tenancy *[agreement]* contratto (m) di locazione

tenancy *[period]* locazione (f)

tenant inquilino (m)

tender (n) *[offer to work]* licitazione (f) *o* offerta (f) d'appalto

tender for a contract fare offerta per un contratto d'appalto

tenderer offerente (m)

tendering licitazione (f)

tenure *[right]* diritto (m) di possesso

tenure *[time]* durata (f) in carica

term *[part of academic year]* trimestre (m) scolastico

term *[time of validity]* periodo (m) *o* durata (f)

term insurance assicurazione (f) temporanea

term loan prestito (m) a termine

terminal (adj) *[at the end]* terminale

terminal (n) *[airport]* terminal (m)

terminal bonus premio (m) (d'assicurazione) finale

terminate terminare

terminate an agreement rescindere un accordo

termination termine (m)

termination clause clausola (f) di rescissione

terms condizioni (fpl)

terms of employment condizioni (fpl) di impiego

terms of payment condizioni (fpl) di pagamento
terms of reference termini (mpl) stabiliti
terms of sale condizioni (fpl) di vendita
territory *[of salesman]* territorio (m)
tertiary industry industria (f) terziaria
tertiary sector settore (m) terziario
test (n) prova (f)
test (v) provare
theft furto (m)
third party terza persona (f)
third quarter terzo trimestre (m)
third-party insurance assicurazione (f) per danni verso terzi
threshold soglia (f)
threshold agreement accordo (m) di indicizzazione
threshold price prezzo (m) d'entrata
throughput produttività (f)
tie-up *[link]* collegamento (m)
tight money denaro (m) scarso
tighten up on restringere
till (n) cassa (f)
time and motion study studio (m) dei tempi e dei movimenti
time deposit deposito (m) a termine
time limit termine (m) ultimo
time limitation perenzione (f)
time rate tariffa (f) a tempo
time scale scala (f) temporale
time: on time puntuale *o* in orario
timetable (n) *[appointments]* programma (m)
timetable (n) *[trains, etc.]* orario (m)
timetable (v) programmare
timing scelta (f) del momento opportuno
tip (n) *[advice]* informazione (f) riservata
tip (n) *[money]* mancia (f)
tip (v) *[give money]* dare la mancia a

tip (v) *[say what might happen]* pronosticare
TIR (= Transports Internationaux Routiers) Trasporto Internazionale su Strada
token simbolo (m)
token charge costo (m) simbolico
token payment pagamento (m) simbolico
toll pedaggio (m)
toll free *[US]* esente da pedaggio
toll free number *[US]* servizio (m) telefonico gratuito
ton tonnellata (f)
tonnage tonnellaggio (m)
tonne tonnellata (f)
tool up attrezzare (una fabbrica)
top (adj) più alto *o* migliore
top (n) *[highest point]* cima (f) *o* vetta (f)
top (n) *[upper surface]* parte (f) superiore
top (v) *[go higher than]* superare
top management direzione (f) al vertice
top quality qualità (f) superiore
top-selling che è in testa alle vendite
total (adj) totale *o* globale
total (n) totale (m)
total (v) ammontare a
total amount importo (m) totale
total assets totale (m) delle attività
total cost costo (m) totale
total expenditure spesa (f) totale
total income reddito (m) totale
total invoice value valore (m) totale della fattura
total output produzione (f) totale
total revenue reddito (m) complessivo
track record curricolo (m)
trade (n) *[business]* commercio (m)
trade (v) commerciare *o* trafficare
trade agreement trattato (m) commerciale
trade association associazione (f) commerciale
trade cycle ciclo (m) economico

trade deficit *or* **trade gap** deficit (m) della bilancia commerciale
trade description descrizione (f) commerciale
trade directory annuario (m) commerciale
trade discount sconto (m) ai rivenditori
trade fair fiera (f) campionaria
trade in *[buy and sell]* commerciare in *o* trafficare in
trade in *[give in old item for new]* farsi ritirare l'usato
trade journal giornale (m) di categoria
trade magazine rivista (f) di categoria
trade mission missione (f) commerciale
trade price prezzo (m) al rivenditore
trade terms sconti (mpl) al rivenditore
trade union sindacato (m)
trade unionist sindacalista (m)
trade-in *[old item in exchange]* permuta (f)
trade-in price prezzo (m) di permuta
trademark *or* **trade name** marchio (m)
trader commerciante (m)
trading commerciale
trading company società (f) commerciale
trading loss perdita (f) d'esercizio
trading partner partner (m) commerciale
trading profit utile (m) d'esercizio
train (n) treno (m)
train (v) *[learn]* fare pratica
train (v) *[teach]* istruire
trainee tirocinante (m)
traineeship apprendistato (m)
training formazione (f)
training levy contributo (m) aziendale per l'addestramento
training officer funzionario (m) addetto all'addestramento
transact business fare affari

transaction transazione (f)
transfer (n) trasferimento (m)
transfer (v) *[move to new place]* trasferire
transfer of funds trasferimento (m) di capitali
transferable trasferibile
transferred charge call telefonata (f) a carico del ricevente
transit transito (m)
transit lounge sala (f) transiti
transit visa visto (m) consolare di transito
translate tradurre
translation traduzione (f)
translation bureau ufficio (m) traduzioni
translator traduttore (m), traduttrice (f)
transport (n) trasporto (m)
transport (v) trasportare
transport facilities servizi (mpl) di trasporto
treasury tesoreria (f)
treble triplo
trend andamento (m)
trial *[court case]* processo (m)
trial *[test of product]* prova (f)
trial and error metodo (m) per tentativi
trial balance bilancio (m) di verifica
trial period periodo (m) di prova
trial sample campione (m) di prova
triple (adj) triplo
triple (v) triplicare
triplicate: in triplicate in triplice copia
troubleshooter mediatore (m)
truck *[lorry]* camion (m)
truck *[railway wagon]* carro (m) merci
trucker camionista (m)
trucking trasporto (m) mediante autocarro
true copy copia (f) autentica
trust company società (f) fiduciaria
turn down rifiutare

turn over (v) *[make sales]* avere un giro d'affari di
turnkey operation operazione (f) chiavi in mano
turnkey operator costruttore (m) chiavi in mano
turnover *[of staff]* ricambio (m)
turnover *[of stock]* movimento (m)
turnover *[sales]* volume (m) d'affari
turnover tax imposta (f) sul volume d'affari
turnround *[goods sold]* rotazione (f)
turnround *[making profitable]* inversione (f) di tendenza
turnround *[of plane]* rotazione (f)

Uu

unaccounted for inspiegato
unaudited non verificato
unaudited accounts contabilità (f) non sottoposta a revisione contabile
unauthorized expenditure spesa (f) non autorizzata
unavailability non disponibilità (f)
unavailable non disponibile
unchanged immutato
unchecked figures cifre (fpl) non verificate
unclaimed baggage bagagli (mpl) non reclamati
unconditional incondizionato
unconfirmed non confermato
undated non datato
undelivered non consegnato
under *[according to]* secondo
under *[less than]* meno di *o* inferiore

under construction in costruzione
under contract sotto contratto
under control sotto controllo
under new management sotto nuova gestione
undercharge far pagare meno
undercut a rival vendere a minor prezzo di un concorrente
underdeveloped countries paesi (mpl) sottosviluppati
underequipped con attrezzatura insufficiente
underpaid malpagato
undersell vendere sotto costo
undersigned sottoscritto
underspend spendere meno
understand capire
understanding intesa (f)
undertake intraprendere
undertaking *[company]* azienda (f) *o* impresa (f)
undertaking *[promise]* compito (m) *o* impegno (m)
underwrite *[guarantee]* garantire
underwrite *[pay costs]* finanziare
underwriting syndicate gruppo (m) di collocamento
undischarged bankrupt fallito (m) non riabilitato
uneconomic rent affitto (m) non redditizio
unemployed disoccupato
unemployment disoccupazione (f)
unemployment pay sussidio (m) di disoccupazione
unfair ingiusto
unfair competition concorrenza (f) sleale
unfair dismissal licenziamento (m) ingiusto
unfavourable sfavorevole
unfavourable exchange rate tasso (m) di cambio sfavorevole
unfulfilled order ordinazione (f) inevasa
unilateral unilaterale
union sindacato (m)
union recognition riconoscimento (m) sindacale

unique selling point *or* **proposition (USP)** proposta (f) unica di vendita
unit *[in unit trust]* azione (f)
unit *[item]* unità (f)
unit cost costo (m) unitario
unit price prezzo (m) unitario
unit trust fondo (m) comune di investimento
unlimited liability responsabilità (f) illimitata
unload *[get rid of]* disfarsi di
unload *[goods]* scaricare
unobtainable non ottenibile
unofficial non ufficiale *o* ufficioso
unpaid non pagato
unpaid invoices fatture (fpl) insolute
unsealed envelope busta (f) aperta
unsecured creditor creditore (m) non garantito
unskilled non specializzato
unsold invenduto
unsubsidized senza sovvenzioni
unsuccessful che non ha successo
up front anticipato
up to fino a *o* conforme a
up to date *[complete]* aggiornato
up to date *[modern]* moderno *o* attuale
up-market rivolto a una fascia alta del mercato
update (n) aggiornamento (m)
update (v) aggiornare *o* mettere al corrente
upset price prezzo (m) d'apertura
upturn miglioramento (m)
upward trend tendenza (f) al rialzo
urgent urgente
use (n) uso (m)
use (v) usare
use up spare capacity impiegare la capacità produttiva inutilizzata
useful utile
user utente (m)
user-friendly facile da usare *o* accessibile
USP (= unique selling point *or* **proposition)** proposta (f) unica di vendita
usual solito *o* abituale
utilization utilizzazione (f)

Vv

vacancy *[for job]* posto (m) vacante
vacant vacante
vacate lasciar vuoto
valid valido
validity validità (f)
valuation valutazione (f)
value (n) valore (m)
value (v) valutare
value added tax (VAT) imposta sul valore aggiunto (IVA)
valuer stimatore (m)
van furgone (m)
variable costs costi (mpl) variabili
variance variazione (f)
variation variazione (f)
VAT (= value added tax) imposta sul valore aggiunto (IVA)
VAT declaration dichiarazione (f) IVA
VAT inspector ispettore (m) IVA
VAT invoice fattura con IVA
vehicle veicolo (m)
vendor venditore (m)
venture (n) *[business]* affare (m) rischioso
venture (v) *[risk]* rischiare
venture capital capitale (m) di rischio
venue luogo (m) di ritrovo
verbal verbale
verbal agreement accordo (m) verbale
verification verifica (f)
verify verificare
vertical communication comunicazione (f) verticale
vertical integration integrazione (f) verticale
vested interest interessi (mpl) costituiti
veto a decision porre il veto a una decisione
via via *o* tramite

viable realizzabile
VIP lounge sala (f) per VIP
visa visto (m) consolare
visible imports importazioni (fpl) visibili
visible trade partite (fpl) visibili
void (adj) *[not valid]* nullo
void (v) invalidare *o* annullare
volume volume (m)
volume discount sconto (m) sul quantitativo
volume of sales volume (m) delle vendite
volume of trade *or* **volume of business** volume (m) degli scambi commerciali
voluntary liquidation liquidazione (f) volontaria
voluntary redundancy cassa (f) integrazione volontaria
vote of thanks ringraziamento (m)
voucher *[document from an auditor]* pezza (f) giustificativa
voucher *[paper given instead of money]* buono (m)

Ww

wage salario (m)
wage claim rivendicazione (f) salariale
wage freeze congelamento (m) salariale
wage levels livelli (mpl) salariali
wage negotiations negoziato (m) salariale
wage scale scala (f) retributiva
waive rinunciare
waive a payment rinunciare ad un pagamento
waiver *[of right]* rinuncia (f)
waiver clause clausola (f) di recessione

warehouse (n) magazzino (m)
warehouse (v) immagazzinare
warehouseman magazziniere (m)
warehousing magazzinaggio (m)
warrant (n) *[document]* autorizzazione (f)
warrant (v) *[guarantee]* garantire
warrant (v) *[justify]* giustificare
warranty (n) garanzia (f)
wastage spreco (m)
waste (n) spreco (m)
waste (v) (use too much) sprecare
waybill lettera (f) di vettura
weak market mercato (m) fiacco
wear and tear deterioramento (m) naturale
week settimana (f)
weekly settimanale
weigh pesare
weighbridge pesa a ponte (f)
weight peso (m)
weight limit limite (m) di peso
weighted average media (f) ponderata
weighted index indice (m) ponderato
weighting ponderazione (f)
well-paid job lavoro (m) ben pagato
wharf molo (m)
white knight 'cavaliere (m) bianco'
whole-life insurance assicurazione (f) sulla vita
wholesale (adv) all'ingrosso
wholesale dealer commerciante (m) all'ingrosso
wholesale discount sconto (m) all'ingrosso
wholesale price index indice (m) dei prezzi all'ingrosso
wholesaler commerciante (m) all'ingrosso
wildcat strike sciopero (m) selvaggio
win a contract vincere un contratto
wind up *[a company]* mettere in liquidazione
wind up *[a meeting]* dichiarare sciolta una riunione

winding up liquidazione (f) *o* scioglimento (m)
window finestra (f)
window display esposizione (f) in vetrina
withdraw *[an offer]* ritirare
withdraw *[money]* prelevare
withdraw a takeover bid ritrattare un'offerta di rilevamento
withdrawal *[of money]* ritiro (m)
withholding tax ritenuta (f) d'acconto
witness (n) testimone (m)
witness (v) *[a document]* firmare come testimone
witness an agreement firmare un accordo come testimone
word-processing videoscrittura (f)
wording dicitura (f)
work (n) lavoro (m)
work (v) lavorare
work in progress lavori in corso
work permit permesso (m) di lavoro
work-to-rule sciopero (m) bianco
worker lavoratore (m), lavoratrice (f)
worker director lavoratore che fa parte del consiglio di amministrazione e che agisce come portavoce del personale
workforce forza (f) lavoro
working (adj) attivo
working capital capitale (m) d'esercizio
working conditions condizioni (fpl) di lavoro
working party commissione (f) di studio
workshop officina (f)
workstation *[at computer]* posto (m) di lavoro
world mondo (m)
world market mercato (m) mondiale
worldwide (adj) mondiale
worldwide (adv) in tutto il mondo
worth (n) *[value]* valore (m)
worth: be worth valere
worthless privo di valore

wrap up *[discussion]* concludere
wrap up *[goods]* impaccare
wrapper confezionatore (m)
wrapping involucro (m) *o* imballaggio (m)
wrapping paper carta (f) da imballaggio
wreck (n) *[company]* impresa (f) fallita
wreck (n) *[ship]* nave (f) naufragata
wreck (v) *[ruin]* distruggere
writ mandato (m)
write scrivere
write down *[assets]* ridurre il valore
write off *[debt]* annullare
write out redigere
write out a cheque compilare un assegno
write-off *[loss]* svalutazione (f)
writedown *[of asset]* svalutazione (f)
writing scrittura (f)
written agreement accordo (m) scritto
wrong sbagliato
wrongful dismissal licenziamento (m) ingiustificato

Xx Yy Zz

year anno (m)
year end fine (f) esercizio
yearly payment pagamento (m) annuale
yellow pages Pagine Gialle (fpl)
yield (n) *[on investment]* rendita (f)
yield (v) *[interest]* rendere
zero zero (m)
zero-rated aliquota (f) nulla
zip code *[US]* codice (m) d'avviamento postale

Italiano-Inglese
Italian-English

Aa

abbandonare [lasciare] abandon; leave

abbassare lower (v)

abbassare [ridurre il prezzo] knock down or knock off or reduce price

abbassare i prezzi lower prices

abbassare il prezzo (di articoli) mark down

abbonato (m) al telefono telephone subscriber

abbozzare [redigere] draft (v)

abile [qualificato] qualified [skilled]

abilità (f) [capacità] capacity or ability

abilità (f) tecnica skill

abitante (m) [residente] inhabitant or resident (n)

abituale (solito) usual or routine

abolire i controlli (mpl) decontrol

abolizione (f) della regolamentazione deregulation

accantonamento (m) shelving or postponing

accantonamento (m) [riserva] provision or money put aside

accantonamento (m) al fondo di ammortamento allowance for depreciation

accantonare (differire) shelve

accantonare [accumulare] accumulate

accantonare fondi (mpl) per un progetto earmark funds for a project

accaparramento (m) hoarding [of goods]

accaparramento (m) [monopolio] corner (n) or monopoly

accaparrarsi il mercato (m) corner the market

accertamento (m) dei danni assessment of damages

accertamento (m) fiscale tax assessment

accertamento (m) patrimoniale means test

accertare [stabilire il valore] assess

accertare i danni assess damages

accessibile [facile da usare] user-friendly

accessori (mpl) fittings

accettabile [soddisfacente] acceptable

accettar accept (v)

accettar accept (v) or agree

accettare di fare qualcosa agree to do something

accettare una cambiale accept a bill

accettazione (f) acceptance

accettazione (f) di un'offerta acceptance of an offer

accidentale [casuale] random

accomodamento (m) composition [with creditors]

accomodamento (m) [accordo] adjustment

acconsentire a fare qualcosa agree to do something

acconto (m) deposit (n) [paid in advance]

accont : in acconto on account

accordare [cedere] allow or give

accordare [concedere] grant (v)

accordo (m) settlement or agreement

accord : essere d'accordo con agree with [be of the same opinion]

accordo (m) [accomodamento] adjustment

accordo (m) [intesa] arrangement or compromise

accordo (m) aperto open-ended agreement

accordo (m) bilaterale reciprocal agreement

accordo (m) creditizio di sostegno standby arrangements

accordo (m) di indicizzazione threshold agreement

accordo (m) di lunga data long-standing agreement

accordo (m) di marketing marketing agreement

accordo (m) in esclusiva exclusive agreement

accordo (m) multilaterale multilateral agreement

accordo (m) parziale one-sided agreement

accordo (m) scritto written agreement

accordo (m) sulla parola (f) gentleman's agreement

accordo (m) sulla produttività productivity agreement

accordo (m) verbale verbal agreement

accord -tipo (m) model agreement

accreditare (un conto) credit (v)

accumulare accumulate

accumularsi *[maturare]* accrue

accurato *[preciso]* accurate

accusa (f) charge (n) *[in court]*

accusare ricevuta di una lettera acknowledge receipt of a letter

accusato (m) defendant

acquirente (m) *[cliente]* shopper

acquirente (m) genuino genuine purchaser

acquisizione (f) *[acquisto]* acquisition

acquisizione (f) di controllo contestata contested takeover

acquisizione (f) di controllo inversa reverse takeover

acquistare *[comperare]* purchase (v)

acquisti (mpl) shopping *[goods bought]*

acquisto (m) purchase (n); purchasing *or* buying

acquisto (m) a termine forward buying

acquisto (m) centralizzato central purchasing

acquisto (m) di una società da parte dei suoi stessi dirigenti management buyout (MBO)

acquisto (m) fatto per impulso impulse purchase

acquisto (m) in massa bulk buying

acquisto (m) per contanti cash purchase

acquisto (m) rateale hire purchase (HP)

acquisto (m) *[acquisizione]* acquisition *or* purchase

ad alta definizione near letter-quality (NLQ)

ad valorem ad valorem

adattamento (m) stagionale seasonal adjustments

adattare *[adeguare]* adjust

addebitare un acquisto charge a purchase

addebitare un conto debit an account

addebitare una telefonata al ricevente reverse the charges

addebiti (mpl) per interessi interest charges

addebito (m) debit (n)

addebito (m) diretto direct debit

addestramento (m) dei dirigenti management training

addestramento (m) interno (alla ditta) in-house training

addestramento (m) sul lavoro on-the-job training

addetto (m) al controllo dell'avanzamento progress chaser

addetto (m) alle pubbliche relazioni public relations man

addetto (m) alle vendite sales clerk

addetto (m) commerciale commercial attaché

addizionale (supplementare) additional

addizione (f) addition *[calculation]*

adeguamento (m) fiscale tax adjustments

adeguare *[adattare]* adjust

adeguato *[sufficiente]* adequate

adempimento (m) fulfilment

adempimento (m) di un contratto completion of a contract

adibire ad altro uso redevelop

aereo (m) plane
aereo (m) da carico freight plane
aeroplano (m) a noleggio charter plane
aeroporto (m) airport
affare (m) business *[discussion]*
affare (m) *[occasione]* bargain (n) *[cheaper than usual]*
affare (m) *[operazione]* deal (n)
affare (m) poco vantaggioso hard bargain
affare (m) rischioso venture (n) or risky deal
affari (mpl) business *[commerce]*
affari: fare affari do business or transact business
affermare claim (v) or suggest
affermativo affirmative
affidare entrust
affidare fondi ad un progetto commit funds to a project
affiliata (f) subsidiary company
affiliato *[associato]* affiliated
affitansi uffici (mpl) offices to let
affittare *[impianti]* lease equipment
affittar let (v)
affittare *[dare in affitto]* lease out (v) *[of landlord]*
affittare *[tenere in affitto]* lease (v) *[of tenant]*
affittare un negozio let an office
affitto (m) lease (n)
affitto (m) rent
affitto (m) alto high rent
affitto (m) nominale nominal rent
affitto (m) non redditizio uneconomic rent
affittuario (m) lessee
affittuario (m) occupante sitting tenant
affrancar frank (v)
affrancare *[mettere francobolli]* stamp (v) a letter
affrancatura (f) pagata postpaid
affrettarsi hurry up
agenda (f) appointments book
agenda (f) da tavolo desk diary
agenda (f) tascabile pocket diary
agente (m) agent *[working in an agency]*

agente (m) *[rappresentante]* agent or representative
agente (m) commissionario commission agent
agente (m) di assicurazione insurance agent
agente (m) di brevetti patent agent
agente (m) di cambio stockbroker
agente (m) di factoring factor (n) *[person]*
agente (m) doganale customs broker
agente (m) in cambi foreign exchange broker
agente (m) marittimo ship broker
agente (m) del credere del credere agent
agenzia (f) agency
agenzia (f) che fornisce personale temporaneo temp agency
agenzia (f) di lavoro employment agency or employment bureau
agenzia (f) di stampa news agency
agenzia (f) immobiliare letting agency
agenzia (f) per il recupero dei crediti debt collection agency
agenzia (f) per reperimento di referenze credit agency
agenzia (f) di pubblicità advertising agency
agevolazione (f) concession *[reduction]*
agevolazione (f) fiscale tax relief
agevolazioni (fpl) creditizie credit facilities
aggiornamento (m) update (n)
aggiornamento (m) *[sollecito]* follow up
aggiornare *[mettere al corrente]* update or bring up to date
aggiornare *[rimandare]* adjourn
aggiornare una riunione adjourn a meeting
aggiornato up to date *[complete]*
aggirare get round *[a problem]*
aggiudicare un contratto a qualcuno award a contract to someone

aggiudicazione (f) *[giudizio]*
adjudication
aggiungere *[sommare]* add
aggiungere il 10% per il servizio
add on 10% for service
aggiunta (f) addition *[thing added]*
aggiustare *[riparare]* repair (v)
agire act (v) *or* do something *or*
take action
agricolo *o* agrario agricultural
aiuto (m) *[assistenza]* assistance
aiuto (m) *[appoggio]* backing
al giorno per day
alla settimana per week
albergo (m) *[hotel]* hotel
albergo (m) selezionato graded
hotel
alimentatore (m) di fogli paper
feed
alimentazione (f) continua
continuous feed
aliquota (f) d'imposta tax rate
aliquota (f) d'imposta base
standard rate (of tax)
all'anno per year *or* per annum
all'avanguardia state-of-the-art
all'estero abroad *or* overseas
all'estero *[offshore]* offshore
all'ingrosso wholesale (adv)
all'ora per hour
allargamento (m) expansion
allegare enclose
allegato (m) enclosure
altamente qualificato highly
qualified
altamente retribuito highly-paid
alternativa (f) alternative (n)
alternativo alternative (adj)
altezza: essere all'altezza cope *or*
be up to
americano American (adj)
Americano, -ana American (n)
ammanco (m) shortfall
ammasso (m) hoard
ammettere admit *or* agree
amministrare *[gestire]* manage
amministrare un patrimonio
manage property
amministrativo administrative
amministratore (m) director

amministratore (m) di società
company director
amministratore (m) delegato
[direttore generale] managing
director (MD)
amministrazione (f) *[gestione]*
administration
ammissione (f) admission
ammontare (m) *[importo]* amount
[of money]
ammontare a amount to *or* total
(v)
ammortamento (m) amortization
or depreciation
**ammortamento (m) a quote
costanti** straight line depreciation
ammortamento (m) accelerato
accelerated depreciation
ammortare *o* ammortizzare
amortize *or* depreciate
ampliare expand
anagrafe (f) registry office
analisi (f) analysis
analisi (f) dei costi cost analysis
analisi (f) dei sistemi systems
analysis
analisi (f) del progetto project
analysis
analisi (f) delle mansioni job
analysis
analisi (f) delle vendite sales
analysis
analisi (f) di mercato market
analysis
**analisi (f) preventiva della
convenienza dei costi**
cost-benefit analysis
analisi (f) statistica statistical
analysis
analista (m) dei costi cost
accountant
analista (m) dei sistemi systems
analyst
analista (m) di mercato market
analyst
analizzare analyse *or* analyze
**analizzare il potenziale del
mercato** analyse the market
potential
andamento (m) trend
andare go

andare in pensione retire *[from one's job]*

andare incontro ad una richiesta meet a demand

anno (m) year

anno (m) di base base year

anno (m) fiscale tax year

anno (m) solare calendar year

annotazione (f) entering

annuale *[annuo]* annual

annualmente annually *or* on an annual basis

annuario (m) directory

annuario (m) commerciale commercial directory *or* trade directory

annullamento (m) invalidation

annullare *[cancellare]* cancel

annullare *[invalidare]* void (v)

annullare un assegno cancel a cheque

annullare un contratto cancel a contract

annullato cancelled *or* off

annunci (mpl) economici (su giornale) classified ads *or* classified advertisements

annunciare announce

annuncio (m) announcement

annuncio (m) pubblicitario *[pubblicità]* advertisement

annuo *[annuale]* annual

anticipato advance (adj) *or* up front

anticipazione (f) su un conto advance on account

anticipo (m) advance (n) *[loan]*

anticipo (m) in contanti cash advance

antiquato obsolete *or* old-fashioned

anziano *[piu vecchio]* senior

aperto open (adj)

aperto ad offerte open to offers

apertura (f) opening (n)

apertura: d'apertura *[iniziale]* opening (adj) *or* initial

apertura (f) sul mercato . gap in the market

appaltare lavoro farm out work

apparecchiatura (f) equipment

apparecchiatura (f) d'ufficio business equipment

apparecchiatura (f) difettosa faulty equipment

apparecchiatura (f) pesante heavy equipment

appartamento (m) flat (n)

appartenere a belong to

appellare *[ricorrere in appello]* appeal (v) *[against a decision]*

appello (m) *[ricorso]* appeal (n) *[against a decision]*

appendice (f) appendix

applicare enforce

appoggio (m) *[aiuto]* backing

apportare bring in

apporto (m) di capitali contribution of capital

apprendista (m) junior clerk

apprendista (m) in direzione aziendale management trainee

apprendistato (m) traineeship

apprezzamento (m) appreciation *[how good something is]*

apprezzare appreciate *[how good something is]*

appropriarsi indebitamente embezzle *or* misappropriate

appropriazione (f) indebita embezzlement *or* misappropriation

approssimativamente approximately

approssimativo approximate *or* rough

approvare approve *or* agree

approvare: far approvare carry *or* approve in a vote

approvare i termini di un contratto approve the terms of a contract

approvvigionare *[fornire]* supply (v)

appuntamento (m) appointment *[meeting]*

aprire open (v) *[start new business]*

aprire fino a notte tarda late-night opening

aprire trattative open negotiations

aprire un conto open an account

aprire un conto bancario open a bank account

aprire una lettera di credito issue a letter of credit

aprire una linea di credito open a line of credit

aprire una seduta open a meeting

arbitrare una vertenza arbitrate in a dispute

arbitrato (m) arbitration

arbitro (m) arbitrator

archivio (m) (di un computer) computer file

archivio (m) [documentazione] records

area (f) o regione (f) area or region

area (f) [campo] field

area (f) del dollaro dollar area

area (f) di carico loading bay

area (f) problematica problem area

area (f) uffici office space

arenarsi (di trattative) break down (v) [of talks]

argomento (m) [questione] item on agenda or matter to be discussed

aria (f) air

armonizzazione (f) harmonization

arredamento (m) per ufficio office furniture

arrestare check (v) or stop

arresto (m) check (n) or stop

arretrati (mpl) arrears

arrivare arrive

arrivare a reach or come to

arrivare ad una decisione reach a decision

arrivi (mpl) arrivals

arrivo (m) arrival

arrotondare aumentando round up

arrotondare diminuendo round down

articoli (mpl) deperibili perishable goods

articoli (mpl) che vendono rapidamente fast-selling items

articoli (mpl) di lusso luxury goods

articoli (mpl) diversi miscellaneous items

articoli (mpl) non ricorrenti non-recurring items

articoli (mpl) vari sundries

articolo (m) [prodotto] article or item

articolo (m) unico one-off item

ascendere [salire] climb

ascensore (m) lift (n)

aspettativa (f) [congedo autorizzato] leave of absence

assalire [attaccare] attack

assegnare award (v)

assegnatario (m) assignee

assegni (mpl) personalizzati personalized cheques

assegno (m) cheque

assegno (m) a copertura garantita certified cheque

assegno (m) al portatore cheque to bearer

assegno (m) circolare banker's draft or bank draft

assegno (m) dello stipendio pay cheque or salary cheque

assegno (m) di cassa cashier's check [US]

assegno (m) in bianco blank cheque

assegno (m) non sbarrato open cheque

assegno (m) sbarrato crossed cheque

assemblea (f) assembly or meeting

assemblea (f) del personale staff meeting

assemblea (f) generale general meeting

Assemblea (f) Generale degli Azionisti annual general meeting (AGM)

assemblaggio (m) [montaggio] assembly [putting together]

assente absent or away from work

assenza (f) [mancanza] absence

assicurabile insurable

assicurare insure

assicurare la vita di qualcuno assure someone's life

assicurarsi contro un rischio
cover a risk
assicuratore (m) insurer
assicuratore (m) marittimo marine
underwriter
assicurazione (f) insurance *or*
(life) assurance
assicurazione (f) *[garanzia]*
indemnity
assicurazione (f) auto motor
insurance
assicurazione (f) contro gli incendi
fire insurance
assicurazione (f) globale
comprehensive insurance
assicurazione (f) malattie health
insurance
assicurazione (f) marittima marine
insurance
**assicurazione (f) per danni verso
terzi** third-party insurance
assicurazione (f) sulla casa house
insurance
assicurazione (f) sulla vita life
assurance *or* life insurance
assicurazione (f) temporanea
term insurance
assistente (mf) *[collaboratore]*
assistant
assistenza (f) *[aiuto]* assistance
**assistenza (f) post-vendita alla
clientela** after-sales service
assistere assist
assistere a attend (meeting)
associato associate (adj)
associato (m) *[socio]* associate (n)
associato *[affiliato]* affiliated
associazione (f) *[circolo]*
association *or* society
associazione (f) commerciale
trade association
associazione (f) in copartnership
compartecipazione
associazione (f) in partecipazione
['joint venture'] joint venture
assoluto outright
assumere *[impiegare]* employ
assumere del personale hire staff
**assumersi la responsabilità di
qualcosa** accept liability for
something

asta (f) auction (n)
attaccare attack
attaccare *[unire]* attach
attendere istruzioni await
instructions
attendibile reliable
attendibilità (f) reliability
attenzione (f) attention
attenzione: all'attenzione di FAO
(for the attention of)
atterrare land (v) *[of plane]*
atteso due *[expected]*
attestato (m) *[referenze]* reference
[report on person]
attestazione (f) ufficiale affidavit
attirare appeal to (v) *or* attract
attività (f) activity
attività (fpl) e passività (fpl) assets
and liabilities
attività (f) bancaria banking
attività (f) commerciale fiorente
flourishing trade
**attività (f) esterna di ricerca e di
studio** field work
attività (f) finanziaria *[finanza]*
finance (n)
attività (f) illegale racketeering
attività (fpl) immateriali intangible
assets
attività (fpl) liquide current assets
attività (fpl) occulte hidden asset
attività (f) previsionale forecasting
attività (f) promozionale
merchandizing
attività (f) secondaria sideline
attività (f) trascurata neglected
business
attivo working (adj)
attivo (m) mobiliare personal
assets
attivo (m) esigibile *[cespiti
realizzabili]* realizable assets
atto (m) deed
atto (m) costitutivo deed of
partnership
atto (m) costitutivo di società
articles of association
atto (m) di cessione deed of
assignment
atto (m) di donazione deed of
covenant

atto (m) di trasferimento deed of transfer

atto (m) di vendita [fattura] bill of sale

attraccare [entrare in porto] dock (v) [ship]

attrarre attract

attrezzare (una fabbrica) tool up (a factory)

attrezzatura (f) per ufficio office equipment

attribuire un diritto a qualcuno assign a right to someone

attuale present (adj) [now]

attuale [moderno] up to date [modern]

attuale: non attuale out of date

attuare [realizzare] implement (v)

attuario (m) actuary

attuazione (f) implementation

aumentare gain or increase or rise [get bigger]

aumentare raise or increase

aumentare di prezzo increase in price

aumentare di valore appreciate or increase in value

aumentare il prezzo (di articoli) mark up (an item)

aumentare proporzionalmente scale up

aumento (m) increase or rise [higher salary]

aumento (m) increase or gain [getting bigger]

aumento: in aumento on the increase or mounting

aumento (m) del costo della vita cost-of-living increase

aumento (m) di paga retroattivo retroactive pay rise

aumento (m) di prezzo mark-up [action]

aumento (m) medio annuale mean annual increase

aumento (m) percentuale percentage increase

aumento (m) salariale pay rise

autenticare [legalizzare] authenticate

autenticare [certificare] certify

autentico [vero] genuine

autobus (m) bus

autobus (m) dell'aeroporto airport bus

autocopiante carbonless

autofinanziamento (m) self-financing (n)

autofinanziarsi: che può autofinanziarsi self-financing (adj)

automobile (f) car

automobile (f) di grande successo best-selling car

automobile (f) a noleggio hire car

autoregolatore self-regulatory

autoregolazione (f) self-regulation

autorità (f) authority

autorità (fpl) portuali port authority

autorizzare authorize or give permission or license

autorizzare (qualcuno a fare qualcosa) allow or permit (someone to do something)

autorizzare un pagamento authorize payment

autorizzato authorized

autorizzazione (f) authorization or permission

autorizzazione (f) warrant (n) [document]

avallante (m) guarantor

avallante (m) [sostenitore] backer

avallare stand security for

avallo (m) [sponsorizzazione] sponsorship

avanzare [fare progressi] progress (v)

avaria (f) average (n) [insurance]

avaria (f) generale general average

aver bisogno di require [need]

avere (v) carry [have in stock]

avere (m) [lato dell'attivo] credit side

avere come risultato result in

avere indietro get back [something lost]

avere lo scopo di aim (v)

avere luogo take place

avere successo *[riuscire]* succeed *[do well]*

avviamento (m) start-up

avviamento (m) commerciale goodwill

avvio (m) start (n)

avvisare *[informare]* advise *[tell what happened]*

avviso (m) notice *or* piece of information

avviso (m) di ricevimento doganale customs receipt

avviso (m) di rinnovo renewal notice

avvocato (mf) lawyer; counsel

avvocato (mf) della parte querelante prosecution counsel

avvocato (mf) difensore defence counsel

azienda (f) *[impresa]* business *or* firm *or* company

azienda (f) autonoma independent company

azienda (f) commerciale business establishment

azienda (f) con forte indebitamento highly-geared company

aziende (f) in concorrenza competing firms

azione (f) share (n) *[in a company]*

azione (f) action *[thing done]*

azione (f) *[causa]* action *or* lawsuit

azioni (fpl) ordinarie ordinary shares *or* equities

azioni (fpl) privilegiate preference shares

azioni (fpl) privilegiate cumulative cumulative preference shares

azioni (fpl) quotate quoted shares

azioni (fpl) trascurate neglected shares

azionista (m) shareholder

azionista (m) di maggioranza majority shareholder

azionista (m) di minoranza minority shareholder

azionista (m) principale major shareholder

Bb

bacheca (f) showcase

bacino (m) dock (n)

bagagli (mpl) non reclamati unclaimed baggage

bagaglio (m) luggage

bagaglio (m) a mano hand luggage

bagaglio (m) in eccesso excess baggage

banca (f) bank (n)

banca (f) centrale central bank

banca (f) d'emissione issuing bank

banca (f) di compensazione clearing bank

banca (f) di sconto discount house *[bank]*

Banca (f) Europea per gli Investimenti (BEI) European Investment Bank (EIB)

banca (f) mercantile merchant bank

banchiere (m) banker

banco (m) counter

banco (m) dei pagamenti pay desk

banco (m) di esposizione display stand

banconota (f) banknote; bill (n) *[US]*

barattare barter (v)

baratto (m) *[scambio]* barter (n)

barriera (f) barrier

barriera (f) *[protezione]* hedge (n)

barriera (f) doganale customs barrier

barriere (fpl) tariffarie tariff barriers

base (f) base (n) *[place]*

base: di base basic (adj)

base (f) *[fondamento]* basis

base (f) di dati database

base (f) monetaria monetary base

basilare *[di base]* basic (adj) *[simple]*

basso *[scadente]* low (adj)

basso: a basso prezzo cheap

basso livello (m) low (n)

battuta (f) d'arresto setback

bene (m) *[cespite]* asset

bene (m) *[merce]* commodity

beneficiario (m) beneficiary

beneficio (m) *[utilità]* benefit (n)

benestare (m) approval

beni (mpl) di consumo consumer goods

beni (mpl) di consumo durevoli consumer durables

beni (mpl) durevoli durable goods

beni (mpl) invisibili invisible assets

beni (mpl) reali tangible assets

beni (mpl) strumentali capital goods

benzina (f) a prezzo ridotto cut-price petrol

biasimare blame (v)

biasimo (m) *[colpa]* blame (n)

biglietto (m) business card; ticket

biglietto (m) aereo privo di prenotazione standby ticket

biglietto (m) aperto (senza data di ritorno) open ticket

biglietto (m) da visita business card

biglietto (m) di andata one-way fare

biglietto (m) di banca note (n)

biglietto (m) omaggio complimentary ticket

bilancia (f) balance (n)

bilancia (f) commerciale attiva favourable balance of trade

bilancia (f) commerciale in dollari dollar balance

bilancia (f) dei pagamenti balance of payments

bilancia (f) commerciale balance of trade

bilanciare balance (v)

bilancio (m) balance (n)

bilancio (m) d'apertura opening balance

bilancio (m) dello Stato budget (n) *[government]*

bilancio (m) di chiusura closing balance

bilancio (m) di verifica trial balance

bilancio (m) preventivo budget (n) *[personal, company]*

bilancio (m) d'esercizio balance sheet

bilaterale bilateral

bilione (m) billion (UK)

binario (m) platform *[in railway station]*

bloccare block (v)

bloccare i salari e i prezzi freeze *or* peg wages and prices

bloccare un assegno stop a cheque

bloccare un conto stop an account

bloccato *[congelato]* frozen

blocco (m) *[commerciale]* freeze (n)

blocco (m) degli affitti rent control

blocco (m) del credito credit freeze

blocco (m) del lavoro straordinario overtime ban

blocco (m) di fogli per lavagna flip chart

boicottaggio (m) boycott (n)

boicottare boycott (v)

bolla (f) di spedizione dispatch note *or* shipping note *or* delivery note

bolletta (f) bill *[list of charges]*

bolletta (f) d'avviso advice note

bollettino (m) bulletin

bonifico (m) bank transfer

boom (m) boom (n)

bordo: a bordo on board

borsa (f) bag

borsa (f) *[cartella]* briefcase

borsa (f) di studio grant (n)

Borsa (f) Merci commodity exchange

Borsa (f) Valori stock exchange

bozza (f) rough draft

bozza (f) di un piano draft plan

bozza (f) di un progetto draft project

breve: a breve *o* a breve termine short-term (adj) *or* on a short-term basis

breve: nel più breve termine as soon as possible (asap)

brevettare un'invenzione patent an invention

brevettato patented

brevetto (m) patent

brevetto (m) richiesto *o* in attesa di brevetto patent applied for *or* patent pending

britannico *[inglese]* British

broker (m) broker

budget (m) *[bilancio preventivo]* budget (n) *[personal, company]*

budget (m) di gestione operational budget

budget (m) generale overhead budget

budget (m) operativo operating budget

budget (m) per le spese di promozione promotion budget

budget (m) provvisorio provisional budget

budget (m) pubblicitario publicity budget *or* advertising budget

budgetario *[relativo al budget]* budgetary

budgettare budget (v)

buon affare (m) good buy

buon guadagno (m) healthy profit

buona gestione (f) good management

buona qualità (f) good quality

buono good

buono (m) coupon *or* voucher

buono (m) premio gift coupon *or* gift voucher

busta (f) aperta unsealed envelope

busta (f) chiusa sealed envelope

bustarella (f) *[tangente]* bribe (n)

Cc

cadere fall (v) *or* go lower

cadere *[calare]* drop (v)

cadere *[crollare]* collapse (v)

caduta (f) *[crollo]* fall (n) *or* collapse

caduta (f) *[ribasso]* drop (n)

calare *[cadere]* drop (v)

calcolare calculate

calcolare 10% per il trasporto allow 10% for carriage

calcolare una media average (v)

calcolatore (m) calculator

calcolatrice (f) tascabile pocket calculator

calcolo (m) calculation

calcolo (m) approssimativo rough calculation

calcolo (m) sbagliato miscalculation

calligrafia (f) handwriting

calo (m) lowering

cambiale (f) bill of exchange

cambiale (f) *[effetto]* bill (n) *[written promise to pay]*

cambiale (f) di favore *[effetto di comodo]* accommodation bill

cambiali (fpl) da incassare *[effetti attivi]* bills receivable

cambiali (fpl) da pagare *[effetti passivi]* bills payable

cambiamento (m) change *or* difference *or* shift

cambiamento (m) *[modifica]* alteration

cambiare change *or* exchange *[money]*

cambiare switch *or* change

cambiare *[modificare]* alter

cambiavalute (m) money changer

cambio (m) exchange (n) *[currency]*

cambio (m) incrociato cross rate

camera (f) room

Camera (f) di Commercio
Chamber of Commerce
camion (m) lorry *or* truck
camion (m) articolato articulated
lorry
camionista (m) lorry driver *or*
trucker
campagna (f) campaign *or* drive
campagna (f) country *[not town]*
campagna (f) aggressiva hard
selling
campagna (f) di vendite sales
campaign
**campagna (f) promozionale a
mezzo posta** mail shot
campagna (f) pubblicitaria
publicity campaign *or* advertising
campaign
campionamento (m) sampling
campionare sample (v) *or* test
campionatura (f) casuale random
sampling
campionatura (f) per accettazione
acceptance sampling
campione (m) sample (n)
campione (m) casuale random
sample
campione (m) di prova trial
sample
campione (m) gratuito free
sample
campione (m) per dimostrazione
demonstration model
**campione (m) (statistico) di
controllo** check sample
campo (m) (area) area *or* field
canale (m) channel (n)
canali (mpl) di distribuzione
distribution channels *or* channels of
distribution
canalizzare channel (v)
cancellare cross out
cancellare *[annullare]* cancel
cancellazione (f) *[disdetta]*
cancellation
cancelleria (f) d'ufficio office
stationery
candidato (m) candidate
candidato (m) a un posto di lavoro
applicant for a job

capace di capable of
capacità (f) capacity *[space]*
capacità (f) *[abilità]* capacity
[ability]
capacità (f) di guadagno earning
capacity
capacità (f) di produzione
manufacturing capacity
capacità (f) in eccedenza
overcapacity
capacità (f) industriale industrial
capacity
capacità (f) produttiva capacity
[production]
capacità (f) produttiva in eccesso
excess capacity
capacità (f) produttiva inutilizzata
spare capacity
caparra (f) rimborsabile
refundable deposit
capi (mpl) d'intesa heads of
agreement
capienza (f) di magazzino storage
capacity
capire (rendersi conto di) realize
or understand
capitale (m) o capitali (mpl)
capital
capitale (m) d'apporto initial
capital
capitale (m) d'esercizio working
capital
capitale (m) di rischio risk capital
capitale (m) di rischio venture
capital
capitale (m) disponibile available
capital
capitale (m) effettivo equity
capital
capitale (m) in fuga flight of
capital
capitale (m) mutuato loan capital
capitale (m) nominale nominal
capital
capitale (m) obbligazionario loan
stock
capitale (m) sociale share capital
capitali (mpl) capital
capitalizzare capitalize
capitalizzazione (f) capitalization

capitalizzazione (f) di mercato market capitalization

capitalizzazione (f) delle riserve capitalization of reserves

capo (m) boss (informal)

capo (m) (direttore) principal (n) *[person]*

capo (m) del personale personnel manager

capo (m) reparto head of department; floor manager

capo (m) servizio departmental manager

capo (m) ufficio chief clerk

carenza (f) di manodopera manpower shortage

caricabile chargeable

caricare *[un camion o una nave]* load a lorry *or* a ship

caricare *[programma]* load (v) *[a computer program]*

carico (m) load (n) *or* cargo

carico (m) di camion lorry-load

carico (m) di coperta deck cargo

carico (m) di ritorno homeward freight

carico (m) lordo deadweight cargo

carico (m) utile payload

carnet (m) carnet *[document]*

caro dear

carovita (m) *[costo della vita]* cost of living

carrello (m) elevatore (a forche) fork-lift truck

carro (m) merci railway goods wagon

carta (f) assegni cheque (guarantee) card

carta (f) carbone carbon paper

carta (f) d'imbarco boarding card *or* boarding pass

carta (f) d'imbarco embarkation card

carta (f) da imballaggio wrapping paper

carta (f) da pacco brown paper

carta (f) di credito credit card; charge card

carta (f) di credito d'oro gold card

carta (f) di credito telefonica phone card

carta (f) di sbarco landing card

carta (f) riciclata recycled paper

cartella (f) *[borsa]* briefcase

cartella (f) *[portfolio]* portfolio

cartellino (m) del prezzo price ticket *or* price tag *or* price label

cartello (m) cartel

cartolina (f) postale card *or* postcard

cartoncino (m) card *[material]*

cartoncino (m) della società compliments slip

cartone (m) cardboard

cartone (m) carton *[material]*

cartone (m) *[imballo di cartone]* carton *[box]*

casa (f) house *[for family]*

casa: di casa in casa house-to-house

casella (f) postale P.O. box number

cassa (f) case *or* crate *or* box

cassa (f) checkout *or* till *[in supermarket]*

cassa (f) automatica prelievi cash dispenser

cassa (f) da imballaggio packing case

cassa (f) integrazione volontaria voluntary redundancy

cassa: in cassa integrazione redundant

cassaforte (f) safe (n)

cassiere (m), cassiera (f) cashier

casuale (accidentale) random

catalogo (m) catalogue *or* list

catalogo (m) di vendita per corrispondenza mail-order catalogue

categoria (f) category *or* class

catena (f) chain *[of stores]*

catena (f) di montaggio assembly line *or* production line

cattiva amministrazione (f) mismanagement *or* maladministration

cattivo acquisto (m) bad buy

causa: a causa di owing to

causa (f) *[azione]* action *[lawsuit]*

causa (f) di forza maggiore act of God; force majeure

causa (f) legale court case

causa (f) per risarcimento action for damages

cavaliere (m) bianco white knight

cavarsela get along

cedente (m) *[parte venditrice]* assignor

cedere *[accordare]* allow *or* give

cedola (f) di dividendo dividend warrant

centrale central

centralino (m) telefonico telephone exchange *or* switchboard

centralizzare centralize

centralizzazione (f) centralization

centro (m) centre

centro (m) (di città) downtown (n)

centro: in centro downtown (adv)

centro (m) assistenza service centre

centro (m) commerciale shopping centre; shopping mall *or* arcade

centro (m) d'affari business centre

centro (m) di costi cost centre

centro (m) di profitto profit centre

centro (m) industriale industrial centre

certificare *[autenticare]* certify

certificato certificated

certificato (m) certificate

certificato (m) azionario share certificate

certificato (m) d'iscrizione certificate of registration

certificato (m) d'origine certificate of origin

certificato (m) di accettazione certificate of approval

certificato (m) di deposito certificate of deposit

certificato (m) di garanzia certificate of guarantee

certificato (m) di sdoganamento clearance certificate

certificato (m) medico doctor's certificate

certificazione (f) *[revisione contabile]* auditing

cespite (m) (bene) asset

cespiti (mpl) congelati frozen assets

cespiti (mpl) realizzabili *[attivo esigibile]* realizable assets

cessare (finire) stop (v) *[doing something]*

cessare di lavorare stop work *or* knock off

cessazione (f) delle consegne suspension of deliveries

cessione (f) *[trasferimento]* cession *or* assignment

cessione (f) di una cambiale delivery *[of bill of exchange]*

check in (m) check-in counter

chiamare call (v) *or* telephone (v)

chiamata (f) telefonica phone call *or* telephone call

chiaro clear (adj) *[easy to understand]*

chiave key (adj) *[important]*

chiave (f) key *[to door]*

chiedere apply for *[ask for]*

chiedere (a qualcuno di fare qualcosa) ask *[someone to do something]*

chiedere *[domandare]* ask for *[something]*

chiedere informazioni enquire *or* inquire

chiedere ulteriori dettagli o particolari ask for further details *or* particulars

chiedere un rimborso ask for a refund

chilo (m) o chilogrammo (m) kilo *or* kilogram

chiudere shut (v)

chiudere *[finire]* close (v) *[after work]*

chiudere *[incollare]* seal (v) *[envelope]*

chiudere *[sospendere un'attività]* close down

chiudere a chiave lock (v)

chiudere a chiave un negozio o un ufficio lock up a shop *or* an office

chiudere un conto close an account

chiudere un conto bancario close a bank account

chiuso closed *or* shut

chiusura (f) closing *or* close *or* end

chiusura (f) *[termine]* closure

ciclico cyclical

ciclo (m) cycle

ciclo (m) economico economic cycle *or* trade cycle

cifra (f) figure *or* digit

cifra (f) preventivata estimated figure

cifre (fpl) *[numeri]* figures

cifre (fpl) destagionalizzate seasonally adjusted figures

cifre (fpl) effettive historical figures

cifre (fpl) non verificate unchecked figures

cima (f) *[vetta]* top (n) *[highest point]*

circolazione (f) circulation *[of money]*

circolo (m) *[associazione]* society *or* club

citare *[intentare causa]* sue

citazione (f) in giudizio summons

classe (f) class

classe (f) business business class

classe (f) turistica economy class *or* tourist class

classificare classify

classificazione (f) classification

clausola (f) clause; article

clausola (f) addizionale rider

clausola (f) condizionale proviso

clausola (f) di esclusione exclusion clause

clausola (f) di penalità penalty clause

clausola (f) di recessione waiver clause

clausola (f) di recupero dell'investimento payback clause

clausola (f) di rescissione cancellation clause *or* termination clause

clausola (f) di salvaguardia escape clause

cliente (mf) client *or* customer

cliente (mf) abituale regular customer

clientela (f) clientele

clienti (mpl) eventuali potential customers

coassicurazione (f) co-insurance

codice (m) code

codice (m) a barre bar code

codice (m) d'avviamento postale postcode *or* zip code *[US]*

codice (m) di etica professionale code of practice

codice (m) di magazzino stock code

codice (m) di zona area code

codice (m) fiscale tax code

codici (mpl) leggibili dal computer computer-readable codes

codifica (f) *o* codificazione (f) coding

coefficiente (m) di redditività profitability *[ratio of profit to cost]*

coefficiente (m) di carico load factor

cogliere *[raccogliere]* collect *or* fetch

coincidenza (f) connection

collaborare collaborate

collaboratore (m) *[assistente]* assistant

collaborazione (f) collaboration

collaterale collateral (adj)

collegamento (m) tie-up *or* link

collegare connect

collegare in rete network (v) *[computers]*

collettivo collective

collocazione (f) *[posizione]* situation *[place]*

colloquio (m) *[intervista]* interview (n)

colmare una lacuna (f) fill a gap

colonna (f) del dare debit column

colonna (f) dell'avere credit column

colpa (f) fault *or* blame

colpevole (mf) di appropriazione indebita embezzler
come consigliato as per advice
come da campione as per sample
come da fattura as per invoice
cominciare *[iniziare]* begin *or* start
comitato (m) commission *or* committee
commerciabile marketable
commerciale commercial (adj)
commercializzare *[vendere]* commercialize *or* market (v)
commercializzazione (f) commercialization
commerciante (m) dealer *or* trader
commerciante (m) all'ingrosso wholesaler *or* wholesale dealer
commerciante (m) in proprio sole trader
commerciare handle *or* deal in *or* sell
commerciare in *o* **trafficare in** trade in *[buy and sell]*
commercio (m) commerce *or* trade *or* business
commercio (m) a senso unico one-way trade
commercio (m) bilaterale reciprocal trade
commercio (m) d'esportazione export trade
commercio (m) estero foreign trade *or* overseas trade
commercio (m) internazionale international trade
commercio (m) interno domestic trade
commercio (m) invisibile invisible trade
commercio (m) legittimo lawful trade
commercio (m) libero fair trading
commercio (m) marittimo maritime trade
commercio (m) multilaterale multilateral trade
commesso (m) *o* **commessa (f) (di negozio)** salesman *or* saleswoman *or* shop assistant

commesso (m) viaggiatore commercial traveller
commettere commit *[crime]*
commissione (f) *[percentuale]* commission *[money]*
commissione (f) di mediazione brokerage *or* broker's commission
commissione (f) di studio working party
comodo convenient
compagnia (f) *[società di capitali]* company
compagnia (f) aerea airline
compagnia (f) di assicurazione insurance company
compagno (m) *o* **compagna (f)** *[socio]* partner
comparabilità (f) comparability
compartecipazione (f) agli utili profit-sharing
compensare compensate; make up for
compensare un assegno clear a cheque
compensazione (f) di un assegno clearance of a cheque
compenso (m) *[ricompensa]* compensation
compenso (m) *[emolumento]* fee *[for services]*
compenso (m) per lavoro straordinario overtime pay
comperare buy *or* purchase
comperare a termine buy forward
comperare in contanti buy for cash
competenza (f) remit (n)
competere con qualcuno *o* **con un'azienda** compete with someone *or* with a company
competitività (f) competitiveness
competitivo competitive
competizione (f) *[concorrenza]* competition
compilare make out *[invoice]*
compilare un assegno write out a cheque
compito (m) *[impegno]* undertaking *or* promise
complementare complementary

complesso (m) produttivo
production unit
completamento (m) completion
completare complete (v) *or*
finalize
completo complete (adj)
comporre (formare) form (v)
comporre un numero dial a
number
compratore (m) purchaser *or* buyer
**compravendita (f) di azioni da
parte degli stessi amministratori
della Società** insider dealing
comprensivo comprehensive
comprese tasse (fpl) inclusive of
tax
compromesso (m) compromise (n)
comproprietà (f) co-ownership *or*
joint ownership *or* part-ownership
comproprietario (m) co-owner *or*
joint owner *or* part-owner
computer (m) computer
computerizzare computerize
comune common
comune: in comune jointly
comunicare communicate
comunicato (m) stampa press
release
comunicazione (f) communication
comunicazione (f) orizzontale
horizontal communication
comunicazione (f) verticale
vertical communication
comunicazioni (fpl)
communications
comunità (f) community
con cum
con coupon (m) cum coupon
con dividendo (m) cum dividend
concedente (m) franchiser
concedere *[accordare]* grant (v)
concedere il diritto di esclusiva
franchise (v)
concessionario (m) franchisee;
licensee; concessionaire
concessione (f) concession *or*
right; franchise
concessione (f) di licenze
licensing

concessione (f) di vendita
distributorship; franchising
concessione (f) fiscale tax
concession
conciliazione (f) conciliation
concludere conclude *[agreement]*
concludere *[finire]* end (v)
concludere definitivamente clinch
concordare *[corrispondere a]*
agree with *or* be the same as
concordato *[convenuto]* agreed
concorrente (m) competitor
concorrenza (f) *[competizione]*
competition
concorrenza: in concorrenza
competing (adj)
concorrenza (f) accanita keen
competition
concorrenza (f) dura stiff
competition
concorrenza (f) sleale unfair
competition
concorrenza (f) spietata cut-throat
competition
condirettore (m) joint managing
director
condirezione (f) joint management
condizionato *[con riserve]*
qualified *[with reservations]*
condizione (f) condition *[terms]*
condizione: a condizione che on
condition that
condizione (f) *[stato]* condition
[state]
condizione (f) sociale status
condizioni (fpl) terms
**condizioni: a condizioni
vantaggiose** on favourable terms
condizioni (fpl) di assunzione
conditions of employment
condizioni (fpl) di impiego terms
of employment
condizioni (fpl) di lavoro working
conditions
condizioni (fpl) di pagamento
terms of payment
condizioni (fpl) di vendita terms of
sale
condizioni (fpl) moderate easy
terms

**condizioni (fpl) per pagamento in
contanti** cash terms; cash price
conducente (m) driver
condurre (guidare) drive (v) *[a
car]*
condurre una trattativa conduct
negotiations
conferenza (f) *[congresso]*
conference
conferenza (f) stampa press
conference
conferire il diritto entitle
conferma (f) confirmation *or*
acknowledgement
confermare confirm
**confermare l'assunzione di una
persona** confirm someone in a job
confermare una prenotazione
confirm a booking
confermato: non confermato
unconfirmed
confezionatore (m) wrapper
**confezione (f) a bolla di plastica
trasparente** bubble pack
confezione (f) finta dummy pack
confezione (f) per esposizione
display pack
conflitto (m) di interessi conflict
of interest
conformarsi a (osservare) comply
with
confrontare (paragonare) compare
confronto (m) comparison
congedo (m) leave (n)
congedo (m) autorizzato
[aspettativa] leave of absence
congedo (m) per maternità
maternity leave
congegno (m) device
congelamento (m) salariale wage
freeze
congelare freeze (v) *[prices]*
congelare un credito freeze
credits
congelato *[bloccato]* frozen
congiunto (unito) joint
congiuntura (f) economic trends
conglomerato (m) conglomerate
congresso (m) *[conferenza]*
conference

consegna (f) di merci delivery of
goods
consegna (f) gratuita free delivery
consegnare deliver; consign
consegnare: non consegnato
undelivered
consegnatario (m) consignee
conseguibile *[ottenibile]*
obtainable
**Conservatore (m) del Registro
delle Società** Registrar of
Companies
**conservazione (f) in ambiente
frigorifero** cold storage
considerare consider
consigliare *[raccomandare]*
advise *or* recommend *[what should
be done]*
Consiglio (m) di Amministrazione
board of directors
consistere in consist of
consocio (m) copartner
consolidamento (m) consolidation
consolidare consolidate
consolidare spedizioni
consolidate *[shipments]*
consolidato consolidated
consorzio (m) consortium
consueto *[fisso]* regular *[always
at same time]*
consulente (m) consultant *or*
adviser
**consulente (m) di direzione
aziendale** management consultant
consulente (m) fiscale tax
consultant
consulente (m) legale legal
adviser
consulente (m) tecnico consulting
engineer
consulenza (f) consultancy
consulenza (f) legale legal advice
consultarsi consult
consumatore (m) consumer
consumo (m) consumption
consumo (m) interno *o* nazionale
home consumption
contabile (mf) *[ragioniere]*
bookkeeper
contabilità (f) accounting;
bookkeeping

contabilità (f) a costi correnti current cost accounting

contabilità (f) basata sui conti cost accounting

contabilità (f) di bilancio budget account *[in bank]*

contabilità (f) di fine mese month-end accounts

contabilità (f) di metà mese mid-month accounts

contabilità (f) non sottoposta a revisione contabile unaudited accounts

contabilità (f) semestrale half-yearly accounts

container (m) container *[for shipping]*

containerizzare containerize *[put into containers]*

containerizzazione (f) containerization *[putting into containers]*

contanti: in contanti in cash

contare count (v) *[add]*

contare su depend on

contatto (m) contact (n)

contenere contain *or* hold

contenitore (m) container; holder

contenitore (m) di contanti cash till

contenuto (m) contents

contenzioso: in contenzioso sub judice

conti (mpl) attivi accounts receivable

conti (mpl) gestione management accounts

conti (mpl) passivi accounts payable

contingente (m) di importazione import quota

contingenza (f) contingency; cost-of-living bonus

continuamente continually

continuare continue

continuazione (f) continuation

continuo continual *or* continuous

conto (m) account; bill *[in restuarant]*

conto: per conto di on behalf of

conto (m) [dell'albergo] hotel bill

conto (m) a garanzia escrow account

conto (m) aperto open account

conto (m) assegni cheque account

conto (m) bancario bank account

conto (m) bloccato account on stop

conto (m) capitale capital account

conto (m) chiuso dead account

conto (m) congelato frozen account

conto (m) congiunto joint account

conto (m) corrente current account

conto (m) creditori credit account

conto (m) delle entrate revenue accounts

conto (m) dettagliato itemized account

conto (m) di cassa cash account

conto (m) di contropartita contra account

conto (m) di deposito deposit account

conto (m) di prestanome nominee account

conto (m) di risparmio savings account

conto (m) in credito account in credit

conto (m) numerato numbered account

conto (m) personale charge account

conto (m) profitti e perdite profit and loss account

conto (m) scoperto overdrawn account

conto (m) spese expense account

contraffare counterfeit (v)

contraffatto [falso] counterfeit (adj)

contraffazione (f) forgery *[action]*

contrapporre set against

contrario contrary

contrarre contract (v)

contrarre debiti incur debts *or* run into debt

contrassegno (m) countersign

contrasto (m) contrast (n)

contrattare *[tirare sul prezzo]* bargain (v)

contrattazione (f) bargaining

contratti (mpl) a termine su materie prime commodity futures

contratto (m) contract (n)

contratto (m) a breve termine short-term contract

contratto (m) a prezzo fisso fixed-price agreement

contratto (m) a termine forward contract

contratto (m) salariale collettivo collective wage agreement

contratto (m) di assicurazione insurance contract

contratto (m) di lavoro contract of employment

contratto (m) di locazione tenancy *[agreement]*

contratto (m) globale package *[of services]*

contrattuale contractual

contrattualmente contractually

contribuente (m) taxpayer

contribuire contribute

contributo (m) contribution

controfferta (f) counter-offer *or* counterbid

controllabile *[trattabile]* manageable

controllante controlling (adj)

controllare control (v)

controllare *[esaminare]* check (v) *or* examine

controlli (mpl) dei prezzi price controls

controlli (mpl) valutari exchange controls

controllo (m) examination *or* check

controllo: a controllo statale government-controlled *or* government-regulated

controllo (m) *[verifica]* control (n) *or* check

controllo (m) budgetario budgetary control

controllo (m) dei materiali materials control

controllo (m) dei prezzi price control

controllo (m) del credito credit control

controllo (m) delle scorte stock control

controllo (m) di magazzino inventory control

controllo (m) di qualità quality control

controllo (m) doganale customs examination

controllo (m) passeggeri check-in *[at airport]*

controllore (m) controller *[who checks]*

controllore (m) della qualità quality controller

controreazione (f) feedback

controrichiesta (f) counter-claim (n)

contumace: essere contumace default (v)

conveniente good value (for money)

convenire covenant (v)

convenuto *[concordato]* agreed

convenzione (f) covenant (n)

conversione (f) conversion

conversione (f) della valuta currency conversion

conversione (f) di fondi conversion of funds

conversione (f) di un prestito refunding of a loan

convertibilità (f) convertibility

convertire convert

convocare call (v) *or* convene *[meeting]*

cooperare co-operate

cooperativa (f) co-operative (n)

cooperativo *[cooperativa]* co-operative (adj)

cooperazione (m) *[collaborazione]* co-operation

cooptare qualcuno co-opt someone

copertura (f) cover (n) *[top]*

copertura (f) assicurativa insurance cover

copia (f) copy (n)
copia (f) *[esemplare]* copy (n) *[book, newspaper]*
copia (f) autentica certified copy *or* true copy
copia (f) carbone carbon copy
copia (f) di riserva backup copy
copia (f) in chiaro hard copy
copiare *[riprodurre]* copy (v)
copiatrice (f) copier *or* copying machine
coprire cover (v)
coprire i costi cover costs
corona (f) (danese, norvegese) krone *[currency used in Denmark and Norway]*
corona (f) (svedese) krona *[currency used in Sweden]*
corporazione (f) corporation
corporazione (f) *[gilda]* guild
correggere correct (v) *or* amend *or* rectify
corrente current *or* ruling
correre un rischio run a risk *or* take a risk
corretto correct (adj) *or* right
correzione (f) correction
correzione (f) strutturale structural adjustment
corriere (m) *[messaggero]* courier *[messenger]*
corrispondente (mf) correspondent *[who writes letters]*
corrispondenza (f) correspondence
corrispondenza: essere in corrispondenza con qualcuno correspond with someone
corrispondere a *[concordare]* agree with *or* be the same as
corrompere (con denaro o doni) bribe (v)
corso (m) a indirizzo commerciale commercial course
corso (m) d'aggiornamento refresher course
corso (m) in amministrazione management course
corso (m) introduttivo induction course *or* induction training

corso (m) per operazioni a termine forward rate
corte (f) di Giustizia court
costante constant
costare cost (v)
costi (mpl) d'esercizio operating costs *or* operating expenses
costi (mpl) di distribuzione distribution costs
costi (mpl) di factoring factoring charges
costi (mpl) di gestione operational costs *or* running costs *or* running expenses
costi (mpl) di lancio launching costs
costi (mpl) di produzione production costs *or* manufacturing costs
costi (mpl) diretti prime cost
costi (mpl) eccessivi excessive costs
costi (mpl) fissi fixed costs
costi (mpl) fondiari landed costs
costi (mpl) indiretti del lavoro indirect labour costs
costi (mpl) per la spedizione marittima shipping charges *or* shipping costs
costi (mpl) sociali social costs
costi (mpl) variabili variable costs
costituire incorporate *[a company]*
costituire una società (f) set up a company
costituzione (f) incorporation
costo (m) cost (n)
costo (m) della manodopera labour costs
costo (m) della vita *[carovita]* cost of living
costo (m) delle vendite cost of sales
costo (m) diretto direct cost
costo (m) effettivo historic(al) cost
costo (m) marginale marginal cost *or* incremental cost
costo (m) più una percentuale cost plus
costo (m) simbolico token charge
costo (m) totale total cost

costo (m) unitario unit cost

costo (m), assicurazione (f) e nolo (m) cost, insurance and freight (c.i.f.)

costoso costly *or* expensive

costruire [sviluppare] develop [build]

costruire riserve [stoccare] stockpile (v)

costruttore (m) chiavi in mano turnkey operator

costruzione: in costruzione under construction

coupon (m) con risposta pagata reply coupon

crediti (mpl) congelati frozen credits

credito (m) credit (n) *or* credit balance

credito: a credito on credit

credito (m) a breve short-term credit

credito (m) a breve termine short credit

credito (m) a lungo termine long credit

credito (m) al consumatore consumer credit

credito (m) aperto open credit

credito (m) bancario bank credit

credito (m) d'imposta tax credit

credito (m) di appoggio standby credit

credito (m) esente da interessi interest-free credit

credito (m) esigibile debts due

credito (m) immediato instant credit

credito (m) inesigibile bad debt

credito (m) prorogato extended credit

credito (m) rinnovabile automaticamente revolving credit

creditore (m) creditor

creditore (m) differito deferred creditor

creditore (m) in solido co-creditor

creditore (m) ipotecario mortgagee

creditore (m) non garantito unsecured creditor

creditore (m) privilegiato preferential creditor *or* secured creditor

crescente increasing

crescita (f) growth

crescita (f) economica economic growth

crisi (f) del dollaro dollar crisis

crisi (f) di mancanza di liquidità liquidity crisis

crisi (f) economica [crollo] slump (n) *or* depression

crisi (f) finanziaria financial crisis

crollare [cadere] collapse (v) *or* crash *or* fail

crollo (m) [crisi economica] slump (n) [depression]

crollo (m) [caduta] fall (n) *or* collapse (n) *or* crash (n)

cronico chronic

cubico cubic

cucire con punti metallici [graffare] staple (v)

cucitrice (f) [graffatrice] stapler

culminare [raggiungere un punto massimo] peak (v)

cumulativo cumulative

curricolo (m) track record

curriculum (m) vitae curriculum vitae (CV)

curva (f) curve

curva (f) delle vendite sales curve

Dd

da non restituire *o* da gettare disposable

da primato record-breaking

da ricevere receivable

danneggiare damage (v)

danneggiato damaged

danni (mpl) *[rotture]* damage; breakages

danni (mpl) causati da un temporale storm damage

danno (m) alla proprietà damage to property

danno (m) causato da un incendio fire damage

dare give

dare corso ad un'ordinazione deal with an order

dare e avere debits and credits

dare in affitto *[affittare]* lease out (v)

dare in prestito *[prestare]* loan (v)

dare in subappalto subcontract (v)

dare istruzioni brief (v)

dare la caccia a chase *[an order]*

dare soldi come anticipo put money down

data (f) date (n)

data (f) d'inizio starting date

data (f) del lancio launching date

data (f) di chiusura *[termine ultimo]* closing date

data (f) di consegna delivery date

data (f) di entrata in vigore effective date

data (f) di ricevimento date of receipt

data (f) di rimborso redemption date

data (f) di scadenza sell-by date; expiry date *or* maturity date

data (f) di scadenza *[termine ultimo]* deadline

data (f) di ultimazione completion date

datare date (v)

datario (m) date stamp

datato dated

datato: non datato undated

dati (mpl) data

dati (mpl) di emissione computer output

datore (m) di lavoro employer

daziere (m) Excise officer

dazio (m) duty *[tax]*

dazio (m) d'esportazione export duty

dazio (m) doganale customs duty *or* import duty

dazio (m) preferenziale preferential duty *or* preferential tariff

debiti (mpl) a lungo termine long-term debts

debiti (mpl) insoluti outstanding debts

debiti (mpl) privilegiati secured debts

debito (m) debt

debito: a debito *[dovuto]* owing

debito (m) *[registrazione]* debit entry

debito (m) inesigibile irrecoverable debt

debitore (m) debtor

debitore: essere debitore owe

debitore (m) autorizzato al concordato preventivo certificated bankrupt

debitore (m) ipotecario mortgager *or* mortgagor

debitore (m) riconosciuto da tribunale judgment debtor

decentramento (m) decentralization

decentrare decentralize

decidere decide *or* resolve

decidere una linea di condotta decide on a course of action

decimale (m) decimal (n)

decisione (f) decision

decisione (f) *[verdetto]* judgement *or* judgment

decisivo deciding

declino (m) decline (n)

decollare take off

decrescente decreasing (adj)

decretare rule (v) *[give decision]*

decreto (m) ruling (n)

decurtare dock (v) *or* deduct money

dedurre *[fare uno sconto di]* take off *or* deduct

deficit (m) *[disavanzo]* deficit

deficit (m) della bilancia commerciale trade deficit *or* trade gap

definire una domanda d'indennizzo settle a claim

deflazione (f) deflation

deflazionistico deflationary

degrado (m) [normale usura] fair wear and tear

delega (f) delegation [action]

delega (f) [procura] proxy [deed]

delegare delegate (v)

delegato (m) delegate (n)

delegato (m) [sostituto] deputy

delegazione (f) delegation

denaro (m) money

denaro (m) a buon mercato cheap money

denaro (m) contante cash (n) [money]

denaro (m) per le piccole spese spending money

denaro (m) scarso tight money

denominazione (f) della mansione job title

denuncia (f) dei redditi tax return *or* tax declaration

depennare cross off

deperibile perishable

deporto (m) backwardation

depositante (m) depositor

depositare documenti file documents

depositare in banca bank (v)

depositare un marchio di fabbrica register a trademark

depositi (mpl) bancari bank deposits

depositi (mpl) fruttiferi interest-bearing deposits

deposito (m) deposit (n) [in bank]

deposito (m) [magazzino] store (n) [place where goods are kept]

deposito (m) [magazzinaggio] storage (n) [in warehouse]

deposito (m) a termine time deposit

deposito (m) a vista demand deposit

deposito (m) in cassetta di sicurezza safe deposit

deposito (m) in contanti cash deposit

deposito (m) merci goods depot

deposito (m) non rimborsabile non-refundable deposit

deposito (m) vincolato fixed deposit

depressione (f) depression

deregolamentazione (f) deregulation

derivare result from

descrivere describe

descrizione (f) description

descrizione (f) commerciale trade description

descrizione (f) dei compiti job description

design (m) [progettazione] design (n)

desktop publishing (m) desk-top publishing (DTP)

destinare appropriate (v) [funds]

destinatario (m) addressee

destinazione (f) destination

destituzione (f) removal *or* sacking [of someone]

destro right (adj) [not left]

deterioramento (m) naturale wear and tear

determinare determine

determinazione (f) del prezzo pricing

determinazione (f) del prezzo di concorrenza competitive pricing

determinazione (f) marginale del prezzo marginal pricing

detraibile deductible

detraibile dal reddito imponibile tax-deductible

detrazione (f) deduction

detrazioni (fpl) d'imposta tax deductions [from salary to pay tax]

detrazioni (fpl) personali personal allowances

dettagli (mpl) particulars

dettagliante (m) retailer *or* retail dealer

dettagliare detail (v) *or* break down (v) *or* itemize

dettagliato detailed

dettaglio (m) detail (n)
dettare dictate
dettatura (f) dictation
di mezzo [medio] medium (adj)
diagramma (m) diagram
diagramma (m) a barre bar chart
diagramma (m) del ciclo di lavorazione flow diagram
diario diary
dichiarare declare or state
dichiarare le merci alla dogana declare goods to customs
dichiarare qualcuno fallito declare someone bankrupt
dichiarare sciolta una riunione wind up a meeting
dichiarare una perdita report a loss
dichiarato declared
dichiarazione (f) declaration
dichiarazione (f) doganale customs declaration
dichiarazione dei redditi declaration of income
dichiarazione di fallimento declaration of bankruptcy
dichiarazione IVA VAT declaration
dicitura (f) wording
difendere defend
difendere una causa defend a lawsuit
difensore (m) civico ombudsman
difesa (f) defence [legal]
difetto (m) defect or mechanical fault
difettoso defective [faulty]
differenza (f) difference
differenza (f) a credito credit balance
differenze (fpl) di prezzo differences in price
differenziale differential (adj)
differire (rinviare) defer or postpone or shelve
differire un pagamento defer payment
differito deferred
diffusione (f) nei mass-media media coverage

digitare keyboard (v)
dilazione (f) [rinvio] postponement
diluizione (f) della partecipazione azionaria dilution of equity
dimensione (f) size
dimensioni: di medie dimensioni medium-sized
dimettersi resign
diminuire decrease (v) or fall off
diminuzione (f) decrease (n)
diminuzione (f) dei prezzi price reduction or reduction in price; mark-down
diminuzione (f) del valore decrease in value
dimissioni (fpl) resignation
dimostrare demonstrate
dimostratore (m) demonstrator
dimostrazione (f) demonstration
dinamismo (m) [energia] human energy
dipartimentale departmental
dipartimento (m) department
dipartimento (m) design design department
dipendente (m) employee
dipendenti (m) pagati a ore hourly-paid workers
diramare istruzioni issue instructions
direttamente direct (adv)
direttiva (f) directive or guideline
direttivo [gestionale] managerial
diretto direct (adj)
direttore (m), direttrice (f) manager; senior executive
direttore (m) commerciale sales manager
direttore (m) d'albergo hotel manager
direttore (m) del progetto project manager
direttore (m) del reparto esportazioni export manager
direttore (m) del servizio marketing sales executive
direttore (m) dell'ufficio acquisti purchasing manager
direttore (m) della pubblicità advertising manager or publicity manager

direttore (m) delle distribuzioni
distribution manager

direttore (m) delle finanze finance
director

direttore (m) delle vendite sales
executive

direttore (m) di banca bank
manager

direttore (m) di filiale branch
manager

direttore (m) di marketing
marketing manager

direttore (m) di produzione
production manager

direttore (m) di zona area manager

direttore (m) esecutivo executive
director

direttore (m) esterno outside
director

direttore (m) facente funzione
acting manager

**direttore (m) generale
[amministratore delegato]**
managing director (MD); chief
executive

direttore (m) generale general
manager

direttore (m) senza poteri esecutivi
non-executive director

direttore (m) vendite esterne field
sales manager

direzione (f) management
[managers]

direzione (f) [istruzione] directions
or instructions

direzione (f) al vertice top
management

**direzione (f) centrale [sede
centrale]** main office

direzione (f) del personale
personnel management

dirigente (m) executive (n)

**dirigente (m) delle pubbliche
relazioni** public relations officer

dirigente (m) delle vendite sales
executive

dirigente (m) di grado inferiore
junior executive or junior manager

dirigente (m) in capo senior
manager or senior executive

dirigere direct (v) or run (v) or
manage

dirigere male mismanage

diritti (mpl) di porto port charges
or port dues

diritti (mpl) portuali harbour dues

**diritti (mpl) speciali di prelievo
(DSP)** special drawing rights
(SDRs)

diritto (m) right or entitlement;
legal title

diritto (m) law [study]

diritto (m) civile civil law

diritto (m) commerciale
commercial law

diritto (m) contrattuale contract
law

diritto (m) della navigazione
maritime law

diritto (m) di concessione royalty

diritto (m) di possesso tenure
[right]

diritto (m) di precedenza right of
way

diritto (m) di veto right of veto

diritto (m) internazionale
international law

diritto (m) societario company law

disavanzo (m) [deficit] deficit

discendente [giù] down or
downward

discesa (f) delle vendite slump in
sales

dischetto (m) diskette

disco (m) disk

discorso (m) di ringraziamento
speech of thanks

discrepanza (f) discrepancy

discussione (f) discussion

discussione (f) [disputa] argument

discussione (f) collettiva joint
discussions

discussione (f) produttiva
productive discussions

discutere discuss

disdetta (f) [cancellazione]
cancellation

disdire un affare call off a deal

disegno (m) industriale industrial
design

disfarsi di get rid of
disoccupato out of work *or* unemployed
disoccupazione (f) unemployment
disoccupazione (f) strutturale structural unemployment
disonestamente fraudulently
disonesto *[fraudolento]* fraudulent
dispari odd *[not even]*
disparità (f) dei prezzi price differential
dispersione (f) leakage
disponibile available
disponibile: non disponibile unavailable
disponibilità (f) availability
disponibilità: non disponibilità (f) unavailability
disponibilità (f) di capitali money supply
disponibilità (fpl) finanziarie financial assets
disporre *[sistemare]* arrange *or* set out
disposizione (m) *[sistemazione]* arrangement *or* system
disposizioni (fpl) *[regolamenti]* regulations
disputa (f) argument
dissentire differ
dissolvere *[risolvere]* dissolve
distinta (f) d'imballaggio packing list *or* packing slip
distinta (f) di versamento paying-in slip *or* deposit slip
distretto (m) commerciale commercial district
distribuire distribute
distributore (m) distributor
distribuzione (f) distribution
distruggere wreck (v) *or* ruin
ditta (f) (impresa) firm (n) *or* business *or* company
ditta (f) a conduzione familiare family company
ditta (f) di consulenza consultancy firm
ditta (f) di vendita a rate hire-purchase company

ditta (f) di noleggio impianti plant-hire firm
dittafono (m) dictating machine
divario (m) gap
diversificare diversify
diversificazione (f) diversification
diverso different
dividendo (m) dividend
dividendo (m) finale final dividend
dividendo (m) in acconto interim dividend
dividendo (m) minimo minimum dividend
dividere share (v)
divieto (m) di importazione import ban
divisa (f) forte strong currency
divise (fpl) *[moneta straniera]* foreign currency
divisione (f) division *[part of a group]*
divulgare *[rivelare]* disclose
divulgare un'informazione disclose a piece of information
divulgazione (f) *[rivelazione]* disclosure
divulgazione (f) di un'informazione riservata disclosure of confidential information
documentario (m) documentary
documentarsi su *[fare ricerche]* research (v)
documentazione (f) documentation; records
documenti (mpl) documents
documenti (mpl) falsi faked documents
documento (m) document
documento (m) provvisorio scrip
dogana (f) customs
doganiere (m) customs officer
dollaro (m) dollar
domanda (f) demand (n)
domanda: fare domanda scritta apply in writing
domanda (f) *[istanza]* application
domanda (f) d'impiego application for a job
domanda d'impiego: fare domanda d'impiego apply for a job

domanda (f) d'indennizzo claim (n)

domanda (f) di lavoro job application

domanda (f) effettiva effective demand

domanda (f) finale final demand

domandare demand (v)

domandare [chiedere] ask for [something]

domandare [richiedere] request (v)

domestico domestic

domicilio (m) domicile

domicilio: a domicilio door-to-door

donna (f) d'affari businesswoman

dono (m) [omaggio] free gift

doppia tassazione (f) double taxation

doppio double (adj)

dorso (m) [retro] back (n)

dossier (m) [pratica] dossier

dover rispondere a qualcuno report to someone

dovere (m) [impegno] obligation or duty

dovutamente [regolarmente] duly or legally

dovuto [a debito] due or owing

dovuto: essere dovuto fall due or be due

dozzina (f) dozen

DSP (diritti speciali di prelievo) special drawing rights (SDRs)

duplicare duplicate (v)

duplicato (m) duplicate (n)

duplicato: fare il duplicato di una fattura duplicate an invoice

duplicazione (f) duplication

durata (f) [periodo] term [of validity]

durata (f) in carica tenure [time]

duty free shop [negozio esente da tasse] duty-free shop

Ee

eccellente excellent

eccessivo excessive

eccesso excess

eccetto [tranne] except

eccezionale [straordinario] exceptional

economia (f) economy

economia (f) [scienze economiche] economics

economia (f) controllata controlled economy

economia (f) dell'offerta supply side economics

economia (f) di massa economies of scale

economia (f) di mercato libero free market economy

economia (f) di tipo misto mixed economy

economia (f) matura mature economy

economia (f) nera black economy

economia (f) solida stable economy

economico [a basso prezzo] economical or cheap

economico [finanziario] economic or financial

economista (mf) economist

economista (mf) di mercato market economist

economizzare economize or save

ecu (m) (Unità di Conto Europea) ecu or ECU (= European currency unit)

edificio (m) facility [building]

edificio (m) principale main building

effetti (mpl) a breve termine short-dated bills

effetti (mpl) all'incasso bills for collection

effetti (mpl) attivi receivables *or* bills receivable

effetti (mpl) bancabili *[strumenti scontabili]* bankable paper

effetti (mpl) passivi *[cambiali da pagare]* bills payable

effettivo effective

effettivo (reale) actual

effetto (m) effect (n)

effetto (m) *[cambiale]* bill (n) *or* promise to pay

effetto (m) a catena knock-on effect

effetto (m) a lunga scadenza long-dated bill

effetto (m) accettato irrevocabilmente irrevocable acceptance

effetto (m) bancario bank bill *[GB]*

effetto (m) di comodo *[cambiale di favore]* accommodation bill

effettuare effect (v)

efficacia (f) effectiveness

efficiente efficient

efficienza (f) efficiency

elaborare cifre process figures

elaborato a mezzo computer computerized

elaboratore (m) ad uso personale *[personal computer]* personal computer (PC)

elaborazione (f) delle ordinazioni order processing

elaborazione (f) dei dati data processing

elaborazione (f) delle informazioni processing of information

elaborazione (f) di massa batch processing

elasticità (f) elasticity

eleggere elect

elementi (m) ciclici cyclical factors

elemento (m) decisivo deciding factor

elencare list (v) *or* index (v)

elencazione (f) scheduling

elenco (m) classificato classified directory

elenco (m) delle cause docket

elenco (m) di indirizzi mailing list

elenco (m) telefonico telephone book *or* telephone directory

elezione (f) election

eliminare delete

eliminare gradualmente phase out

eliminare le scorte in eccesso dispose of excess stock

embargo (m) embargo (n)

emendamento (m) *[rettifica]* amendment

emergenza (f) emergency

emettere issue (v) *[shares]*

emettere allo scoperto overdraw

emettere un assegno draw *[a cheque]*

emettere una fattura raise an invoice

emissione (f) azionaria share issue

emissione (f) di certificati azionari provvisori scrip issue

emissione (f) di diritti rights issue

emissione (f) gratuita di azioni bonus issue

emolumento (m) *[compenso]* fee *[for services]*

energia (f) elettrica energy *[electricity]*

energia (f) *[dinamismo]* human energy

ente (m) locale local government

entrare enter *or* go in

entrare: far entrare admit *or* let in

entrare in porto *[attraccare]* dock (v) *[ship]*

entrare in possesso di una società acquire a company

entrare in vigore run (v) *or* be in force

entrata (f) entry *[going in]*

entrate (fpl) receipts

equalizzazione (f) equalization

equipaggiare equip

equivalere a qualcosa correspond with something

equo (giusto) fair (adj)

erodere erode

errore (m) error *or* mistake

errore (m) casuale random error

errore (m) di computer computer error

errore (m) di trascrizione clerical error

esame (f) examination

esame: in esame on approval

esaminare examine *or* inspect

esaminare [controllare] check (v) *or* examine

esatto exact (adj)

esattamente exactly

esattore (m) dei crediti debt collector

esattore (m) delle imposte tax collector

esattore (m) di affitti rent collector

esaurire [vendere tutto] sell out *[all stock]*

esaurire run out of

esaurito out of stock

esborso (m) outlay *or* disbursement

escludere exclude

esclusione (f) exclusion

esclusività (f) exclusivity

escluso excluding; exclusive of

esecutivo executive (adj)

esecuzione (f) execution

eseguire execute

esemplare (m) [copia] copy (n) *[of book, newspaper]*

esentare exempt (v)

esentasse tax-exempt

esente exempt (adj)

esente da canone d'affitto rent-free

esente da dazio duty-free

esente da pedaggio toll free *[US]*

esente da tassa exempt from tax

esente da tasse tax-free *or* free of tax

esenzione (f) exemption

esenzione (f) fiscale tax exemption *or* exemption from tax

esercitare exercise (v)

esercitare il commercio di un prodotto merchandise a product

esercitare un'opzione exercise an option *or* take up an option

esercizio (m) exercise (n)

esercizio (m) di un'opzione exercise of an option

esercizio (m) finanziario financial year

esibire exhibit (v)

esigenza (f) di manodopera manpower requirements

esigere exact (v)

espansione (f) industriale industrial expansion

esperto experienced

esperto (m) [professionista] expert (n) *or* professional (n)

esperto (m) di statistica statistician

esplorare explore

esporre display (v)

esportare export (v)

esportatore exporting (adj)

esportatore (m) exporter

esportazione (f) export (n)

esportazioni (fpl) exports

espositore (m) [standista] exhibitor

esposizione (f) [mostra] exhibition *or* display

esposizione (f) in vetrina window display

espresso express (adj)

esprimere express (v) *[state]*

espropriazione (f) per pubblica utilità compulsory purchase

essere in ritardo (nel fare una cosa) fall behind *or* be late

essere valido run (v) *or* be in force

estendersi [variare] range (v)

esteriore outside

esterno external *[outside a company]*

estero [straniero] external *or* foreign

estero (m) [i paesi stranieri] overseas (n)

estero: all'estero abroad *or* overseas

estinguere [un debito] redeem *or* pay off *or* clear *[a debt]*

estratto (m) conto statement of account

estratto (m) conto bancario bank statement

età (f) della pensione retirement age

etichetta (f) label (n)

etichetta (f) di posta aerea airmail sticker

etichetta (f) indirizzata address label

etichettare label (v)

etichettatura (f) labelling

ettaro (m) hectare

euro (m) euro

euroassegno (m) Eurocheque

eurodollaro (m) Eurodollar

euromercato (m) Euromarket

euromoneta (f) Eurocurrency

evadere evade

evadere un'ordinazione fulfil an order

evasione (f) d'imposta evasion

evasione (f) di un'ordinazione order fulfilment

evasione (f) fiscale tax avoidance *or* tax evasion

evidenziatore (m) marker pen

ex cedola (f) ex coupon

ex dividendo (m) ex dividend

expertise (f) *[perizia]* expertise

extra extra

Ff

fabbrica (f) factory *or* plant

fabbricante (m) *[produttore]* manufacturer

fabbricare *[produrre]* manufacture (v) *or* produce *or* make

fabbricazione (f) *[lavorazione]* manufacture (n)

faccenda (f) *[problema]* matter (n) *or* problem

facente funzione di *[sostituto]* acting

facile easy

facile da usare *[accessibile]* user-friendly

facilitazioni (fpl) di scoperto overdraft facility

facoltativo optional

factoring (m) factoring

factoring: fare del factoring factor (v)

fallimento (m) bankruptcy

fallire fail

fallire: fare fallire ruin (v) *or* bankrupt (v)

fallire *[non arrivare a compimento]* fall through

fallito bankrupt (adj)

fallito (m) bankrupt (n)

fallito (m) non riabilitato undischarged bankrupt

falsificare falsify *or* fake (v) *or* forge

falsificazione (f) falsification

falso (m) forgery *[copy]*

falso *[contraffatto]* false *or* counterfeit (adj)

falso *[fittizio]* dummy

far entrare admit *[let in]*

far pagare charge (v) *[money]*

far pagare meno undercharge

far pagare troppo overcharge (v)

fare pratica train (v) *[learn]*

fare progressi *[avanzare]* progress (v)

fare riferimento a refer *[to item]*

fare soldi make money

fare un'ordinazione place an order

farsi ritirare l'usato trade in *[give in old item for new]*

fascia (f) tax bracket

fascicolo (m) file (n) *[documents]*

fascicolo (m) dello schedario card-index file

fascicolo (m) supplementare (in una rivista) magazine insert

fattibilità (f) feasibility

fatto appositamente custom-built *or* custom-made

fattore (m) factor (n) *[influence]*
fattore (m) costo cost factor
fattore (m) negativo minus factor *or* downside factor
fattore (m) positivo plus factor
fattori (mpl) di produzione factors of production
fattorino (m) deliveryman *or* messenger
fattura (f) invoice (n) *or* bill
fattura (f) [atto di vendita] bill of sale
fattura (f) con IVA VAT invoice
fattura (f) dettagliata itemized invoice
fattura (f) proforma pro forma (invoice)
fatturare invoice (v) *or* bill (v)
fatturato (m) [vendite] sales (revenue)
fatturazione (f) invoicing *or* billing
fatture (fpl) insolute unpaid invoices
favorevole favourable
fax (m) fax (n)
fedeltà (f) alla marca brand loyalty
fede: in buona fede bona fide; in good faith
fedeltà (f) dei clienti customer loyalty
fermare countermand
fermarsi stay (v)
fermo (stabile) stable
fermoposta (m) poste restante
ferrovia (f) railway *or* rail *or* railroad *[US]*
festa (f) nazionale public holiday; bank holiday
fiasco: fare fiasco fail (v) *or* flop (v)
fiducia (f) confidence
fiera (f) campionaria trade fair
file (m) [archivio] computer file
filiale (f) branch office; subsidiary
finale final
finanza (f) [attività finanziaria] finance (n)
finanza (f) pubblica public finance
finanze (fpl) finances
finanziamento (m) financing

finanziamento (m) del disavanzo (m) deficit financing
finanziare finance (v) *or* fund (v) *or* pay costs
finanziare un'operazione finance an operation
finanziariamente financially
finanziario [economico] financial
finanziatore (m) moneylender
fine fine (adv) *[very small]*
fine (f) [scadenza] expiry
fine (f) [termine] end (n)
fine (f) del mese month end
fine (f) esercizio year end
finestra (f) window
finire [concludere] end (v)
finire [portare a termine] complete (v)
finire [cessare] stop (v) *[doing something]*
finito finished
fino a [conforme a] up to
fiorente booming *or* flourishing
firma (f) signature
firmare sign (v)
firmare come testimone witness (v) *[a document]*
firmare il registro check in *or* register *[at hotel]*
firmare un accordo come testimone witness an agreement
firmare un assegno sign a cheque
firmare un contratto sign a contract
firmatario (m) signatory
firmatario (m) congiunto joint signatory
fiscale fiscal
fissaggio (m) fixing
fissare fix *or* arrange
fissare obiettivi set targets
fissare una riunione per le 3 del pomeriggio fix a meeting for 3 p.m.
fissato fixed
fissato (m) bollato contract note
fisso fixed *or* flat
fisso (consueto) regular *[always at same time]*
fittizio (falso) dummy
flessibile flexible

flessibilità (f) flexibility
fluire flow (v)
flusso (m) flow (n)
flusso (m) di cassa cash flow
flusso (m) di cassa positivo positive cash flow
fluttuante fluctuating
fluttuante [galleggiante] floating
fluttuare [oscillare] fluctuate
fluttuare: far fluttuare float (v) [a currency]
fluttuazione (f) fluctuation
foglietto (m) slip (n) [piece of paper]
foglio (m) di calcolo elettronico spreadsheet [computer]
foglio (m) di carta sheet of paper
fondamentale [di base] basic or most important
fondamento (m) [base] basis
fondi (mpl) insufficienti insufficient funds [US]
fondi (mpl) pubblici public funds
fondo (m) fund or reserve (n)
fondo (m) comune di investimento unit trust
fondo (m) di cassa cash float; cash in hand
fondo (m) di previdenza contingency fund
fondo (m) pensioni pension fund
Fondo Monetario Internazionale (FMI) International Monetary Fund (IMF)
fonte (f) di reddito source of income
formale formal
formalità (f) formality
formalità (fpl) doganali customs formalities
formare (comporre) form (v)
formare un numero telefonico dial (v) a number
formato (m) normale regular size
formazione (f) training
formulazione (f) form of words
fornire (approvvigionare) supply (v)
fornire di personale staff (v)
fornitore (m) supplier

fornitore (m) allo stato o statale government contractor
fornitura (f) supply (n) [action]
forte strong
forte richiesta (f) keen demand
forti costi (mpl) heavy costs
forza (f) lavoro labour force or workforce
forza (f) vendita [personale addetto alle vendite] sales force
forzato forced
forze (fpl) di mercato market forces
fotocopia (f) photocopy (n)
fotocopiare photocopy (v)
fotocopiatrice (f) photocopier
fotocopiatura (f) photocopying
fragile fragile
franco [senza spese] franco
franco a bordo free on board (f.o.b.)
franco di porto carriage free
franco di spese [gratuito] free of charge
franco dogana free of duty
franco posta post free
franco su rotaia free on rail
francobollo (m) postage stamp
fraudolento fraudulent
frequente frequent
frode (f) fraud
fronte: far fronte a una spesa meet an expense
frontiera (f) border
fruttare [rendere] earn or bear or produce (v) [interest]
fuga (f) [di denaro] flight [of money]
fungere da interfaccia interface (v)
funzionamento (m) [marcia] running (n) [of machine]
funzionare [operare] act or operate or work
funzionare: far funzionare operate (v) or run a machine
funzionario (m) official (n)
funzionario (m) addetto all'addestramento training officer
funzionario (m) di banca banker

fuoco (m) *[incendio]* fire (n)

fuori controllo out of control

fuori orario d'ufficio outside office hours

fuori stagione off-season

furgone (m) van

furgone (m) per le consegne delivery van

furto (m) theft

furto (m) di scarsa entità pilferage or pilfering

fusione (f) merger

futura consegna (f) future delivery

Gg

galleria (f) *[con negozi]* shopping mall *or* shopping arcade

gamma (f) range (n) *or* series of items

gamma (f) dei prezzi price range

gamma (f) di prodotti product mix

garante (m) surety; sponsor (n)

garantire guarantee (v)

garantire *[sponsorizzare]* sponsor (v)

garantire per qualcuno stand surety for someone

garantire un debito guarantee a debt

garanzia (f) guarantee (n) *or* security

garanzia (f) collaterale collateral (n)

generale general

generi (mpl) di consumo consumables

gestionale *[direttivo]* managerial

gestione (f) *[amministrazione]* administration *or* management

gestione (f) del portafoglio portfolio management

gestire *[amministrare]* manage

gettare throw away

gettare: da gettare disposable

giacenze (fpl) finali alla chiusura dell'esercizio closing stock

gilda (f) *[corporazione]* guild

giornale (m) newspaper

giornale (m) di categoria trade journal

giorno (m) day

giorno (m) festivo legale statutory holiday

giorno (m) per giorno day-to-day

giovane *[junior]* junior (adj)

girante (m) endorser

girare un assegno endorse a cheque

girata (f) endorsement *[action]*

giratario (m) endorsee

giroconto (m) giro system

giù *[discendente]* down

giudicare judge (v)

giudice (m) adjudicator

giudice (m) *[magistrato]* judge (n)

giudizio (m) *[aggiudicazione]* adjudication

giudizio (m) arbitrale award (n)

giungere ad un accordo reach an agreement

giungere al punto di pareggio break even (v)

giuridico legal *[referring to law]*

giurisdizione (f) jurisdiction

giustificare justify *or* warrant (v)

giusto rightful

giusto *[equo]* fair (adj)

globale *[totale]* all-in *or* total (adj)

governativo *[del governo]* government (adj)

governo (m) government (n)

grado (m) di solvibilità credit rating

graduale gradual

graduato graduated

graffare *[cucire con punti metallici]* staple (v)

graffare insieme fogli staple papers together

graffatrice (f) *[cucitrice]* stapler

graffetta (f) paperclip
grafico (m) a settori pie chart
grafico (m) delle vendite sales chart
grammo (m) gram *or* gramme
grande magazzino (m) department store
grande quantità (f) [massa] mass *[of things]*
grande quantità (f) [volume] bulk
grande supermercato (m) superstore
gratifica (f) (premio) bonus
gratifica (f) di bilancio incentive bonus
gratifica (f) natalizia [tredicesima] Christmas bonus
gratis gratis *or* free
gratuitamente free (adv) *[no payment]*
gratuito [franco di spese] free of charge
gravare d'imposta [tassare] tax (v)
grave heavy *[important]*
griglia (f) [reticolo] grid
grinta (f) drive (n) *[energy]*
grossa (f) [dodici dozzine] gross (n) (= 144)
gru (f) crane
gruppi (mpl) socioeconomici socio-economic groups
gruppo (m) batch (n) *[of orders]*; group *[of people]*
gruppo (m) di collocamento underwriting syndicate
gruppo (m) industriale group *[of businesses]*
gruppo (m) selezionato di consumatori consumer panel
guadagnare earn *[money]*
guadagni (mpl) earnings *[salary]*
guadagno (m) gain (n) *[increase in value]*
guadagno (m) [profitto] return (n) *[profit]*
guadagno (m) lordo gross earnings
guardia (f) giurata security guard
guasto (m) breakdown (n) *[machine]*

guerra (f) dei prezzi price war
guerra (f) della diminuzione dei prezzi price-cutting war
guida (f) (turistica) courier *[guide]*
guida (f) stradale street directory
guidare [condurre] drive (v) *[a car]*

Hh Ii

hard disk (m) hard disk
holding (f) [società controllante] holding company
hotel (m) [albergo] hotel
illecito illicit
illegale illegal
illegalità (f) illegality
illegalmente illegally
imballaggio (m) packing *or* packaging; wrapping
imballaggio (m) ermetico airtight packaging
imballaggio (m) termocontrattile shrink-wrapping
imballare [impacchettare] pack (v)
imballare (merce) in casse crate (v) *or* pack goods into cartons
imballato con metodo termocontrattile shrink-wrapped
imballo (m) a perdere non-returnable packing
imballo (m) di cartone carton *or* box
imbarcare o imbarcarsi embark *or* board
imbarcarsi in embark on
imbarco (m) embarkation
imbonimento (m) sales pitch
imbrogliare fiddle (v)
imbroglio (m) [truffa] fiddle (n)
imitazione (f) imitation *or* fake (n)

mmagazzinare store *or* stock up *or* keep in warehouse

mmagine (f) aziendale corporate image

mmagine (f) del prodotto brand image

mmagine (f) pubblica public image

mmediatamente immediately

mmediato *[istantaneo]* immediate *or* instant

mmetere *[informazioni nel computer]* input information *[on computer]*

mmissione (f) mediante tastiera keyboarding

mmobile (m) con chiusura di sicurezza lock-up premises

mmobilizzazioni (fpl) capital assets

mmobilizzi (mpl) fixed assets

mmobilizzi (mpl) tecnici capital equipment

mmutato unchanged

mpaccare wrap up *[goods]*

mpacchettare *[imballare]* pack (v) *or* parcel (v)

mpacchettatore (m) packer

mpadronirsi capture

mpegni (mpl) commitments

mpegno (m) *[compito]* undertaking *or* promise

mpegno (m) *[dovere]* obligation *or* duty

mperfetto imperfect

mperfezione (f) imperfection

mpianti (mpl) plant (n) *or* machinery

mpianti (mpl) di magazzinaggio storage facilities

mpianti (mpl) portuali harbour facilities

mpianto (m) di magazzinaggio storage unit

mpiegare *[assumere]* employ

mpiegatizio *[d'ufficio]* clerical

mpiegato employed

mpiegato (m) clerk

mpiegato (m) addetto al partitario delle vendite sales ledger clerk

impiegato (m) addetto alle informazioni information officer

impiegato (m) alla biglietteria booking clerk

impiegato (m) di spedizioniere shipping clerk

impieghi (mpl) disponibili appointments vacant

impiego (m) *[lavoro]* job *or* employment

impiego (m) *[posto]* position *or* post *or* job

impiego (m) a tempo pieno full-time employment

imporre impose

imporre *[una tassa]* levy (v) *[a duty]*

importante important

importanza (f) importance

importanza: avere importanza be important *or* matter (v)

importanza: di scarsa importanza petty *or* minor

importare *[merci]* import (v)

importatore (m) importer

importatore, -trice importing (adj)

importazione (f) importation

importazioni (fpl) imports

importazioni (fpl) visibili visible imports

importazioni-esportazioni import-export (adj)

importo (m) *[ammontare]* amount *[of money]*

importo (m) aggiuntivo premium *[on lease]*

importo (m) dovuto amount owing

importo (m) fisso flat rate

importo (m) forfettario lump sum

importo (m) maturato accrual

importo (m) pagato amount paid

importo (m) totale total amount

imposizione (f) enforcement

imposta (f) *[tassa]* tax (n) *or* duty

imposta (f) arretrata back tax

imposta (f) di bollo stamp duty

imposta (f) diretta direct tax

imposta (f) generale sugli acquisti purchase tax

imposta (f) indiretta excise duty

imposta (f) pagata tax paid
imposta (f) progressiva graded tax
imposta (f) progressiva sul reddito
graduated income tax
imposta (f) sul reddito income tax
**imposta (f) sul valore aggiunto
(IVA)** value added tax (VAT)
imposta (f) sul volume di affari
sales tax *or* turnover tax
imposta (f) sulla società
corporation tax
imposta (f) sulle plusvalenze
capital gains tax
imposta (f) trattenuta alla fonte
tax deducted at source
imposte (f) indirette indirect tax
imposte (f) progressive
progressive taxation
imprenditore (m) contractor;
entrepreneur
imprenditoriale entrepreneurial
impresa (f) business *or* company
**impresa (f) di trasporti
[trasportatore]** carrier *or* haulage
contractor
impronta (f) mark (n)
impulso (m) impulse
in acconto on account
in aumento on the increase *or*
mounting
in buona fede bona fide
in comune jointly
in concorrenza competing (adj)
in contanti cash (adv)
in media on an average
in orario [puntuale] on time
in ritardo [tardi] late (adv)
in scala naturale full-scale (adj)
in scala ridotta small-scale (adj)
in vendita for sale
inabile [privo di validità] invalid
inabilità (f) [invalidità] invalidity
inadempiente (m) defaulter
inadempienza (f) default (n)
inadempienza (f) nel pagamento
default on payments
inadempimento (m) del contratto
breach of contract
incapace incompetent
incarico (m) assignment *[work]*

incartamenti (mpl) papers
incassabile cashable
incassare cash (v) *or* encash
incassare un assegno cash a
cheque
incassi (mpl) takings *or* returns
incassi (mpl) netti net receipts
incasso (m) take (n) *[money
received]*
incendio (m) *[fuoco]* fire (n)
incentivo (m) incentive
incidente (m) accident *or* crash (n)
incidente (m) professionale
occupational accident
includere count (v) *or* include
incluso inclusive
incollare *[chiudere]* seal (v) *[an
envelope]*
incondizionato unconditional
incontrare meet *[someone]*
incorporare merge
incorporato *[inserito]* built-in
incorrere (in) incur
incrementativo incremental
incremento (m) increment
indagare inquire
indagine (f) *[analisi]* investigation
or examination
indebitamento (m) indebtedness
indebitamento (m) a breve
short-term debts
indebitarsi get into debt
indebitato indebted
indennità (f) *[indennizzo]*
indemnification
indennità (f) di contingenza
cost-of-living allowance
indennizzare *[risarcire]*
indemnify; make good *[a defect or
loss]*
indennizzo (m) *[indennità]*
indemnification
indicare un prezzo *[quotare]*
quote (v) *or* estimate costs
indicare un profitto show a profit
indicatore (m) indicator
indicatori (mpl) economici
economic indicators
indice (m) index (n)

indice (m) dei prezzi al consumo consumer price index

indice (m) dei prezzi al dettaglio retail price index

indice (m) dei prezzi all'ingrosso wholesale price index

indice (m) del costo della vita cost-of-living index

indice (m) di crescita growth index

indice (m) di rendimento rate of return

indice (m) economico index number

indice (m) ponderato weighted index

indicizzato index-linked

indicizzazione (f) indexation *or* index-linking

indipendente independent

indiretto indirect

indirizzare una lettera o un pacco address a letter *or* a parcel

indirizzo (m) *[recapito]* address (n)

indirizzo (m) cablografico cable address

indirizzo (m) d'inoltro forwarding address

indirizzo (m) d'ufficio business address

indirizzo (m) del mittente return address

indirizzo (m) di comodo accommodation address

indirizzo (m) personale home address

indiscriminato *[uniforme]* across-the-board

indispensabile essential

indossatrice (f) model (n) *[person]*

industria (f) industry

industria (f) a forte assorbimento di capitali capital-intensive industry

industria (f) che si è sviluppata rapidamente boom industry

industria (f) chiave key industry

industria (f) di base staple industry

industria (f) pesante heavy industry

industria (f) primaria primary industry

industria (f) secondaria secondary industry

industria (f) statalizzata nationalized industry

industria (f) terziaria tertiary industry

industriale industrial

industriale (m) industrialist

industrializzare industrialize

industrializzazione (f) industrialization

inefficiente inefficient

inefficienza (f) inefficiency

inferiore *[più basso]* lower (adj)

inferiore *[meno di]* under *or* less than

inflazione (f) inflation

inflazione (f) da costi cost-push inflation

inflazionistico inflationary

influenza (f) influence (n)

influenzare influence (v)

informare *[avvisare]* inform *or* advise

informazione (f) riservata tip (n) *[advice]*

informazioni (fpl) commerciali status inquiry

informazioni (fpl) di volo flight information

infortunio (m) sul lavoro industrial accident

infrangere infringe

infrangere un accordo break an agreement

infrastruttura (f) infrastructure

infrazione (f) fiscale tax offence

ingegnere (m) edile site engineer

ingiusto unfair

inglese *[britannico]* English *or* British

ingranaggio (m) gear

ingrosso: all'ingrosso wholesale (adv)

ininterrotto *[senza scalo]* non-stop

iniziale initial (adj) *or* starting *or* opening
iniziare [cominciare] begin *or* start (v) *or* initiate
iniziare un dibattito (m) initiate discussions
iniziativa (f) initiative
iniziativa (f) commerciale commercial undertaking
iniziativa (f) privata private enterprise
iniziativa (f) su scala ridotta small-scale enterprise
inizio (m) beginning
innovare innovate
innovativo innovative
innovatore (m) innovator
innovazione (f) innovation
inoltrare file (v) *[a request]*
inoltrare una domanda di brevetto file a patent application
inoltro (m) forwarding
inondare flood (v)
inondazione (f) flood (n)
inquilino (m) tenant
insegna (f) sign (n)
inseguire chase *or* follow up
inserimento (m) in un nuovo lavoro induction
inserire insert *or* put in
inserire in una lista di proscrizione blacklist (v)
inserito [incorporato] built-in
inserzione (m) advertisement
inserzione: pubblicare un'inserzione per un impiego disponibile advertise a vacancy
inserzioni (fpl) [annunci economici su giornale] classified ads
inserzionista (m) advertiser
insolvente insolvent
insolvenza (f) insolvency
inspiegato unaccounted for
insuccesso (m) failure *or* flop
insuccesso (m) commerciale commercial failure
intangibile intangible
integrazione (f) orizzontale horizontal integration

integrazione (f) verticale vertical integration
intendere propose to *[do something]*
intensificare escalate
intentare azione legale take legal action
intentare causa [citare] sue
intentare causa civile bring a civil action
interdire [vietare] ban (v)
interdizione (f) ban (n)
interessare interest (v)
interessarsi di concern (v) *or* deal with
interesse (m) interest (n)
interesse (m) alto high interest
interesse (m) composto cumulative interest
interesse (m) composto compound interest
interesse (m) fisso fixed interest
interesse (m) maturato accrued interest
interesse (m) semplice simple interest
interessi (mpl) costituiti vested interest
interfaccia (f) interface (n)
intermediario (m) intermediary *or* intermediary
internazionale international
interno internal *or* in-house
interno (m) telephone extension
interno (del territorio nazionale) inland
intero (pieno) full
interpretare interpret
interprete (mf) interpreter
interrompere discontinue
intervallo (m) [fra ordinazione e consegna] lead time
intervista (f) [colloquio] interview (n)
intervistare interview (v)
intervistato (m) interviewee
intervistatore (m) interviewer
intesa (f) understanding

intesa (f) *[accordo]* arrangement *or* understanding *or* compromise

intraprendente go-ahead (adj)

intraprendere undertake

introdurre introduce

introdurre gradualmente phase in

introduzione (m) introduction *or* bringing into use

invalidare *[annullare]* invalidate *or* void (v)

invalidità (f) *[inabilità]* invalidity

invecchiamento (m) obsolescence

invenduto unsold

inventariare *[fare l'inventario]* take stock *or* inventory (v)

inventario (m) stocklist; inventory

inventario (m) *[stock]* stock *or* *[US]* inventory

inventario (m) stocktaking

inventario: fare l'inventario inventory (v) *or* take stock

inversione (f) reversal

inversione (f) di tendenza turnround *[making profitable]*

inverso reverse (adj)

invertire reverse (v)

investigare investigate

investimenti (mpl) ad interessi fissi fixed-interest investments

investimenti (mpl) esteri foreign investments

investimenti (mpl) in titoli di prim'ordine blue-chip investments

investimento (m) investment

investimento (m) garantito secure investment

investimento (m) privo di rischio risk-free investment

investimento (m) sicuro safe investment

investire invest

investire capitali invest in *or* lock up capital

investito invested *or* employed *[money]*

investitore (m) investor

investitori (mpl) istituzionali institutional investors

inviare send

inviare per fax fax (v)

inviare rimessa a mezzo assegno remit by cheque

inviato (m) correspondent *[journalist]*

invio (m) consignment *[things sent, received]*

invio (m) *[per posta]* mailing

invio (m) di riviste per posta magazine mailing

invitare invite *or* call *[on someone to do something]*

invito (m) invitation

involucro (m) *[imballaggio]* wrapping

ipermercato (m) hypermarket

ipoteca (f) mortgage (n)

ipotecare mortgage (v)

irregolare irregular

irregolarità (fpl) irregularities

irrevocabile irrevocable

iscrivere una società register a company

iscriversi register (v) *[in official list]*

iscrizione (f) membership *[being a member]*

ispettivo *[di supervisione]* supervisory

ispettore (m) aziendale factory inspector

ispettore (m) delle tasse tax inspector

ispettore (m) IVA VAT inspector

ispezionare *[esaminare]* survey (v) *or* inspect

ispezione (f) inspection

istantaneo *[immediato]* instant (adj) *or* immediate

istanza (f) *[domanda]* application

istituire institute (v) *or* establish

istituto (m) institute (n)

istituto (m) di credito credit bank

istituto (m) di credito fondiario building society

istituto (m) finanziario financial institution

istituzionale institutional

istituzione (f) institution

istruire train (v) *or* teach
istruzione (f) instruction
istruzioni (fpl) per l'uso directions for use
istruzioni (fpl) per la spedizione shipping instructions *or* forwarding instructions
itinerario (m) itinerary
IVA (imposta sul valore aggiunto) VAT (= value added tax)

Jj Ll

joint venture (f) *[associazione in partecipazione]* joint venture
junior *[giovane]* junior (adj)
lanciare launch (v) *or* bring out
lanciare una società float a company
lancio (m) launch (n) *or* launching
lancio (m) di una società flotation *or* floating of a company
lasciar vuoto vacate
lasciare *[abbandonare]* leave (v) *[resign]*
lasciare *[partire]* leave (v) *or* go away
lasciare libera la camera dell'albergo check out of hotel
lato (m) side
lato (m) dell'attivo *[avere]* credit side
laureato (m) che fa tirocinio come dirigente graduate trainee
lavorare work (v)
lavorare al nero moonlight (v)
lavorare: che lavora in proprio self-employed
lavorare *[trattare]* process (v) *[raw materials]*

lavoratore (m), lavoratrice (f) worker
lavoratore (m) a domicilio homeworker
lavoratore (m) al nero moonlighter
lavoratore (m) a orario ridotto part-timer
lavoratore (m) saltuario casual worker
lavoratore che fa parte del consiglio di amministrazione e che agisce come portavoce del personale worker director
lavoratori (mpl) parzialmente qualificati semi-skilled workers
lavorazione (f) *[fabbricazione]* manufacture (n)
lavoro (m) labour; job *or* piece of work
lavoro (m) *[impiego]* position *or* job
lavoro (m) a contratto contract work
lavoro (m) a contratto a termine temporary employment
lavoro (m) a cottimo piecework
lavoro (m) a orario ridotto part-time work *or* part-time employment
lavoro (m) arretrato backlog
lavoro (m) ben pagato well-paid job
lavoro (m) con turni shift work
lavoro (m) d'ufficio clerical work
lavoro (m) di routine routine work
lavoro (m) in corso work in progress
lavoro (m) manuale manual work
lavoro (m) nero moonlighting
lavoro (m) saltuario casual work
lavoro (m) stabile secure job
lavoro (m) straordinario overtime
lavoro (m) urgente rush job
leasing (m) leasing
leasing (m) immobiliare lease-back
legale legal *or* according to the law
legalizzare *[autenticare]* authenticate

legge (f) law *[rule]*
legge (f) del rendimento decrescente law of diminishing returns
legge (f) dell'offerta e della domanda law of supply and demand
leggibile dal computer computer-readable
legislazione (f) legislation
legittimazione (f) standing
legittimo lawful
lento slow
lento *[stagnante]* slack
lettera (f) letter
lettera: fare una lettera raccomandata register (v) *[letter]*
lettera (f) aerea air letter
lettera (f) circolare circular letter
lettera (f) circolare circular (n)
lettera (f) d'affari business letter
lettera (f) di accompagnamento covering letter
lettera (f) di assunzione letter of appointment
lettera (f) di credito letter of credit (L/C)
lettera (f) di credito circolare circular letter of credit
lettera (f) di credito irrevocabile irrevocable letter of credit
lettera (f) di intenti letter of intent
lettera (f) di presentazione letter of introduction
lettera (f) di reclamo letter of complaint
lettera (f) di referenze letter of reference
lettera (f) di sollecito follow-up letter
lettera (f) di vettura consignment note; waybill
lettera (f) espresso express letter
lettera (f) standard standard letter
leva (f) finanziaria leverage
levata (f) postal collection
libbra (f) *[peso]* pound *[weight: 0.45kg]*
liberare free (v) *or* release
liberarsi di qualcosa get rid of something

libero free (adj)
libero professionista (m) freelancer
libero scambio (m) free trade
libretto (m) assegni cheque book
libretto (m) di versamento bank book
libro (m) book (n)
libro (m) cassa cash book
libro (m) contabile *[registro]* register (n) *or* journal
libro (m) giornale journal *or* accounts book
libro (m) mastro ledger
libro (m) mastro degli acquisti purchase ledger
libro (m) vendite sales book
licenza (f) licence
licenza (f) d'esportazione export licence *or* export permit
licenza (f) di importazione import licence *or* import permit
licenziamento (m) dismissal
licenziamento (m) ingiustificato wrongful dismissal
licenziamento (m) ingiusto unfair dismissal
licenziare discharge or sack *or* dismiss *[employees]*
licenziare: essere licenziato get the sack
licitazione (f) tendering
licitazione (f) *[offerta d'appalto]* tender (n) *[offer to work]*
limitare limit (v) *or* restrict
limitare il credito restrict credit
limitato limited
limitazione (f) agli scambi commerciali restraint of trade
limite (m) limit (n)
limite (m) del prestito lending limit
limite (m) di credito credit limit
limite (m) di peso weight limit
limite (m) massimo ceiling
linea (f) line (n)
linea: in linea on line *or* online
linea (f) aerea *[compagnia aerea]* airline
linea (f) di carico load line

linea (f) di navigazione shipping line

linea (f) di prodotti product line

linea (f) esterna outside line

linea (f) gerarchica line management

linea (f) telefonica telephone line

linguaggio (m) burocratico officialese

linguaggio (m) di computer computer language

linguaggio (m) di programmazione programming language

liquidare clear (v) *[stock]*

liquidare (pagare) una fattura settle *[an invoice]*

liquidare le ordinazioni inevase release dues

liquidatore (m) liquidator *or* official receiver

liquidazione (f) liquidation *or* winding up

liquidazione (f) coatta compulsory liquidation

liquidazione (f) volontaria voluntary liquidation

liquidità (f) liquid assets *or* liquidity

lira (f) lira *[currency used in Turkey]*

lira (f) sterlina pound sterling

lista (f) list (n)

lista (f) di indirizzi address list

lista (f) di selezione picking list

lista (f) nera black list (n)

lista (f) ristretta (di candidati) shortlist (n)

listino (m) *[catalogo]* list (n) *or* catalogue

listino (m) prezzi price list

litro (m) litre

livelli (mpl) salariali wage levels

livello (m) level (n)

livello (m) di livello inferiore low-level

livello (m) delle scorte stock level

livello (m) di organico manning levels

livello (m) di riordinazione reorder level

livello (m) massimo di produzione peak output

locale *[del luogo]* local

locali (mpl) premises

locali (mpl) d'azienda *o* locali commerciali business premises

locatore (m) landlord

locazione (f) tenancy *[period]*

logogramma (m) logo

lordo gross (adj)

lungaggine (f) burocratica red tape

lungo *[per molto tempo]* long

lungo: a lungo termine long-term

luogo (m) site *or* place

luogo: avere luogo take place

luogo (m) d'incontro meeting place

luogo (m) di ritrovo venue

Mm

macchina (f) machine; car

macchina (f) affrancatrice franking machine

macchina (f) che cambia denaro in spiccioli change machine

macchinario (m) pesante heavy machinery

macroeconomia (f) macro-economics

magazzinaggio (m) *[deposito]* warehousing *or* storage (n) *[in warehouse]*

magazziniere (m) warehouseman

magazzino (m) warehouse (n); stockroom *or* storeroom; store

magazzino (m) a prezzi scontati discount store

magazzino (m) doganale bonded warehouse

magazzino (m) frigorifero cold store

maggioranza (f) majority

maggiorazione (f) premium *or* extra charge

maggiore major

magistrato (m) *[giudice]* magistrate *or* judge (n)

malinteso (m) misunderstanding

malpagato underpaid

mancanza (f) *[assenza]* absence

mancanza (f) di fondi lack of funds

mancare miss

mancare il bersaglio miss a target

mancata consegna (f) non-delivery

mancia (f) tip (n) *[money]*

mandare indietro *[respingere]* return (v) *or* send back

mandare un carico per mare send a shipment by sea

mandatario (m) proxy *[person]*

mandato (m) mandate; writ

mandato (m) di pagamento *[vaglia]* money order

maneggevole *[pratico]* handy

maneggio (m) *[gestione]* handling

manifatturiero manufacturing

manifesto (m) manifest

manodopera (f) manpower

manodopera (f) qualificata skilled labour

manodopera (m) a basso prezzo cheap labour

manodopera (m) locale local labour

manovale (m) manual worker

mantenere maintain *[keep at same level]*

mantenere una promessa keep a promise

mantenimento (m) maintenance

mantenimento (m) delle provvigioni maintenance of supplies

mantenimento (m) di contatti maintenance of contacts

manuale manual (adj)

manuale (m) manual (n)

manuale (m) di manutenzione service manual

manuale (m) operativo operating manual

manufatti (mpl) manufactured goods

manutenzione (f) *[revisione]* maintenance *or* service (n) *[of machine]*

marca (f) *[nome del prodotto]* brand name

marca (f) *[marchio]* brand

marchio (m) trademark *or* trade name *or* brand

marchio (m) di fabbrica depositato registered trademark

marchio (m) di qualità quality label

marcia (f) *[funzionamento]* running (n) *[of machine]*

marginale marginal

margine (m) margin *[profit]*

margine (m) di errore margin of error

margine (m) di utile profit margin

margine (m) lordo gross margin

margine (m) netto net margin

marina (f) mercantile merchant navy

marittimo marine *or* maritime

marketing (m) marketing

marketing (m) di massa mass marketing

mass-media (m) *[mezzi di comunicazione di massa]* mass media

massa (f) mass

massimale (m) di credito credit ceiling

massimizzare maximize

massimizzazione (f) maximization

massimo maximum (adj)

massimo (m) maximum (n)

master (m) in gestione d'impresa Master's degree in Business Administration (MBA)

mastro (m) dei conti dei creditori bought ledger

mastro (m) nominale nominal ledger

materiale (m) d'imballaggio packaging material

materiale (m) da esposizione display material

materiale (m) di recupero salvage (n) *or* things saved

materiale (m) illustrativo delle vendite sales literature

materiale (m) per punto di vendita point of sale material (POS material)

materiale (m) pubblicitario con buono coupon ad

materie (fpl) prime raw materials

matrice (f) counterfoil

matrice (f) dell'assegno cheque stub

maturare *[accumularsi]* accrue

maturazione (f) degli interessi accrual of interest

media (f) average (n) *or* mean (n)

media: in media on an average

media (f) ponderata weighted average

mediare mediate

mediatore (m) mediator *or* troubleshooter

mediatore (m) assicurativo insurance broker

mediazione (f) mediation

mediazione (f) di cambio stockbroking

medio average (adj) *or* medium

medio: a medio termine medium-term

meglio: il meglio best (n)

memorandum (m) memorandum *or* memo

memoria (f) del computer computer memory

meno *[negativo]* minus

meno di *[inferiore]* under *or* less than

meno: a meno di short of

mensile monthly (adj)

mensilmente monthly (adv)

mercanteggiare haggle

mercante (m) merchant

mercati (mpl) esteri overseas markets

mercati (mpl) monetari money markets

mercato (m) market (n)

mercato (m) a termine forward market

mercato (m) al rialzo bull market

mercato (m) al ribasso buyer's market

mercato (m) azionario stock market

mercato (m) chiuso closed market

mercato (m) controllato da un solo fornitore captive market

mercato (m) dei cambi foreign exchange market

mercato (m) delle materie prime commodity market

mercato (m) favorevole ai venditori seller's market

mercato (m) fiacco weak market

mercato (m) interno domestic market

mercato (m) libero open market

mercato (m) limitato limited market

mercato (m) mondiale world market

mercato (m) nazionale home market

mercato (m) nero black market

mercato (m) potenziale potential market

mercato (m) prescelto target market

Mercat (m) Europeo Unico Single European Market

merce (f) merchandise (n) *or* goods

merce (f) a prezzo ridotto cut-price goods

merce (f) con dazio pagato duty-paid goods

merce (f) danneggiata da incendio fire-damaged goods

merce (f) in transito goods in transit

merce (f) non venduta returns *or* unsold goods

merce (f) per la vendita al dettaglio retail goods

merchant bank (f) *[banca mercantile]* merchant bank

merci (fpl) deperibili perishable goods

merci (fpl) vendute sottocosto distress merchandise

merito (n) merit

mese (m) month

mese (m) solare calendar month

messaggero (m) *[corriere]* courier *or* messenger

messaggio (m) message

metà (f) half (n)

metà settimana (f) mid-week

metodo (m) LIFO (ultimo a entrare, primo a uscire) LIFO (= last in first out)

metodo (m) per tentativi trial and error

mettere put (v) *or* place

mettere *[posare]* place (v)

mettere a verbale *[verbalizzare]* minute (v)

mettere al corrente *[aggiornare]* update (v)

mettere da parte denaro save up

mettere francobolli *[affrancare]* stamp (v) *[a letter]*

mettere in liquidazione scorte di magazzino liquidate stock

mettere in liquidazione una società liquidate *or* wind up *[a company]*

mettere in ordine put in a certain order

mettere in serbo store (v) *[keep for future]*

mettere in vendita release (v) *or* put on the market

mettere insieme batch (v)

mettere insieme le risorse pool resources

mettere l'embargo su embargo (v)

mettere per iscritto put in writing

mettersi in affari go into business *or* set up in business

mettersi in contatto con contact (v)

mezza dozzina (f) half a dozen *or* a half-dozen

mezzi (mpl) means *[money]*

mezzi (mpl) *[strumenti]* means *[ways]*

mezzi (mpl) di comunicazione di massa mass media

mezzo half (adj)

mezzo (m) medium (n)

microeconomia (f) micro-economics

microelaboratore (m) microcomputer

miglior offerente (m) successful bidder

miglioramento (m) upturn

migliore best (adj)

migliore *[piu alto]* top (adj)

migliore offerente (m) highest bidder

miliardario (m) millionaire

miliardo billion *[US]*

milione (m) million

millantato credito (m) false pretences

minimo minimum (adj)

minimo (m) minimum (n)

ministero (m) ministry *or* government department

Ministero del Tesoro Treasury

ministro (m) government minister *or* secretary

minoranza (f) minority

minuto (m) minute (n) *[time]*

miscellaneo *[vario]* miscellaneous

missione (f) commerciale trade mission

misto mixed

misura (f) della redditività measurement of profitability

misura (f) standard stock size

misure (fpl) measurements

misure (fpl) cubiche cubic measure

misure (fpl) di sicurezza safety measures *or* safety precautions

mittente (m) sender *or* consignor

mobilità (f) mobility

mobilizzare mobilize

mobilizzare capitali mobilize capital

modalità (fpl) di pagamento mode of payment

modello (m) model (n)
modello (m) economico economic model
modello (m) in scala scale model *or* mock-up
modem (m) modem
moderare moderate (v)
moderato moderate (adj)
moderno [attuale] modern *or* up to date
modifica (f) [cambiamento] alteration
modificare [cambiare] alter
modo (m) mode
moduli (mpl) a striscia continua continuous stationery
modulo (m) form (n)
modulo (m) d'iscrizione registration form
modulo (m) delle tasse tax form
modulo (m) di dichiarazione doganale customs declaration form
modulo (m) per domanda di assunzione application form
molo (m) quay *or* wharf
moltiplicare multiply
moltiplicazione (f) multiplication
molto bene fine (adv) *or* very good
mondiale worldwide (adj)
mondo (m) world
mondo: in tutto il mondo worldwide (adv)
moneta (f) (metallica) coin
moneta (f) a corso legale legal tender
moneta (f) inflazionata inflated currency
moneta (f) legale legal currency
moneta (f) spicciola small change
moneta (f) stabile stable currency
moneta (f) straniera foreign currency
monetario monetary
monitor (m) monitor (n) *or* screen
monopolio (m) monopoly
monopolio perfetto (m) absolute monopoly
monopolizzare monopolize

monopolizzazione (f) monopolization
montacarichi (m) goods elevator
montaggio (m) [assemblaggio] assembly [putting together]
montatura (f) giornalistica hype (n)
moratoria (f) moratorium
morto dead (adj) [person]
mostra (f) [esposizione] exhibition *or* display
mostrare show (v)
motivato motivated
motivazione (f) motivation
movimentazione (f) dei materiali materials handling
movimenti (m) di capitali movements of capital
movimento (m) movement *or* turnover [of stock]
multa (f) (penale) fine *or* penalty
multare fine (v)
multilaterale multilateral
multinazionale (f) multinational (n)
multiplo multiple (adj)
mutuare borrow; lend
mutuatario (m) borrower
mutuo (m) borrowing
mutuo (m) [prestito] loan (n)
mutuo (m) a breve scadenza short-term loan
mutuo (m) a lunga scadenza long-term loan
mutuo (m) garantito secured loan
mutuo (reciproco) mutual (adj) *or* reciprocal

Nn

nastro (m) magnetico magnetic tape *or* mag tape

navale (marittimo) maritime

nave (f) ship (n)

nave (f) da carico cargo ship *or* freighter

nave (f) di salvataggio salvage vessel

nave (f) gemella sister ship

nave (f) mercantile merchant ship *or* merchant vessel

nave (f) per trasporto di container container ship

nazionale national

nazionale: di dimensioni nazionali nationwide

nazionalizzazione (f) nationalization

nazione (f) [paese] country [state]

nazione (f) più favorita most-favoured nation

necessario necessary

negativo (meno) minus

negligente negligent

negligenza (f) negligence

negoziabile negotiable

negoziante (m) shopkeeper

negoziare negotiate

negoziare [commerciare] deal in (v)

negoziato (m) [negoziazione] negotiation

negoziato (m) salariale wage negotiations

negoziatore (m) negotiator

negoziazione (f) [negoziato] negotiation

negozio (m) shop *or* store

negozio (m) appartenente a una catena multiple store

negozio (m) che fa parte di una catena chain store

negozio (m) con merce a prezzi ridotti cut-price store

negozio (m) d'angolo corner shop

negozio (m) di vendita a prezzi ridotti discount store

negozio (m) esente da tasse duty-free shop

negozio (m) per articoli da regalo gift shop

netto net (adj)

nicchia (f) niche

nodo (m) della questione bottom line

noleggiare charter (v)

noleggiare un aeroplano charter an aircraft

noleggiare un'automobile hire a car

noleggiatore (m) (di navi, aerei) charterer

noleggio (m) chartering *or* charter (n)

noleggio (m) in blocco block booking

nome (m) name

nome: a nome di on behalf of

nome (m) del prodotto [marca] brand name

nomina (f) appointment [to a job]

nomina (f) del personale staff appointment

nomina (f) di amministratore giudiziario letters of administration

nominare appoint

non datato undated

non disponibile unavailable

non disponibilità (f) unavailability

non pagato outstanding *or* unpaid

non specializzato unskilled

non ufficiale [ufficioso] unofficial

non verificato unaudited

norma (f) standard (n) *or* rule (n) *or* norm

normale [regolare] regular *or* ordinary

normale usura e degrado fair wear and tear

norme (fpl) antincendio fire regulations

norme (fpl) di sicurezza safety regulations

nota (f)   note (n)
nota (f) di accredito   credit note
nota (f) di addebito   debit note
notaio (m)   notary public
notare   note (v) *or* mark (v)
[details]
notificare   notify
notificazione (f)   notification
notte (f)   night
nulla (m) *[zero]*   nil
nullo   null *or* void *or* not valid
numerare   number (v)
numeri (mpl) *[cifre]*   figures
numeri (m) dispari   odd numbers
numerico   numeric *or* numerical
numero (m)   number (n) *or* figure
numero (m) dell'assegno   cheque number
numero (m) di conto corrente di corrispondenza   giro account number
numero (m) di fattura   invoice number
numero (m) di matricola   registration number
numero (m) di partita   batch number
numero (m) di riferimento   reference number
numero (m) di serie   serial number
numero (m) di telefono   phone number
numero (m) minimo legale   quorum
numero (m) telefonico   telephone number *or* phone number
nuova domanda (f)   reapplication
nuova ordinazione (f)   reorder (n)
nuovo accertamento (m)   reassessment
nuovo di zecca   brand new
nuovo orientamento (m)   departure *[new venture]*

Oo

obbligatorio   compulsory
obbligazione (f)   bond *[borrowing by government]*
obbligazione (f) *[di società private]*   debenture
obbligazione (f) al portatore   bearer bond
obbligazione (f) irredimibile   irredeemable bond
obbligazione (f) redimibile   callable bond
obbligazioni (fpl) 'cartastraccia'   junk bonds
obbligazioni (fpl) convertibii   convertible loan stock
obbligazionista (m)   debenture holder
obbligo (m)   liability
obiettivi (mpl) di produzione   production targets
obiettivo (m)   objective (n) *or* target (n)
obiettivo (m) di rilevamento   takeover target
obiettivo (m) di vendita   sales target
obiettivo *[oggettivo]*   objective (adj)
obsolescente   obsolescent
occasione (f) *[affare]*   bargain (n) *[cheaper than usual]*
occultamento (m) di beni   concealment of assets
occupante (m)   occupant
occupare   occupy
occupare: chi occupa   occupant
occuparsi di   attend to *or* handle (v) *or* deal with
occupato   busy; engaged *[telephone]*
occupazionale *[professionale]*   occupational
occupazione (f)   occupancy

offerente (m) tenderer; bidder

offerta (f) offer (n); bid

offerta (f) d'apertura opening bid

offerta (f) d'appalto tender (n)
[offer to work]

offerta (f) d'occasione bargain
offer

offerta (f) di propaganda
introductory offer

offerta (f) di vendita offer for sale

offerta (f) e domanda supply and
demand

offerta (f) in busta chiusa sealed
tenders

offerta (f) per contanti cash offer

offerta (f) premio premium offer

offerta (f) pubblica d'acquisto
takeover bid

offerta (f) reale cash offer

offerta (f) speciale special offer

offerte (fpl) d'impiego situations
vacant

officina (f) workshop

offrire [proporre] offer (v) *[to buy]*

offrire [presentare] present (v) *or*
give

offshore [all'estero] offshore

olio (m) edible oil *or* cooking oil

omaggio (m) [dono] free gift

omaggio: in omaggio
complimentary

**omesso pagamento (m) di un
debito** non-payment *[of a debt]*

omettere [trascurare] omit

omissione (f) omission

onorare honour (v)

non onorare dishonour

non onorare un effetto dishonour
a bill

onorare una cambiale honour a
bill

onorare una firma honour a
signature

onorario (m) honorarium

operativo operational *or* operative
(adj)

operatore (m) operator *or*
operative (n)

operatore (m) in cambi foreign
exchange dealer

operatore (m) su tastiera
keyboarder

operazione (f) operation

operazione (f) [affare] deal (n)

**operazione (f) a denominazione
valutaria multipla** multicurrency
operation

operazione (f) chiavi in mano
turnkey operation

operazione (f) disonesta
fraudulent transaction

operazioni (fpl) [transazioni]
dealing

opinione (f) pubblica public
opinion

opportunità (f) opportunity

opuscoli (mpl) pubblicitari junk
mail

opzione (f) d'acquisto call (n)
[stock exchange]

opzione (f) per l'acquisto option to
purchase

ora (f) hour

ora (f) di accettazione check-in
time

ora (f) di chiusura closing time

ora (f) di punta rush hour

ora (f) lavorativa man-hour

orario hourly

orario (m) timetable (n) *[trains,
etc.]*

orario: in orario [puntuale] on
time

orario (m) d'apertura opening hours

orario (m) d'ufficio office hours

orario (m) di banca banking hours

orario (m) pieno full-time

orario (m) ridotto part-time

ordinare order (v) *[goods]*

ordinaria amministrazione (f)
routine (n)

ordinario ordinary

ordinato on order

ordinazione (f) order (n) *[for
goods]*

ordinazioni (fpl) inevase back
orders *or* dues *or* unfulfilled orders

ordinazione (f) rinnovata repeat
order

ordinazione (f) urgente rush order

ordinazioni (fpl) da evadere
outstanding orders
ordinazioni (fpl) per corrispondenza mail-order
ordine (m) order (n)
ordine (m) alfabetico alphabetical order
ordine (m) bancario banker's order
ordine (m) cronologico chronological order
ordine (m) d'acquisto purchase order
ordine (m) del giorno agenda
ordine (m) di consegna delivery order
ordine (m) di pagamento di valuta estera foreign money order
ordine (m) permanente standing order
ore (fpl) d'ufficio business hours
organico (m) manning
organigramma (m) organization chart
organizzare organize or arrange or plan
organizzativo organizational
organizzazione (f) organization
Organizzazione (f) dei paesi esportatori di petrolio Organization of Petroleum Exporting Countries (OPEC)
organizzazione (f) e metodo (m) organization and methods
organizzazione (f) gerarchica line organization
Organizzazione (f) Internazionale del Lavoro (OIL) International Labour Organization (ILO)
originale (m) original (n)
originario original (adj)
origine (f) origin
ormeggiare berth (v)
ormeggio (m) berth (n)
oro (m) in verghe gold bullion
oscillare *[fluttuare]* fluctuate
osservare *[conformarsi]* comply with
ottenere obtain or gain or get
ottenere la liberazione (su cauzione) di qualcuno

bail someone out
ottenibile *[conseguibile]*
obtainable
ottenibile: non ottenibile
unobtainable
output (m) *[dati di emissione]*
computer output

Pp

pacchetto (m) packet
pacchetto (m) *[azionistico]* block (n) *[of shares]*
pacchetto (m) di buste pack of envelopes
pacchetto (m) di sigarette packet of cigarettes
pacchetto (m) rivendicativo package deal
pacco (m) package or pack or parcel
paese (m) *[nazione]* country *[state]*
paese (m) d'origine country of origin
paese (m) in via di sviluppo developing country
paesi (mpl) esportatori di petrolio oil-exporting countries
paesi (mpl) industrializzati industrialized societies
paesi (mpl) produttori di petrolio oil-producing countries
paesi (mpl) sottosviluppati underdeveloped countries
paesi (mpl) stranieri *[l'estero]* overseas (n)
paga (f) *[salario]* pay (n) *[salary]*
pagabile payable
pagabile a sessanta giorni payable at sixty days

pagabile alla consegna payable on delivery
pagabile anticipatamente payable in advance
pagabile su richiesta payable on demand
pagamenti (mpl) ipotecari mortgage payments
pagamenti (mpl) mensili monthly payments
pagamenti (mpl) scaglionati staged payments
pagamento (m) payment *or* settlement
pagamento (m) [esborso] disbursement
pagamento (m) a carico del destinatario charges forward
pagamento (m) a saldo o totale full payment
pagamento (m) alla consegna cash on delivery (c.o.d.)
pagamento (m) annuale yearly payment
pagamento (m) anticipato advance payment *or* prepayment
pagamento (m) degli arretrati back payment
pagamento (m) di un debito discharge (n) *[of debt]*
pagamento (m) differito deferred payment
pagamento (m) in acconto payment on account
pagamento (m) in base al lavoro effettuato payment by results
pagamento (m) in contanti payment in cash *or* cash payment; prompt payment
pagamento (m) in natura payment in kind
pagamento (m) in più overpayment
pagamento (m) minimo minimum payment
pagamento (m) parziale partial payment
pagamento (m) progressivo progress payments

pagamento (m) provvisiorio interim payment
pagamento (m) semestrale half-yearly payment
pagamento (m) simbolico token payment
pagamento (m) tramite assegno payment by cheque
pagare [remunerare] pay (v) *[worker]*
pagare [saldare] pay (v) *[bill]*
pagare: far pagare charge someone
pagare: far pagare meno undercharge (v)
pagare: far pagare troppo overcharge (v)
pagare a rate pay in instalments
pagare anticipatamente pay in advance
pagare con carta di credito pay by credit card
pagare con un assegno pay by cheque
pagare gli interessi pay interest
pagare in anticipo prepay
pagare in contanti pay cash
pagare un conto pay a bill
pagare un debito service a debt
pagare un dividendo pay a dividend
pagare una fattura pay *or* settle an invoice
pagato paid *[invoice]*
pagato [remunerato] paid *[for work]*
pagato: non pagato outstanding *or* unpaid
pagato in anticipo prepaid
pagatore (m) tardivo slow payer
pagherò (m) promissory note *or* IOU
pagherò (m) cambiario note of hand
Pagine Gialle (fpl) yellow pages
palazzo (m) block (n) *or* large building
paletta (f) pallet
palettizzare [trasportare a mezzo di palette] palletize

pannello (m) panel
paragonabile comparable
paragonabile: essere paragonabile compare with
paragonare [confrontare] compare
pareggiare un budget balance (v) [a budget]
pari par
parità (f) parity
parte (f) part (n)
parte (f) [leg] party
parte (f) contraente contracting party
parte (f) querelante prosecution [party in legal action]
parte (f) superiore top (n) or upper surface
parte (f) venditrice [cedente] assignor
partecipazione (f) investment or interest (n)
partecipazione (f) azionaria shareholding
partenza (f) departure or going away
partenze (fpl) departures
partire (lasciare) leave (v) or go away
partita (f) (di merci) batch or lot [of items]
partitario (m) delle vendite sales ledger
partite (fpl) varie sundry items
partite (fpl) visibili visible trade
partner (m) commerciale trading partner
parziale one-sided
passare a switch over to
passare il tempo a spend [time]
passibile di liable to
passività (fpl) liabilities
passività (fpl) a lungo termine long-term liabilities
passività (fpl) correnti current liabilities
passivo (m) patrimoniale equity
patto: a patto che provided that or providing
pausa (f) break (n)
pavimento (m) floor [surface]

pedaggio (m) toll
penale (f) penalty
penalità (f) [multa] forfeit (n)
penalizzare penalize
pendente pending
pendolare (m) commuter
pendolare: fare il pendolare commute [travel]
penetrazione (f) di mercato market penetration
pensionamento (m) retirement
pensione (f) pension
per affari on business
per cento per cent
per conto di on behalf of
per persona per head
percentuale (f) percentage
percentuale (f) d'errore error rate
percentuale (f) di crescita growth rate
percentuale (f) di occupazione occupancy rate
percentuale (f) per il servizio service charge
percorso (m) run (n) or regular route
perdere miss [train, plane]
perdere [un diritto] forfeit (v) [a right]
perdere denaro lose money
perdere un deposito forfeit a deposit
perdere un'ordinazione lose an order
perdita (f) loss
perdita (f) [di un diritto] forfeiture [of a right]
perdita (f) d'esercizio trading loss
perdita (f) di capitale capital loss
perdita (f) di clientela loss of customers
perdita (f) di un'ordinazione loss of an order
perdita (f) netta net loss
perdita (f) parziale partial loss
perdita (f) secca dead loss
perdita (f) sulla carta paper loss
perdite (fpl) record record losses
perenzione (f) time limitation
perfetta sintonia (f) fine tuning

periferiche (fpl) peripherals

periodico periodic *or* periodical
adj]

periodico (m) *[rivista]* journal *or*
magazine

periodico *[stagionale]* seasonal

periodo (m) period *or* term

periodo (m) *[stagione]* season
time for something]

periodo (m) di avviamento
make-ready time

periodo (m) di massima attività
peak period

periodo (m) di preavviso period
of notice

periodo (m) di prova trial period

periodo (m) di recupero payback
period

periodo (m) di validità period of
validity

periodo (m) medio di permanenza
di un prodotto shelf life of a
product

perito (m) surveyor

perizia (f) d'avaria damage survey

permanenza (f) stay (n) *[time]*

permesso (m) permit (n)

permesso (m) di lavoro work
permit

permesso (m) di soggiorno
residence permit

permettere allow *or* permit

permuta (f) come pagamento
parziale part exchange; trade-in

perseguire *[legalmente]* prosecute

persona (f) addetta al controllo
delle scorte stock controller

persona (f) che prende decisioni
decision maker

persona (f) che risolve problemi
problem solver

personal computer (m)
[elaboratore] personal computer
(PC)

personale personal

personale (m) staff (n) *or*
personnel

personale (m) addetta alle vendite
[forza vendita] sales force *or* sales
team

personale (m) al banco counter
staff

personale (m) alberghiero hotel
staff

personale (m) avventizio
temporary staff

personale (m) d'ufficio office staff

personale (m) di ruolo regular
staff

personale (m) dirigente
managerial staff

personale (m) impiegatizio
clerical staff

personale-chiave key personnel *or*
key staff

personalizzato personalized

pesa a ponte (f) weighbridge

pesante heavy *[weight]*

pesare weigh

peso (m) weight

peso (m) lordo gross weight

peso (m) morto deadweight

peso (m) netto net weight

petroliera (f) tanker

petrolio (m) oil *or* petroleum

pezza (f) giustificativa di cassa
cash voucher

pezzo (m) piece

pezzo (m) di ricambio spare part

pianificare investimenti plan
investments

pianificatore (m) planner

pianificazione (f) planning

pianificazione (f) a lunga scadenza
long-term planning

pianificazione (f) strategica
strategic planning

piano (m) *[di edificio]* floor

piano (m) *[progetto]* plan (n) *or*
project

piano (m) continuo rolling plan

piano (m) di contingenza
contingency plan

piano (m) globale overall plan

piano (m) pensioni pension
scheme

piano *[livello]* level

pianta (f) plan (n) *or* drawing

piatto flat *or* dull

piazza (f) del mercato marketplace *[in town]*

piccola cassa (f) petty cash

piccole imprese (fpl) small businesses

piccole spese (fpl) petty expenses

piccoli annunci (mpl) small ads

piccolo small

piccolo affarista o uomo d'affari small businessman

pieno *[intero]* full

pieno scarico (m) di un debito full discharge of a debt

PIL (prodotto interno lordo) gross domestic product (GDP)

pilota pilot (adj)

pilota (m) pilot (n) *[person]*

pioniere (m) pioneer (n)

pioniere: fare da pioniere in pioneer (v)

più alto *[migliore]* top (adj)

più basso *[inferiore]* lower (adj)

planimetria (f) floor plan

plusvalenza (f) capital gains

PNL (prodotto nazionale lordo) gross national product (GNP)

politica (f) policy *[way of working]*

politica (f) creditizia credit policy

politica (f) dei prezzi flessibile flexible pricing policy

politica (f) della determinazione dei prezzi pricing policy

politica (f) di budget budgetary policy

polizza (f) policy *[insurance]*

polizza (f) contro tutti i rischi all-risks policy

polizza (f) di assicurazione insurance policy

polizza (f) di carico bill of lading

polizza (f) provvisoria covering note

ponderazione (f) weighting

popolare popular

porta (f) door

porta (f) di computer computer port

portafoglio (m) portfolio *or* shareholding

portare bring *or* bear *or* carry

portare *[trasportare]* carry *or* transport

portare qualcuno in tribunale take someone to court

portata (f) lorda deadweight tonnage

portatile portable

portatore (m), portatrice (f) bearer

portfolio (m) *[cartella]* portfolio

portiere (m) reception clerk

portineria (f) reception (desk)

porto (m) port *or* harbour

porto (m) assegnato carriage forward *or* freight forward

porto (m) d'armamento port of registry

porto (m) d'imbarco port of embarkation

porto (m) di scalo port of call

porto (m) di transito entrepot port

porto (m) franco free port

porto (m) pagato carriage paid *or* postage paid

posare (mettere) place (v) *or* put

positivo positive

posizione (f) *[collocazione]* situation *or* place

posizione (f) *[situazione]* position *[state of affairs]*

posizione (f) finanziaria financial position

posporre hold over

possedere possess *or* own (v)

possibile acquirente (m) prospective buyer

possibilità (f) possibility

possibilità (fpl) di mercato market opportunities

possibile possible

possibile: se non è possibile failing that

posta (f) post (n) *or* mail (n)

posta (f) aerea airmail (n)

posta (f) elettronica electronic mail *or* e-mail

posta (f) in arrivo incoming mail

posta (f) in partenza outgoing mail

posta (f) ordinaria surface mail

postale postal

postdatare postdate

posticipare put back *[till later]*

posto (m) *[impiego]* place (n) or position or job

posto (m) *[luogo]* spot or place

posto (m) chiave key post

posto (m) di lavoro place of work; computer workstation

posto (m) vacante job vacancy

potenziale potential (adj)

potenziale (m) potential (n)

potere (m) *[controllo]* power or control (n)

potere (m) contrattuale bargaining power

potere (m) d'acquisto purchasing power; spending power

potere (m) per ricorrere al prestito borrowing power

pranzo (m) d'affari business lunch

pratica (f) *[dossier]* dossier

pratica (f) spregiudicata sharp practice

pratiche (fpl) restrittive restrictive practices

pratica: fare pratica train (v) *[learn]*

pratico *[maneggevole]* practical or handy

preavviso (m) notice *[time allowed]*

precedente previous or prior

precisare *[dichiarare]* state (v)

preciso *[accurato]* precise or accurate

preconfezionare prepack or repackage

predere parte in enter into *[discussion]*

referenza (f) preference

referenziale preferential

referire prefer

refinanziamento (m) re-financing

refisso (m) telefonico dialling code

relevare withdraw *[money]*

relievo (m) sulle importazioni import levy

remio (m) *[gratifica]* bonus

premio (m) addizionale additional premium

premio (m) agli assicurati che non hanno denunciato sinistri no-claims bonus

premio (m) d'operosità incentive payments

premio (m) di assicurazione insurance premium

premio (m) di merito merit award or merit bonus

premio (m) di produttività productivity bonus

premio (m) di rinnovo renewal premium

premio (m) di rischio risk premium

premio (m) finale terminal bonus

prendere a prestito *[mutuare]* borrow

prendere in affitto rent (v) *[pay money for]*

prendere in consegna un carico di merce accept delivery of a shipment

prendere l'iniziativa take the initiative

prendere nota take note

prendere un carico (m) a bordo take on freight

prendere una telefonata take a call

prendersi giorni di ferie take time off work

prenotare book (v)

prenotare una camera *o* un tavolo *o* un posto reserve a room *or* a table *or* a seat

prenotazione (f) *[registrazione]* booking or reservation

prenotazione anticipata (f) advance booking

prenotazioni (fpl) di camera room reservations

preoccupazione (f) concern (n) or worry

preparare lo schema di un contratto draft a contract

preparazione (f) del budget budgeting

prescrizione (f) statute of limitations
presentare present (v) *[show a document]*
presentare *[un modello]* model (v) *[clothes]*
presentare *[introdurre]* introduce
presentare *[offrire]* present (v) *or* give *[a gift]*
presentare (produrre) produce (v) *or* bring out
presentare un conto render an account
presentare un effetto (m) per il pagamento present a bill for payment
presentare un effetto (m) per l'accettazione present a bill for acceptance
presentare una controrichiesta counter-claim (v)
presentarsi report (v) *[go to a place]*
presentarsi al check in check in *[at airport]*
presentarsi per un colloquio di lavoro report for an interview
presentazione (f) production *or* presentation
presentazione (f) in cofanetto boxed set
presente present (adj) *[being there]*
presidente (m) chairman
presidente e amministratore delegato chairman and managing director
presso care of (c/o)
prestanome (m) nominee
prestare lend *or* advance *[money]*
prestatore (m) lender
prestazione (f) performance
prestigio (m) prestige
prestiti (mpl) bancari bank borrowings
prestito (m) *[mutuo]* loan (n)
prestito (m) a termine term loan
prestito (m) agevolato soft loan
prestito (m) bancario bank loan
presto: al più presto possibile as soon as possible (asap)

pretendente (m) di diritto rightful claimant
prevedere forecast (v)
prevenire prevent
preventivo preventive
preventivo (m) estimate (n) *or* quote (n)
prevenzione (f) prevention
previdenza (f) sociale social security
previsione (f) forecast (n)
previsione (f) a lungo termine long-term forecast
previsione (f) della necessità di manodopera manpower forecasting
previsione (f) provvisoria delle vendite provisional forecast of sales
previsione (f) di vendita sales budget
previsione (f) di vendita sales forecast
previsioni (fpl) del flusso di cassa cash flow forecast
previsioni (fpl) di mercato market forecast
prezzi (mpl) concorrenziali keen prices
prezzi (mpl) correnti common pricing
prezzi (mpl) effettivi di vendita actuals
prezzi (mpl) equi fair price
prezzi (mpl) flessibili flexible prices
prezzi (mpl) franco banchina price ex quay
prezzi (mpl) franco magazzino price ex warehouse
prezzi (mpl) franco stabilimento price ex works
prezzi (mpl) inflazionati inflated prices
prezzi (mpl) popolari popular prices
prezzi (mpl) stabili stable prices
prezzo (m) price (n)
prezzo: ad alto prezzo highly-priced

prezzo (m) al dettaglio retail price

prezzo (m) al rivenditore trade price

prezzo (m) allineato competitive price

prezzo (m) concordato agreed price

prezzo (m) consigliato di fabbrica manufacturer's recommended price

prezzo (m) corrente current price

prezzo (m) d'acquisto purchase price

prezzo (m) d'apertura opening price

prezzo (m) d'entrata threshold price

prezzo (m) d'intervento intervention price

prezzo (m) d'occasione bargain price

prezzo (m) d'offerta supply price

prezzo (m) del coperto cover charge

prezzo (m) del petrolio oil price

prezzo (m) del trasporto haulage costs *or* haulage rates

prezzo (m) di catalogo catalogue price

prezzo (m) di chiusura closing price

prezzo (m) di fabbrica factory price

prezzo (m) di fattura invoice value

prezzo (m) di listino list price

prezzo (m) di mercato market price *or* market rate

prezzo (m) di permuta trade-in price

prezzo (m) di rivendita resale price

prezzo (m) di sostegno support price

prezzo (m) di vendita selling price

prezzo (m) eccessivo overcharge (n)

prezzo (m) franco delivered price

prezzo (m) intero full price

prezzo (m) massimo maximum price *or* ceiling price

prezzo (m) medio average price

prezzo (m) minimo reserve price

prezzo (m) netto net price

prezzo (m) per contanti cash price

prezzo (m) per merce pronta spot price

prezzo (m) ridottissimo rock-bottom prices

prezzo (m) ridotto cut price (n)

prezzo ridotto: a prezzo ridotto cut-price (adj)

prezzo (m) scontato discount price

prezzo (m) sotto costo cost price

prezzo (m) stabile firm price

prezzo (m) stabilito set price

prezzo (m) tutto compreso all-in price

prezzo (m) unitario unit price

prima classe first class

prima: di prima classe first-class (adj) *or* A1

prima: di prima qualità prime *or* top grade

prima opzione (f) first option

primario primary

primato (m) record (n) *[better than before]*

primo first

primo *[di prima qualità]* prime

primo ad entrare primo ad uscire first in first out (FIFO)

primo giorno (m) del trimestre quarter day

primo trimestre (m) first quarter

principale principal (adj) *or* main *or* chief

principio (m) principle

privatizzare privatize

privatizzazione (f) privatization

privato private

privilegio (m) lien

privo di validità (inabile) invalid

privo di valore worthless

pro-capite per capita

probabile prospective

probatorio probationary

problema (m) problem

procacciare canvass

procedere proceed

procedimenti (mpl) legali judicial processes

procedimento (m) giudiziario
prosecution *[legal action]*

procedura (f) procedure

procedura (f) di selezione
selection procedure

processi (mpl) industriali
industrial processes

processo (m) process (n)

processo (m) trial *[court case]*

processo (m) decisionale decision making

procura (f) power of attorney; proxy

procurarsi get

procurarsi fondi secure funds

procuratore (m) attorney

procuratore (m) legale solicitor

prodotti (mpl) agricoli agricultural produce

prodotti (mpl) che si fanno concorrenza competing products

prodotti (mpl) competitivi
competitive products

prodotti (mpl) con etichetta propria own label goods

prodotti (mpl) con marchio proprio
own brand goods

prodotti (mpl) di alta qualità
high-quality goods

prodotti (mpl) di seconda qualità
seconds

prodotti (mpl) essenziali staple product

prodotti (mpl) finiti finished goods

prodotti (mpl) semilavorati
semi-finished products

prodotto (m) product or article

prodotto (m) derivato by-product

prodotto (m) di prestigio prestige product

prodotto (m) finito end product

prodotto (m) nazionale lordo (PNL) gross national product (GNP)

prodotto (m) per il mercato di massa mass market product

prodotto (m) sensibile ai cambiamenti di prezzo
price-sensitive product

prodotto (m) interno lordo (PIL)
gross domestic product (GDP)

prodotto-guida (m) del mercato
market leader

produrre *[fabbricare]* produce (v)
or manufacture *or* make

produrre *[presentare]* produce *or*
show *or* bring out

produrre in eccesso overproduce

produrre in serie mass-produce

produrre automobili in serie
mass-produce cars

produttività (f) productivity

produttivo productive

produttore (m) *[fabbricante]*
producer *or* manufacturer

produzione (f) production *or*
making *or* output

produzione (f) in eccesso
overproduction

produzione (f) in serie mass production

produzione (f) totale total output

produzione (f) nazionale domestic production

professionale professional *or*
occupational

professionista (m) *[esperto]*
professional (n) *or* expert

proficuo profitable

profitto (m) (utile) profit *or*
earnings

proforma: fattura (f) proforma pro forma (invoice)

progettare design (v)

progettare *[organizzare]* plan (v)

progettato projected

progettazione (f) *[design]* design (n)

progettazione (f) del prodotto
product design

progetto (m) *[piano]* project *or*
plan

progetto (m) di legge bill (n) *[in Parliament]*

progetto (m) edilizio di ricostruzione redevelopment

progetto (m) pilota pilot scheme

progetto (m) redditizio
money-making plan

programma (m) programme *or*
timetable

programma (m) aziendale corporate plan

programma (m) di computer computer program

programma (m) di ricerca research programme

programmare timetable (v)

programmare un computer program a computer

programmatore (m) di computer computer programmer

programmazione (f) aziendale corporate planning

programmazione (f) delle assunzioni di manodopera manpower planning

programmazione (f) di computer computer programming

programmazione (f) economica economic planning

progresso (m) *[sviluppo]* progress *or* development

progresso: fare progressi progress (v) *or* make progress

proibire forbid

proibitivo prohibitive

prolungamento (m) extension *[making longer]*

prolungare extend *[make longer]*

promessa (f) promise (n)

promettere promise (v)

promozionale promotional

promozione (f) promotion *[better job, publicity]*

promozione (f) delle vendite sales promotion

promozione (f) di un prodotto promotion of a product

promuovere promote *[give better job, advertise]*

promuovere un'immagine aziendale promote a corporate image

pronosticare tip (v) *[say what might happen]*

pronta cassa (f) ready cash

pronto ready

pronunciarsi in una vertenza adjudicate in a dispute

propaganda (f) canvassing

propagandista (m) canvasser

proporre propose *or* move *[a motion]*

proporre *[offrire]* offer (v) *[to buy]*

proporzionale proportional *or* pro rata

proporzione (f) proportion

proposito (m) *[scopo]* aim (n)

proposta (f) proposal *or* suggestion

proposta (f) *[di assicurazione]* insurance proposal

proposta (f) unica di vendita unique selling point *or* proposition (USP)

proprietà (f) ownership

proprietà (f) collettiva collective ownership

proprietà (f) comune common ownership

proprietà (f) immobiliare real estate

proprietà (f) multipla multiple ownership

proprietà (f) privata private property; private ownership

proprietaria (f) proprietress

proprietario (m) proprietor *or* owner

proprietario (m) legittimo rightful owner

prorata *[proporzionale]* pro rata

prosperare flourish *or* prosper

prospettive (fpl) prospects

prospetto (m) prospectus

prossimo early

protesta (f) *[reclamo]* protest *or* complaint

protesta (f) con occupazione sit-down protest

protestare *[reclamare]* complain (about)

protestare contro qualcosa protest (v) *[against something]*

protestare una cambiale protest a bill

protesto (m) *[per mancato pagamento]* protest (n) *[official document]*

protettivo protective

protezione (f) protection

protezione (f) *[barriera]* hedge (n)
protezione (f) del consumatore consumer protection
prova (f) test (n); protection; proof; trial
prova: in prova on approval
prova (f) documentata documentary proof
prova (f) gratuita free trial
provare test (v)
proventi (mpl) da partite invisibili invisible earnings
provvedere provide
provvedere a provide for; make provision for
provvedere di generi alimentari cater for
provvedimenti (mpl) fiscali fiscal measures
provvisorio provisional
provvista (f) supply (n) *or* stock of goods
prudente *[sicuro]* safe (adj)
pubblicazione (f) periodica periodical (n)
pubbliche relazioni (fpl) public relations (PR)
pubblicità (f) (reclame) publicity *or* advertising
pubblicità: fare pubblicità *[reclamizzare]* advertise
pubblicità (f) (spot) TV commercial
pubblicità (f) *[annuncio pubblicitario]* advertisement
pubblicità (f) a mezzo posta direct-mail advertising
pubblicità (f) di un prodotto product advertising
pubblicità (f) su tutto il territorio nazionale national advertising
pubblicizzare publicize
pubblicizzare un nuovo prodotto promote a new product
pubblico public (adj)
punto (m) point
punto (m) di pareggio fra costi e ricavi breakeven point
punto (m) di partenza starting point

punto (m) di riferimento benchmark
punto (m) di vendita point of sale (p.o.s. *or* POS)
punto (m) di vendita al dettaglio retail outlets
punto (m) di vendita diretta della fabbrica factory outlet
punto (m) di vendita elettronico electronic point of sale (EPOS)
punto (m) metallico staple (n)
punto (m) morto deadlock (n)
punto: essere a un punto morto be deadlocked
punto (m) per la dichiarazine doganale d'entrata customs entry point
punto (m) percentuale percentage point
puntuale on time

Qq

quadri (mpl) direttivi management team
quadri (mpl) intermedi middle management
quadro (m) generale survey (n) *or* general report
qualificarsi qualify as
qualificato *[abile]* qualified *or* skilled
qualifiche (fpl) professionali professional qualifications
qualità (f) quality
qualità (f) extra premium quality
qualità: di qualità inferiore low-grade *or* low-quality
qualità (f) scadente poor quality
qualità (f) superiore top quality
qualità superiore di qualità superiore high-quality

quantità (f) quantity
quartiere (m) *[zona]* area *or* quarter *or* district *[of town]*
quarto (m) quarter *[25%]*
quarto trimestre (m) fourth quarter
querelante (m) plaintiff
questione (f) *[argomento]* item *[on agenda]* or matter (n) *[to be discussed]*
quietanza (f) finale final discharge
quota (f) quota
quota (f) (tariffa) rate (n) *or* price
quota (f) d'ammortamento depreciation rate
quota (f) d'iscrizione admission fee
quota (f) di mercato market share
quotare quote (v) *[a reference number]*
quotare *[indicare un prezzo]* quote (v) *[estimate costs]*
quotazione (f) quotation *or* quote *[estimate of cost]*
quotidiano daily

Rr

raccogliere *[cogliere]* collect (v) *or* fetch
raccogliere fondi raise (v) *or* obtain money
raccoglitore (m) collector
raccomandare *[consigliare]* recommend *or* advise *[what should be done]*
raccomandata (f) registered letter
raccomandazione (f) recommendation
raddoppiare double (v)

raduno (m) dei venditori sales conference
rafforzarsi rally (v)
raggiungere reach *or* arrive at
raggiungere un obiettivo meet a target
raggruppare bracket together
ragione (f) sociale corporate name
ragioniere (m) o ragioniera (f) *[contabile]* accountant
ragioniere (m) iscritto all'albo *[revisore ufficiale dei conti]* certified accountant
rallentamento (m) slowdown
rallentare slow down
rammentare remind
rampa (f) di carico loading ramp
rapidamente *[velocemente]* fast (adv)
rapporto (m) report (n); ratio
rapporto (m) corso/utili price/earnings ratio (P/E ratio)
rapporto (m) di indebitamento gearing
rapporto (m) fra utile e dividendo dividend cover
rapporto (m) riservato confidential report
rappresentante (m) sales representative
rappresentante (m) *[agente]* agent *or* representative
rappresentante (m) commissionario commission rep
rappresentante (m) (di commercio) salesman *or* representative
rappresentante (m) esclusivo sole agent
rappresentanza (f) esclusiva sole agency
rappresentare represent
rappresentare qualcuno deputize for someone
rappresentativo representative (adj)
rata (f) instalment
ratifica (f) ratification
ratificare ratify
razionalizzare rationalize
razionalizzazione (f) rationalization

reale real
realizzabile viable
realizzare realize *or* sell for money
realizzare (attuare) implement (v) *or* put into practice
realizzare beni realize property
realizzare la penetrazione di un mercato penetrate a market
realizzare un piano *o* un progetto realize a plan
realizzazione (f) di cespiti realization of assets
reato (m) di omissione nonfeasance
reazione (f) response
recapito (m) *[indirizzo]* address (n)
recentissimo latest
recessione (f) recession
reciproco *[mutuo]* reciprocal *or* mutual
reclamare *[protestare]* complain (about)
reclame (f) *[pubblicità]* advertising
reclamizzare un nuovo prodotto advertise a new product
reclamo (m) *[domanda d'indennizzo]* claim (n)
reclamo (m) *[protesta]* complaint
recuperabile recoverable
recuperare collect (v) *[money]*
recuperare repossess
recuperare *[salvare]* salvage (v)
recuperare un debito collect a debt
recupero (m) collection *[of money]*; salvage *[of goods]*
recupero (m) dell'investimento payback
recupero (m) di crediti debt collection
redditività (f) profitability
redditività (f) dei costi cost-effectiveness
redditizio paying (adj); money-making *or* cost-effective
reddito (m) revenue *or* income
reddito (m) complessivo total revenue
reddito (m) da affittanze rental income

reddito (m) da dividendi dividend yield
reddito (m) da investimenti investment income
reddito (m) effettivo real income *or* real wages
reddito (m) fisso fixed income *or* regular income
reddito (m) imponibile taxable income
reddito (m) lordo gross income
reddito (m) netto net income *or* net salary
reddito (m) non imponibile non-taxable income
reddito (m) personale personal income
reddito (m) societario negativo negative cash flow
reddito (m) sugli investimenti return on investment (ROI)
reddito (m) totale total income
reddito (m) ufficiale official return
redigere *[abbozzare]* draw up *or* draft (v)
redimibile redeemable
referenze (fpl) *[attestato]* reference *[on person]*
regalare give (away) *[as gift]* or present (v)
regalo (m) gift *or* present (n)
regionale regional
regione (f) *[area]* region *or* area
registrare record (v) *or* write in
registrare chiamate log calls
registrare una voce *[contabile]* post an entry
registrato registered (adj)
registratore (f) di cassa cash register
registrazione (f) registration; registry
registrazione (f) *[prenotazione]* booking
registrazione (f) a credito credit entry
registrazione (f) a debito debit entry
registrazione (f) di storno contra entry

registrazione (f) sul computer computer listing

registro (m) register (n) or official list

registro (m) [libro contabile] register (n)

registro (m) degli amministratori register of directors

registro (m) degli azionisti o registro (m) delle azioni register of shareholders

registro (m) delle ordinazioni order book

registro (m) delle ricevute receipt book

Registro (m) delle SPA companies' register

regolamenti (mpl) [disposizioni] regulations

regolamento (m) regulation

regolamento (m) finanziario financial settlement

regolare (v) regulate or adjust

regolare [normale] regular or normal or ordinary

regolarizzare regulate [by law]

regolarmente [dovutamente] duly [legally]

regresso (m) downturn

reimportare reimport (v)

reimportazione (f) reimportation; reimport (n)

reinvestimento (m) reinvestment

reinvestire reinvest

relativo relevant

relativo a relating to

relazione (f) annuale al bilancio annual report

relazione (f) provvisoria interim report

relazione (f) sull'avanzamento progress report

relazioni (fpl) relations

relazioni (fpl) industriali industrial relations

remunerare (pagare) pay (v) [worker]

remunerativo [redditizio] profitable

remunerato [pagato] paid [for work]

rendere [apportare] bring in or yield

rendere [fruttare] produce (v) [interest]

rendere conto account for

rendere effettivo un accordo implement an agreement

rendere saturo il mercato saturate the market

rendersi conto di [capire] realize [understand]

rendiconti (mpl) annuali annual accounts

rendiconto (m) statement

rendiconto (m) del flusso di cassa cash flow statement

rendiconto (m) delle spese statement of expenses

rendimento (m) effettivo effective yield

rendimento (m) immediato current yield

rendimento (m) lordo gross yield

rendimento (m) netto net yield

rendita (f) yield (n) [on investment]

rendita (f) vitalizia [usufrutto] life interest

reparto (m) department [in shop]; division [of company]

reparto (m) esportazioni export department

reparto (m) marketing marketing division

reparto (m) contabilità accounts department

reperimento (m) retrieval

reperire retrieve

replica (f) repeat

rescindere rescind

rescindere [invalidare] void or invalidate

rescindere un accordo terminate an agreement

residente resident (adj)

residente (m) [abitante] resident (n) or inhabitant

residenza (f) residence

resoconto (m) dettagliato detailed account

resoconto (m) mensile monthly statement

resoconto (m) semestrale half-yearly statement

respingere *[mandare indietro]* return (v) or send back

respingere *[rifiutare]* reject (v)

responsabile (m) dei reclami claims manager

responsabile (m) del mastro dei conti dei creditori bought ledger clerk

responsabile (m) di un prodotto product engineer

responsabile (m) di un ufficio acquisti buyer *[for a store]*

responsabile di *o* per responsible or liable (for)

responsabilità (f) responsibility or responsibilties

responsabilità (f) *[obbligo]* liability

responsabilità (f) contrattuale contractual liability

responsabilità (f) illimitata unlimited liability

responsabilità (f) limitata limited liability

restare remain

resti in linea per favore hold the line please or please hold

restituibile returnable

restituire *[consegnare]* hand in or deliver or consign

restringere tighten up on

restringimento (m) shrinkage

restrittivo restrictive

restrizione (f) restraint or restriction or limitation

restrizione (f) endorsement *[on insurance]*

restrizioni (fpl) alle importazioni import restrictions

rete (f) network (n)

rete (f) di distribuzione distribution network

reticolo (m) grid

retribuire remunerate

retribuzione (f) remuneration

retribuzione (f) *[stipendio]* pay (n) or salary

retribuzione (f) a cottimo piece rate

retribuzione (f) a ore hourly rate

retribuzione (f) ferie holiday pay

retro (m) (dorso) back (n)

retroattivo retroactive

retrodatare antedate

rettifica (f) *[emendamento]* rectification or amendment

revisionare service (v) *[a machine]*

revisione (f) *[manutenzione]* service (n) *[of machine]*

revisione (f) contabile audit (n)

revisione (f) contabile periodica general audit

revisione (f) dello stipendio salary review

revisione (f) esterna external audit

revisione (f) interna internal audit

revisore (m) esterno external auditor

revisore (m) interno internal auditor

revisore (m) ufficiale dei conti auditor

revoca (f) di una nomina cancellation of an appointment

revocare revoke

riacquistare buy back

riadattare readjust

riaddestramento (m) retraining

riaddestrare retrain

riassestamento (m) readjustment

riassicurare reinsure

riassicuratore (m) reinsurer

riassicurazione (f) reinsurance

riassumere *[una persona]* re-employ *[someone]*

riassunzione (f) re-employment

ribassista (m) bear (n) *[on Stock Exchange]*

ribasso (m) *[caduta]* reduction or drop (n)

ribasso: in ribasso falling

ribasso (m) delle vendite drop in sales

icambio (m) turnover *[of staff]*

icavare al netto net (v)

icavi (mpl) netti net sales

icavo (m) dalla pubblicità revenue from advertising

icavo (m) nullo nil return

icerca (f) research (n)

icerca: fare ricerche do research or research (v)

icerca (f) automatica dell'informazione data retrieval

icerca (f) di mercato market esearch

icerca (f) e sviluppo (RS) research and development (R & D)

icercatore (m), ricercatrice (f) esearch worker or researcher

icettività (f) alberghi hotel accommodation

icevente receiving

icevere receive

icevimento (m) receipt *[receiving]*

icevuta (f) receipt *[piece of paper]*

icevuta (f) (di vendita) sales eceipt

icevuta (f) in duplicato duplicate eceipt or duplicate of a receipt

ichiamo (m) appeal (n) or attraction

ichiamo (m) per i clienti customer appeal

ichiedere *[domandare]* demand or request (v)

ichiedere *[volere]* take (v) or need

ichiesta (f) request (n); inquiry

ichiesta: su richiesta on request

ichiesta (f) *[domanda]* demand n) *[for payment]*

ichiesta (f) di indennizzo assicurativo insurance claim

ichiesta (f) di informazioni enquiry

ichiesta (f) di iscrizione letter of application

ichiesta (f) di pagamento call (n) *[for money]*

ichiesta (f) stagionale seasonal demand

ichieste (fpl) requirements

riciclare recycle; launder *[money]*

ricollocamento (m) reappointment

ricollocare reappoint

ricompensa (f) *[compenso]* compensation

riconciliare reconcile

riconciliazione (f) reconciliation

riconciliazione (f) dei conti reconciliation of accounts

riconoscere un sindacato recognize a union

riconoscimento (m) recognition

riconoscimento (m) scritto di un debito *[pagherò]* IOU (= I owe you)

riconoscimento (m) sindacale union recognition

ricorrente recurrent

ricorrere a consulenza legale take legal advice

ricorrere in appello *[appellare]* appeal (v) *[against a decision]*

ricorso (m) *[appello]* appeal (n) *[against a decision]*

ricuperare recover or get something back

ricuperare mediante tassazione clawback

ricupero (m) recovery *[getting something back]*

ridistribuire redistribute

ridurre *[abbassare]* reduce or knock down (v) *[price]*

ridurre il valore write down *[assets]*

ridurre le spese reduce expenditure

ridurre un prezzo reduce a price

riduzione (f) *[sconto]* rebate or price reduction

riduzione (f) d'imposta tax allowance

riduzione (f) dei costi cost-cutting

riduzione (f) delle spese retrenchment

riduzione (f) di posti lavorativi job cuts

riduzione (f) di prezzi knockdown prices

riduzioni (fpl) d'imposta tax reductions

rieleggere re-elect

rielezione (f) re-election

riesaminare revise

riesportare re-export (v)

riesportazione (f) re-export (n)

rifarsi delle perdite recoup one's losses

riferimento (m) reference *[dealing with]*

riferimento: fare riferimento a refer *[to item]*

riferire report (v)

riferirsi (fare riferimento a) refer (to)

rifinanziamento (m) di un prestito refinancing *or* restructuring of a loan

rifiutare fall *or* decline (v)

rifiutare *[respingere]* refuse *or* reject (v) *or* turn down

rifiutare un accordo repudiate an agreement

rifiuto (m) refusal *or* rejection

rifornimento (m) restocking

rifornire restock

rifugio (m) fiscale tax haven

riguardante regarding

riguardare apply to *or* affect

rilasciare release (v) *[make public]*

rilascio (m) release (n) *or* issue *[of shares]*

rilevamento (m) takeover

rimandare *[aggiornare]* adjourn

rimandare una lettera al mittente return a letter to sender

rimanenze (fpl) iniziali opening stock

rimanere indietro fall behind *[be in a worse position]*

rimborsabile refundable

rimborsabile repayable *or* repayable

rimborsare pay back

rimborsare un'obbligazione redeem a bond

rimborso (m) reimbursement *or* refund *or* repayment

rimborso (m) delle spese reimbursement of expenses

rimborso (m) totale full refund

rimessa (f) remittance

rimetterci out of pocket

rimettere remit (v)

rimuovere remove

ringraziamento (m) vote of thanks

rinnovare renew

rinnovare un abbonamento renew a subscription

rinnovare un contratto d'affitto renew a lease

rinnovare una cambiale renew a bill of exchange

rinnovo (m) renewal

rinnovo (m) di un contratto d'affitto renewal of a lease

rinnovo (m) di un abbonamento renewal of a subscription

rinnovo (m) di una cambiale renewal of a bill

rinuncia (f) renunciation; waiver *[of right]*

rinunciare waive

rinunciare ad un pagamento waive a payment

rinunciare ad un'azione (f) abandon an action

rinviare *[differire]* postpone

rinvio (m) return (n); deferment *or* postponement

rinvio (m) di pagamento deferment of payment

riordinare reorder (v)

riorganizzare reorganize

riorganizzazione (f) reorganization

riorganizzazione (f) di una società restructuring of the company

ripagare repay

riparare *[aggiustare]* repair (v) *or* fix *or* mend

riparazione (m) repair (n)

riparo (m) shelter

ripartire un rischio spread a risk

ripartizione (f) breakdown (n) *[of items]*

ripetere un'ordinazione repeat an order

riportare a nuovo carry forward

riportare un pareggio carry over a balance

riprendere resume

riprendere le trattative resume negotiations

riprendersi recover *or* get better *or* stage a recovery

ripresa (f) recovery *or* getting better; rally

riprodurre *[copiare]* copy (v)

ripudiare repudiate

risarcimento (m) di danni damages *or* compensation for damage

risarcire *[indennizzare]* indemnify

risarcire qualcuno per una perdita indemnify someone for a loss

riscattare surrender (v) *[an insurance]*

riscattare un pegno redeem a pledge

riscattare una polizza surrender a policy

riscatto (m) surrender (n) *[of an insurance policy]*

riscatto (m) *[di un prestito]* redemption *[of a loan]*

rischiare risk (v) *[money]*

rischio (m) risk (n)

rischio (m) d'incendio fire risk

rischio (m) finanziario financial risk *or* exposure

rischioso risky

riscossione (f) delle imposte tax collection

riserva (f) store *[of items kept]* *or* reserve *[of supplies]*

riserva (f) *[accantonamento]* reserve *or* provision *[money put aside]*

riserva: di riserva backup (adj) *[copy]*

riserva (f) di cassa cash reserves

riserva (f) di materia prima stock of raw materials

riservare reserve (v)

riservatezza (f) confidentiality

riservato confidential

riserve (fpl) reserves

riserve: con riserve *[condizionato]* with reservations

riserve (fpl) d'emergenza emergency reserves

riserve (fpl) occulte hidden reserves

riserve (fpl) valutarie currency reserves

risoluzione (f) resolution

risoluzione (f) di problemi problem solving

risolvere un problema solve a problem

risorse (fpl) resources

risorse (fpl) finanziarie financial resources

risorse (fpl) naturali natural resources

risparmi (mpl) savings

risparmiare *[economizzare]* save (v)

risparmiare: che risparmia energia energy-saving (adj)

rispettare respect (v)

rispettare una scadenza (f) meet a deadline

rispondere answer (v) *or* reply (v)

rispondere: dover rispondere a qualcuno report to someone

rispondere: che deve rispondere a qualcuno responsible to someone

rispondere a una lettera answer a letter

rispondere al telefono answer the telephone

risposta (f) answer (n) *or* reply (n)

ristagno (m) stagnation

ristrutturare restructure

ristrutturazione (f) restructuring

risultati (mpl) results *[company's profit or loss]*

risultato (m) result *[in general]*

risultato: avere come risultato result in

ritaglio (m) (di campioni) swatch

ritardare delay (v)

ritardo (m) delay (n) *or* hold-up (n)

ritardo: in ritardo late (adv)

ritardo: essere in ritardo *[nel fare una cosa]* fall behind *or* be late *[in doing something]*

ritelefonare phone back
ritenuta (f) d'acconto withholding tax
ritirare withdraw *[an offer]*
ritirare la propria candidatura stand down
ritiro (m) collection *[of goods]*; withdrawal *[of money]*
ritorno (m) return (n) *or* going back
ritrattare un'offerta di rilevamento withdraw a takeover bid
riunione (f) meeting; conference
riunione (f) del consiglio di amministrazione board meeting
riuscire *[avere successo]* succeed *or* do well
riuscire a manage to
riuscire: non riuscire fail *[not to do something]*
rivalutare revalue (v)
rivalutazione (f) revaluation; appreciation *[in value]*
rivelare (divulgare) reveal *or* disclose
rivelazione (f) *[divulgazione]* revelation *or* disclosure
rivendicare claim (v) *[insurance]*
rivendicazione (f) salariale wage claim
rivendita (f) resale
rivenditore (m) stockist
rivista (f) (periodico) magazine *or* journal
rivista (f) aziendale house magazine
rivista (f) di categoria trade magazine
rivolgere la parola a qualcuno address (v) *or* speak to someone
rivolto a una fascia alta del mercato up-market
roll on/roll off *[traghetto per automezzi]* roll on/roll off ferry
rompere break (v) *[a contract]*
rompersi break down (v) *[of machine]*
rotazione (f) turnround *[goods sold]*
rotazione (f) delle scorte stock turnover

rottura (f) breakdown (n) *[of talks]*
rotture (fpl) *[danni]* breakages
routine (f) *[ordinaria amministrazione]* routine (n)
rovinare (viziare) spoil
RS (ricerca e sviluppo) R&D (= research and development)

Ss

sacchetto (m) di carta paper bag
saggio (m) *[campione]* sample (n)
sala (f) di esposizione showroom
sala (f) di vendita all'asta auction rooms
sala (f) esposizioni exhibition hall
sala (f) per VIP VIP lounge
sala (f) riunioni boardroom; conference room
sala (f) transiti transit lounge
salario (m) wage
salario (m) minimo minimum wage
salario (m) minimo garantito guaranteed minimum wage
salario (m) orario hourly wage
saldare *[pagare]* pay (v) *or* settle *[bill]*
saldare un conto settle an account
saldezza (f) steadiness
saldi (mpl) per inventario stocktaking sale
saldo (m) sale (n) *[at a low price]*
saldo (m) a metà prezzo half-price sale
saldo (m) da riportare balance brought down *or* brought forward
saldo (m) debitore debit balance
saldo (m) di cassa cash balance
saldo (m) di un debito clearing *or* paying *[of a debt]*

saldo (m) dovuto balance due to us

saldo (m) in banca bank balance

saldo (m) riportato balance carried down or carrried forward

salire [ascendere] climb

salire alle stelle soar

salone (m) delle partenze departure lounge

salvaguardia (f) safeguard

salvare [su disco] save (v) [on computer]

salvare [recuperare] salvage (v)

salvo errori e omissioni (S.E. & O) errors and omissions excepted (e. & o.e.)

salvo vista e verifica on approval

saturare saturate or glut (v)

saturare di prodotti overstock (v)

saturazione (f) saturation or glut

sbagliato wrong

sbarcare land (v) [passengers, cargo]

sbarrare un assegno cross a cheque

sbocco (m) outlet

sborsare pay out

scadente [basso] low (adj)

scadenza (f) [fine] expiry

scadere [terminare] expire or mature or lapse

scaduto overdue

scaffalatura (f) shelving or shelves

scaffale (m) shelf

scaglionare stagger

scala (f) scale [system]

scala: in scala naturale full-scale (adj) or full-size

scala: in scala ridotta small-scale

scala (f) [variazioni] range (n) or variation

scala (f) incrementale incremental scale

scala (f) retributiva wage scale

scala (f) temporale time scale

scalo (m) merci freight depot

scalo (m) per container container port

scambiabile exchangeable

scambiare swap (v) or exchange

scambiare con exchange (v) [one thing for another]

scambio (m) swap (n) or exchange

scambio (m) [baratto] barter (n)

scambio (m) di merci e prodotti bartering

scappatoia (f) fiscale tax shelter

scaricare unload [goods]

scaricare merce in un porto land goods at a port

scaricatore (m) (di porto) [stivatore] stevedore

scarsità (f) shortage

scarto (m) reject (n)

scatola (f) di cartone cardboard box

scatola (f) per la piccola cassa petty cash box

scegliere choose

scegliere la strada più facile take the soft option

scelta (f) choice (n)

scelta (f) del momento opportuno timing

scendere [diminuire] fall off

scheda (f) filing card or index card

schedare card-index (v)

schedario (m) card index; filing cabinet

schedatura (f) filing [action]; card-indexing

schema (m) del ciclo flow chart

scienze (fpl) economiche [economia] economics [study]

sciogliere una società di persone dissolve a partnership

scioglimento (m) [liquidazione] winding up

sciolto loose

scioperante (m) striker

scioperare strike (v)

sciopero (m) strike (n)

sciopero (m) bianco go-slow or work-to-rule

sciopero (m) con occupazione sit-down strike

sciopero (m) di protesta protest strike

sciopero (m) di solidarietà sympathy strike

sciopero (m) generale general strike

sciopero (m) selvaggio wildcat strike

scontabile discountable

sconti (mpl) al rivenditore trade terms

scontista (m) discounter

sconto (m) [riduzione] discount or rebate or price reduction

sconto: con sconto di off [reduced by]

sconto: fare uno sconto di take off or deduct

sconto (m) ai rivenditori trade discount

sconto (m) all'ingrosso wholesale discount

sconto (m) cassa cash discount

sconto (m) del valore attuale discounted cash flow (DCF)

sconto (m) di base basic discount

sconto (m) percentuale percentage discount

sconto (m) per pagamento in contanti cash discount

sconto (m) sul quantitativo quantity discount or volume discount

scontrarsi con crash (v) into

scoperto (di c/c) overdraft

scopo (m) [proposito] aim (n)

scopo: avere lo scopo di aim (v)

scorrettamente incorrectly

scorretto incorrect

scorta (f) [di materie prime] stockpile (n)

scorte (fpl) stock (n) or goods or inventory (n)

scritto a mano handwritten

scrittura (f) writing

scrittura (f) contabile entry [writing]

scrivania (f) desk

scrivere write

scuola (f) per segretarie d'azienda secretarial college

scuola (m) superiore di commercio commercial college

scusa (f) apology

scusarsi apologize

S. E. & O. (salvo errori e omissioni) e. & o.e. (errors and omissions excepted)

seconda categoria o seconda classe second-class

seconda mano: di seconda mano secondhand

secondo second (adj)

secondo: a secondo di according to or under

secondo i termini convenuti according to the terms agreed; on agreed terms

secondo trimestre (m) second quarter

sede (f) head office

sede (f) legale registered office

sede (f) centrale headquarters (HQ); main office

segnale (m) di linea libera dialling tone

segnale (m) di linea occupata engaged tone

segno (m) place (n) [in a text]

segretaria (f), segretario (m) secretary

segretaria (f) personale personal assistant (PA)

segretaria (f) temporanea temp (n)

segretario (m) del consiglio d'amministrazione company secretary

segreteria (f) telefonica answering machine

segreto secret (adj)

segreto (m) secret (n)

seguire follow

seguito: fare seguito follow

seguito: in seguito a further to

selezionare candidati screen candidates

selezione (f) selection

sembrare appear

semestre (m) half-year

senza scalo [ininterrotto] non-stop

senza scopo di lucro non profit-making

senza sovvenzioni unsubsidized

senza spese [franco] franco

senza tener conto di regardless of

separare separate (v)
separato separate (adj)
sequela (f) *[serie]* run (n) *[work routine]*
sequestrare sequester *or* sequestrate *or* seize
sequestratario (m) sequestrator
sequestro (m) sequestration *or* seizure
serie (f) set (n); run (n)
serratura (f) lock (n)
servire serve
servire un cliente serve a customer
servizi (mpl) facilities
servizi (mpl) di elaborazione elettronica computer services
servizi (mpl) di trasporto transport facilities
servizio (m) service (n)
servizio (m) di marketing marketing department
servizio (m) in camera room service
servizio (m) pacchi postali parcel post
servizio (m) postale postal service
servizio (m) scadente poor service
servizio (m) segreteria telefonica answering service
servizio (m) sollecito prompt service
servizio (m) spedizioni dispatch department
servizio (m) stralci giornalistici clipping service
servizio (m) telefonico gratuito toll free number *or* 0800 number
settimana (f) week
settimanale weekly
settore (m) sector *or* branch
settore (m) privato private sector
settore (m) pubblico public sector
settore (m) terziario tertiary sector
sezione (f) *[reparto]* department *[in office]*
sfavorevole unfavourable
sforzo (m) effort
sfruttare exploit

sgravio (m) per doppia tassazione double taxation agreement
sicurezza (f) security *or* safety
sicurezza (f) del posto di lavoro job security
sicurezza (f) dell'impiego security of employment
sicurezza (f) di possesso security of tenure
sicuro (prudente) safe (adj)
sigillare seal (v) *[attach a seal]*
sigillo (m) seal (n)
sigillo (m) doganale customs seal
siglare initial (v)
silo (m) grain elevator
simbolo (m) token
simbolo (m) di successo status symbol
sindacalista (m) trade unionist
sindacato (m) (trade) union
sindacato (m) degli inquilini rent tribunal
sindrome (f) della fenice phoenix syndrome
sinergia (f) synergy
singolo single
sinistro left *[not right]*
sistema (m) system
sistema (m) *[rete]* network (n)
sistema (m) di acquisti a rate hire purchase (HP)
sistema (m) di controllo control systems
sistema (m) di recupero delle informazioni retrieval system
sistema (m) di sorveglianza dell'ufficio office security
sistema (m) elettronico di elaborazione computer system
sistema (m) in tempo reale real-time system
Sistema (m) Monetario Europeo (SME) European Monetary System (EMS)
sistema (m) operativo operating system
sistema (m) tributario tax system
sistemare settle *or* arrange things
sistemare (disporre) arrange *or* set out

sistemazione (f) *[disposizione]*
system *or* arrangement
situato situated
situazione (f) *[posizione]* situation
or position *or* state of affairs
situazione (f) contrattuale
bargaining position
SME (Sistema Monetario Europeo)
EMS (= European Monetary
System)
smentita (f) disclaimer
sociale social
società (f) society *[in general]*
**società (f) a responsabilità limitata
(Srl)** private limited company
società (f) collegata (f) associate
company
società (f) commerciale trading
company
società (f) controllante parent
company; holding company
società (f) cooperativa cooperative
society
società (f) (di capitali) company
**società (f) di capitali a
responsabilità limitata** limited
(liability) company (Ltd)
**società (f) di capitali a
sottoscrizione pubblica (SpA)**
Public Limited Company (Plc)
società (f) di factoring factor (n)
[company]
società (f) di medie dimensioni
middle-sized company
società (f) di navigazione shipping
company
società (f) di persone partnership
società (f) di servizi service (n)
(business)
**società (f) di vendita per
corrispondenza** mail-order
business *or* mail-order firm
società (f) esistente solo di nome
shell company
società (f) fiduciaria trust company
società (f) finanziaria finance
company
**società (f) in accomandita
semplice** limited partnership
società (f) mutua (di assicurazioni)
mutual (insurance) company

società (f) orientata al profitto
profit-oriented company
società (f) quotata in Borsa
quoted company
società (f) rivale rival company
società (f) sorella sister company
socio (m) member *[of a group]*
socio (m) *[compagno]* partner
socio (m) *[associato]* associate (n)
socio (m) accomandante sleeping
partner
socio (m) anziano senior partner
soddisfacente *[accettabile]*
satisfactory *or* acceptable
soddisfare satisfy *[customer]*;
meet *[a need]*
soddisfare una richiesta satisfy a
demand
soddisfazione (f) satisfaction
soddisfazione (f) dei clienti
customer satisfaction
soddisfazione (f) sul lavoro job
satisfaction
software (m) software
soggetto a subject to
soggetto a condizioni conditional
soglia (f) threshold
soldi (mpl) in anticipo money up
front
solido *[stabile]* solid *or* firm (adj)
solito *[abituale]* usual *or* normal
sollecitare ordinazioni solicit
orders
sollecito prompt
sollecito (m) reminder *or*
follow-up
sollevare raise (v) *[a question]*
solo *[unico]* sole
soluzione (f) solution
solvente solvent (adj)
solvibile credit-worthy
solvibilità (f) solvency
somma (f) sum *[of money]*
somma (f) *[addizione]* sum *or*
addition *[calculation]*
sommare *[aggiungere]* add
sommare una colonna di cifre add
up a column of figures
sondaggio (m) random check

sondaggio: fare un sondaggio sample (v) *or* ask questions

sondaggio (m) d'opinione opinion poll

soprattassa (f) di importazione import surcharge

sopravvalutare overvalue *or* overestimate (v)

sorpassare *[superare]* exceed *or* go higher than

sorvegliare supervise

sospendere suspend

sospendere i pagamenti stop payments

sospendere le trattative break off negotiations

sospendere un'attività *[chiudere]* close down

sospensione (f) suspension *or* stoppage

sospensione (f) dei pagamenti suspension of payments

sospensiva (f) stay of execution

sostegno (m) *[contenitore]* holder *[thing]*

sostegno (copia) backup copy

sostenere bear (v) *or* pay for

sostenere le spese di qualcuno defray someone's expenses

sostenere spese incur *[costs]*

sostenitore (m) *[avallante]* backer

sostituire replace

sostituto (m) *[delegato]* replacement *or* deputy

sostituto *[facente funzione di]* acting

sostituzione (f) replacement *[of an item]*

sotterfugio (m) fiscale tax loophole

sotto contratto under contract

sotto controllo under control

sotto nuova gestione under new management

sottoporre refer *or* pass to someone

sottoprodotto (m) spinoff

sottoscritto undersigned

sottoscrittore (m) contributor

sottoscrivere una polizza take out a policy

sottrarsi al pagamento delle tasse evade tax

sovraccarico (m) di scorte overstocks

sovrappiù (m) *[surplus]* surplus

sovrapprezzo (m) surcharge

sovrapprofitti (mpl) excess profits

sovvenzionare subsidize

sovvenzione (f) *[sussidio]* subvention *or* subsidy

spaiato odd *[not a pair]*

spartire *[dividere]* share (v) *or* divide among

spartire un ufficio share an office

spazio (m) space *or* room

spazio (m) *[vuoto]* blank (n)

spazio (m) pubblicitario advertising space

speciale special

specialista (m) specialist

specializzato skilled

specializzato: essere specializzato specialize in

specializzato: non specializzato unskilled

specializzazione (f) specialization

specifica (f) specification

specificare specify

specificare *[dettagliare]* itemize

specificazione (f) delle mansioni job specification

speculatore al rialzo bull *[on stock exchange]*

spedire dispatch (v) *or* send *or* forward *or* ship (v)

spedire merce in container ship in containers

spedire per espresso express (v) *or* send fast

spedire per posta post (v) *or* mail (v)

spedire per posta aerea airmail (v)

spedire un pacco per posta ordinaria send a package by surface mail

spedire un pacco per via aerea send a package by airmail

spedire una fattura (per posta)
send an invoice by post
spedizione (f) dispatch (n) *or*
sending
spedizione (f) consolidata
consolidated shipment
spedizione (f) in massa bulk
shipments
spedizione (f) marittima shipping
spedizione (f) per espresso
express delivery
spedizioniere (m) (per via terra)
forwarding agent
spedizioniere (m) marittimo
shipper *or* shipping agent
spendere spend *[money]*
spendere meno underspend
spendere oltre il proprio budget
overspend one's budget
**spendere oltre le proprie
possibilità** overspend
spesa (f) shopping
spesa (f) (conto) expense
spesa (f) compresa inclusive
charge
spesa (f) non autorizzata
unauthorized expenditure
spesa (f) postale postage
spesa (f) totale total expenditure
spese (fpl) expenditure *or*
expenses *or* outgoings
spese (fpl) bancarie bank charges
spese (fpl) conto capitali capital
expenditure
**spese (fpl) d'ammissione o spese
(fpl) d'entrata** admission charge *or*
entrance charge
spese (fpl) d'esercizio running
costs *or* running expenses *or*
operating costs *or* operating
expenses
spese (fpl) d'imballo packing
charges
spese (fpl) d'incasso collection
charges *or* collection rates
spese (fpl) di amministrazione
administrative expenses
spese (fpl) di avviamento start-up
costs
**spese (fpl) di confezione o
spedizione** handling charges

spese (fpl) di consumo consumer
spending
spese (fpl) di immagazzinamento
storage cost
spese (fpl) di scarico (da nave)
landing charges
spese (fpl) di trasporto freight
costs
spese (fpl) extra extra charges
spese (fpl) generali overhead costs
or overheads
spese (fpl) generali di produzione
manufacturing overheads
spese (fpl) impreviste incidental
expenses
spese (fpl) legali legal costs *or*
legal charges *or* legal expenses
spese (fpl) postali postal charges
or postal rates
spese (fpl) postali e imballo
postage and packing (p & p)
spese (fpl) pubblicitarie publicity
expenditure
spese (fpl) straordinarie
below-the-line expenditure
spese (fpl) supplementari
additional charges *or* extras
**spese (fpl) trasporto merci via
aerea** air freight charges *or* rates
spiccioli (mpl) change (n) *or* cash
spiegare explain
spiegazione (f) explanation
spina (f) elettrica electric plug
spinta (f) boost (n)
spionaggio (m) industriale
industrial espionage
sponsor (m) *[garante]* sponsor (n)
sponsorizzare *[patrocinare]*
sponsor (v)
sponsorizzato dal governo
government-sponsored
sponsorizzazione (f) *[avallo]*
sponsorship
sportellista (m) teller
sportello (m) di cassa cash desk
spot (m) *[pubblicità]* TV
commercial (n)
sprecare waste (v) (use too much)
spreco (m) waste (n) *or* wastage
stabile *[solido]* firm (adj) *or* stable

stabilimento (m) *[fabbrica]* plant (n) *or* factory

stabilire *[istituire]* establish

stabilire *[organizzare]* arrange *[meeting]*

stabilire come obiettivo target (v)

stabilire il prezzo price (v) *or* fix a price

stabilire il valore *[accertare]* assess

stabilità (f) stability

stabilità (f) dei prezzi price stability

stabilizzare stabilize

stabilizzarsi level off *or* level out

stabilizzazione (f) stabilization

stadio (m) stage (n)

stagionale *[periodico]* seasonal

stagione (f) season

stagnante stagnant

stampa (f) press

stampante (f) printer *[machine]*

stampante (f) a matrice d'aghi dot-matrix printer

stampante (f) con testina a margherita daisy-wheel printer

stampante (f) laser laser printer

stampante (f) lineare line printer *or* computer printer

stampare print out

stampato (m) printout

stand (m) stand (n) *[at exhibition]*

standard standard (adj) *or* stock (adj) *or* normal

standard (mpl) di produzione production standards

standardizzare standardize

standardizzazione (f) standardization

standista (m) *[espositore]* exhibitor

stanziamento (m) promozionale promotional budget

stanziare allocate

star del credere del credere

stare al passo con la richiesta keep up with the demand

statistica (f) statistics

statistico statistical

stato (m) *[nazione]* state (n) *or* country

stato (m) *[condizione]* state (n) *or* condition

stato (m) giuridico legal status

stato (m) ordinato: essere stato ordinato on order

statutario statutory

statuto (m) societario articles of association

stazione (f) ferroviaria railway station

sterlina (f) pound sterling

stima: fare una nuova stima reassess

stimare *[valutare]* estimate (v) *or* value (v)

stimatore (m) valuer

stimolare l'economia stimulate the economy

stimolo (m) stimulus

stipendiato salaried

stipendio (m) salary

stipendio (m) iniziale starting salary

stipendio (m) interessante attractive salary

stipendio (m) lordo gross salary

stipula (f) stipulation

stipulare stipulate

stipulare un contratto draw up a contract

stiva (f) hold (n) *[of ship]*

stivatore (m) *[scaricatore di porto]* stevedore

stoccare *[costruire riserve]* stockpile (v)

stock (m) *[scorte]* stock (n) *[goods]*

stop (m) *[fine]* stop (n)

stornare una registrazione contra an entry

strada (f) road

straniero *[estero]* foreign *or* external

straordinario extraordinary; outstanding *or* unusual

strategia (f) strategy

strategia (f) commerciale business strategy

strategia (f) di marketing
marketing strategy
strategico strategic
strozzatura (f) *[nel processo aziendale]* bottleneck
strumenti (mpl) *[mezzi]* ways *or* means
strumenti (mpl) scontabili *[effetti bancabili]* bankable paper
strumento (m) instrument *or* implement (n)
strumento (m) *[documento]* instrument *[document]*
strumento (m) negoziabile negotiable instrument
strumento (m) non negoziabile non-negotiable instrument
struttura (f) structure (n)
struttura a rete grid structure
strutturale structural
strutturare structure (v) *or* arrange
studiare study (v)
studio (m) study (n)
studio (m) dei tempi e dei movimenti time and motion study
studio (m) della fattibilità feasibility report
su richiesta on request
subaffittante (m) sublessor
subaffittare sublease (v) *or* sublet
subaffitto (m) sublease (n)
subaffittuario (m) sublessee
subappaltatore (m) subcontractor
subappalto (m) subcontract (n)
subire un danno suffer damage
subire una forte flessione slump (v)
succedere succeed *or* take over *[from someone else]*
successo (m) success
successo: avere successo *[riuscire]* succeed *[do well]*
successo: che non ha successo unsuccessful
successo: di successo successful
sufficiente sufficient; adequate
superare (sorpassare) exceed *or* go higher than
superficie (f) area *[surface]*
superficie (f) di pavimento floor space

superiore superior (adj) *[better quality]*
superiore (m) superior (n) *[person]*
supermercato (m) supermarket
supermercato (m) all'ingrosso cash and carry
supervisione (f) *[vigilanza]* supervision
supervisione: di supervisione supervisory
supervisore (m) supervisor
supplementare supplementary; additional
surplus (m) *[sovrappiù]* surplus
sussidiario subsidiary (adj)
sussidio (m) *[sovvenzione]* subsidy
sussidio (m) di disoccupazione unemployment pay
svalutare devalue *or* depreciate *or* lose value
svalutazione (f) devaluation *or* depreciation *or* loss of value
svendere sell off
svendere merci sul mercato dump goods on a market
svendita (f) per chiusura d'esercizio closing-down sale
svendite (fpl) di fine stagione end of season sales
sviluppare develop *or* plan
sviluppare *[costruire]* develop *or* build
sviluppo (m) *[progresso]* development
sviluppo (m) del prodotto product development
sviluppo (m) economico economic development
svincolo (m) doganale customs clearance
svolgere esercizio d'impresa carry on a business

Tt

tabella (f) fissa dei prezzi fixed scale of charges
tabellone (m) hoarding *[for posters]*
tabulare tabulate
tabulato (m) computer printout
tabulatore (m) tabulator
tabulazione (f) tabulation
taccheggiare shoplifting
taccheggiatore (m) shoplifter
tachigrafo (m) tachograph
tacito consenso (m) tacit approval
taglia (f) size
taglia (f) standard stock size
taglia: di taglia forte outsize (OS)
tagliare cut (v)
tagliare i prezzi o le condizioni di credito slash prices *or* credit terms
taglio (m) cut (n)
tangente (f) *[bustarella]* bribe (n)
tangibile tangible
tappare plug (v) *or* block
tara (f) tare
tardi *[in ritardo]* late (adv)
tariffa (f) tariff; fare; scale of charges *or* rate
tariffa (f) a tempo time rate
tariffa (f) doganale customs tariff
tariffa (f) in vigore going rate
tariffa (f) notturna night rate
tariffa (f) protezionistica protective tariff
tariffa (f) ridotta cheap rate
tariffe (fpl) delle inserzioni pubblicitarie advertising rates
tariffe (fpl) di assicurazione insurance rates
tariffe (fpl) di nolo freight rates
tariffe (fpl) differenziali differential tariffs
tariffe (fpl) pubblicitarie differenziali graded advertising rates

tasca (f) pocket (n)
tassa (f) (imposta) tax (n)
tassa (f) ad valorem ad valorem tax
tassa (f) di base basic tax
tassa (f) di circolazione road tax
tassa (f) di registrazione registration fee
tassa (f) esclusa exclusive of tax
tassabile taxable
tassare *[gravare d'imposta]* tax (v)
tassazione (f) taxation
tassazione (f) alta high taxation
tassazione (f) diretta direct taxation
tassazione (f) indiretta indirect taxation
tasse (fpl) aeroportuali airport tax
tassi (mpl) monetari money rates
tasso (m) rate (n) *or* amount
tasso (m) d'inflazione rate of inflation
tasso (m) d'interesse interest rate
tasso (m) di base prime rate
tasso (m) di cambio exchange rate *or* rate of exchange
tasso (m) di cambio corrente current rate of exchange
tasso (m) di cambio sfavorevole unfavourable exchange rate
tasso (m) di cambio stabile stable exchange rate
tasso (m) di conversione conversion price *or* conversion rate
tasso (m) di produzione rate of production
tasso (m) di sconto discount rate
tasso (m) fisso di cambio fixed exchange rate
tasso (m) fluttuante di cambio floating exchange rates
tasso (m) ridotto reduced rate
tasso (m) su prestiti a breve call rate
tasso (m) ufficiale di sconto bank base rate
tastiera (f) keyboard (n)
tastierino (m) numerico numeric keypad

tasto (m) key *[on keyboard]*
tasto (m) delle maiuscole shift key
tasto (m) di comando control key
tavole (fpl) attuariali actuarial tables
tecnica (f) di vendita selling technique
tecniche (fpl) di marketing marketing techniques
tecniche (fpl) di propaganda canvassing techniques
tecniche (fpl) gestionali management techniques
telecomando (m) remote control
telefonare phone (v) *or* telephone (v)
telefonata (f) a carico del ricevente reverse charge call *or* collect call *[US]*
telefonata (f) d'affari business call
telefonata (f) di routine routine call
telefonata (f) in arrivo incoming call
telefonata (f) internazionale international call
telefonata (f) urbana local call
telefonista (mf) telephonist
telefono (m) phone (n) *or* telephone (n)
telefono (m) a gettoni pay phone
telefono (m) a schede card phone
telefono (m) cellulare cellular phone
telefono (m) interno internal telephone
telefono (m) per conferenze conference phone
telescrivente (f) *[telex]* telex (n)
teleselezione (f) dial direct
teleselezione (f) internazionale international direct dialling
telex (m) telex (n)
tempo (m) di elaborazione computer time
tempo (m) improduttivo down time
tempo (m) libero spare time
tendenza (f) al rialzo upward trend

tendenza (f) di mercato market trends
tenere hold (v) *or* keep; stock *[goods]*
tenere in affitto *[affittare]* lease (v) *[of tenant]*
tenere in efficienza maintain *or* keep going
tenere su keep up
tenere una seduta hold a meeting *or* a discussion
terminal (m) airport terminal
terminal (m) della compagnia aerea air terminal
terminal (m) per container container terminal
terminale terminal (adj) *[at the end]*
terminale (m) di computer computer terminal
terminare *[scadere]* terminate; expire
termine (m) termination; expiration
termine (m) *[chiusura]* closure
termine (m) *[fine]* end (n)
termine (m) ultimo *[data di chiusura]* closing date *or* time limit
termine (m) ultimo *[data di scadenza]* deadline
termini (mpl) stabiliti terms of reference
terra (f) o terreno (m) land (n)
territorio (m) territory *[of salesman]*
terza persona (f) third party
terzo trimestre (m) third quarter
tesoreria (f) treasury
tessera (f) card
tessera (f) *[di abbonamento ferroviario]* season ticket
tessera (f) prelievo contanti cash card
testa: che è in testa alle vendite top-selling
testimone (m) witness (n)
tetto (m) dei prezzi price ceiling
tetto (m) salariale credit ceiling
timbrare stamp (v) *[mark]*
timbro (m) stamp (n) *[device]*

tipografia (f) printer *or* printing company

tirare sul prezzo *[contrattare]* bargain (v)

tiratura (f) circulation *[of newspaper]*

tirocinante (m) trainee

titolare (m) holder *[person]*

titoli (mpl) securities

titoli (mpl) di prim'ordine gilt-edged securities *or* gilts

titoli (mpl) di stato government stock *or* government bonds

titolo (m) di prim'ordine blue chip

togliere lift (v) *or* remove

togliere l'embargo lift an embargo

togliere la seduta close a meeting

tonnellaggio (m) tonnage

tonnellaggio (m) lordo gross tonnage

tonnellata (f) ton *or* tonne

totale total (adj) *or* overall

totale (m) total (n) *or* sum

totale (m) corrente running total

totale (m) delle attività total assets

totale (m) generale grand total

totale (m) parziale subtotal

totale *[globale]* total (adj) *or* all-in

tradurre translate

traduttore (m), traduttrice (f) translator

traduzione (f) translation

traente (m) drawer

trafficare *[commerciare]* trade (v)

trafficare in *[commerciare in]* trade in *[buy and sell]*

traghetto (m) ferry

traghetto (m) per automezzi car ferry *or* roll on/roll off ferry

tramite (via) via

tranne (eccetto) except

transazione (f) transaction

transazione (f) a pronti spot purchase

transazione (f) commerciale business transaction

transazione (f) sul disponibile cash transaction *or* cash deal

transazioni (fpl) *[operazioni]* stock exchange dealing

transito (m) transit

trarre vantaggio da benefit from (v) *or* capitalize on

trascurabile negligible

trascurare *[omettere]* omit

trasferibile transferable

trasferimento (m) transfer (n) *or* assignment *or* cession

trasferimento (m) di capitali transfer of funds

trasferire transfer (v)

traslocare move *[house, office]*

trasloco (m) move *[to new house]*

trasmissione (f) conveyance; drive (n) *[part of machine]*

trasportare transport (v) *or* ship (v)

trasportare *[portare]* carry

trasportare a mezzo di palette palletize

trasportare merci via aerea airfreight (v)

trasportatore (m) haulage contractor

trasportatore (m) su strada road haulier

trasporti (mpl) pubblici public transport

trasporto (m) transport (n); carriage *or* freight

trasporto (m) di merci freightage

trasporto (m) di ritorno homeward freight

trasporto (m) ferroviario rail transport

trasporto (m) in container containerization *or* shipping in containers

trasporto (m) in superficie surface transport

trasporto (m) marittimo shipment

trasporto (m) mediante autocarro trucking

trasporto (m) merci via aerea air freight

trasporto (m) su strada road transport *or* road haulage

Trasporto Internazionale su Strada Transports Internationaux Routiers (TIR)

tratta (f) (bank) draft (n)
tratta (f) a vista sight draft
trattabile *[controllabile]* manageable
trattabile *[negoziabile]* negotiable
trattamento (m) equo fair dealing
trattare process (v) *or* deal with *or* negotiate
trattare *[lavorare]* process (v) *[raw materials]*
trattare con qualcuno deal with someone
trattario (m) drawee
trattativa (f) negotiation
trattative (fpl) difficile hard bargaining
trattato (m) commerciale trade agreement
trattenere hold up (v) *or* delay *or* keep back
tredicesima (f) *[gratifica natalizia]* Christmas bonus
treno (m) train (n)
treno (m) merci goods train *or* freight train
tribunale (m) law courts
tribunale (m) arbitrale arbitration board *or* arbitration tribunal
tribunale (m) del lavoro industrial tribunal
tribunale (m) di arbitrato adjudication tribunal
tribunale (m) di arbitrato industriale industrial arbitration tribunal
trimestrale quarterly (adj)
trimestralmente quarterly (adv)
trimestre quarter *[three months]*
triplicare triple (v)
triplice: in triplice copia in triplicate
triplo triple (adj)
truffa (f) *[imbroglio]* fiddle (n)
turno (m) *[di lavoro]* shift (n) *[team of workers]*
turno (m) di giorno day shift
turno (m) di notte night shift
tutte le spese pagate all expenses paid

Uu

UE (Unione Europea) EU (European Union)
ufficiale official (adj)
ufficiale: non ufficiale unofficial
ufficiale (m) di dogana customs official
ufficiale (m) di stato civile registrar
ufficio (m) office
ufficio: d'ufficio clerical
ufficio (m) a pianta aperta open-plan office
ufficio (m) acquisti buying department or purchasing department
ufficio (m) addetto alla fatturazione invoicing department
ufficio (m) assistenza service department
ufficio (m) assistenza ai clienti customer service department
ufficio (m) cambio bureau de change
ufficio (m) computer computer department
Ufficio (m) Dazio e Dogana Customs and Excise Department
ufficio (m) del personale personnel department
ufficio (m) della pubblicità publicity department
ufficio (m) delle pubbliche relazioni public relations department
ufficio (m) deposito bagagli left luggage office
ufficio (m) design design department
ufficio (m) di rappresentanza representative company
ufficio (m) indennità claims department

ufficio (m) informazioni information bureau

ufficio (m) legale legal department

ufficio (m) prenotazioni booking office

ufficio (m) produzioni production department

ufficio (m) pubblico general office

ufficio (m) reclami complaints department

ufficio (m) traduzioni translation bureau

ufficio (m) vendite sales department

ufficiosamente off the record

ufficioso *[non ufficiale]* unofficial

uguagliare equal (v)

uguale equal (adj)

ultima offerta (f) *[di licitazione]* closing bid

ultimo a entrare, primo a uscire last in first out (LIFO)

ultimo trimestre (m) last quarter

unico one-off *or* unique

unico proprietario (m) sole owner

uniforme *[indiscriminato]* general *or* across-the-board

unilaterale unilateral

unione (f) doganale customs union

Unione (f) Europea (UE) European Union (EU)

unire join

unire *[attaccare]* attach *or* join

unità (f) unit *or* item

unità (f) a dischi magnetici disk drive

unità (f) monetaria monetary unit

unito *[congiunto]* joint; united

uomo (m) man (n)

uomo (m) d'affari businessman

uomo (m) delle consegne deliveryman

uomo (m) di fiducia right-hand man

urgente urgent

usare use (v)

usato *[di seconda mano]* secondhand

uscente retiring

uscita (f) exit

uscita: in uscita outgoing

uso (m) use (n)

usuale *[comune]* common *or* frequent

usuale *[standard]* stock (adj) *or* normal

usufrutto (m) *[rendita vitalizia]* life interest

usurpare un brevetto infringe a patent

usurpazione (f) di brevetto infringement of patent

utente (m) user

utente (m) finale end user

utile useful

utile (m) *[profitto]* profit

utile (m) al lordo delle imposte pretax profit *or* profit before tax

utile (m) al netto delle imposte profit after tax

utile (m) d'esercizio operating profit *or* trading profit

utile (m) in aumento increasing profits

utile (m) lordo gross profit

utile (m) netto net profit

utile (m) per azione earnings per share *or* earnings yield

utili (mpl) distribuibili distributable profit

utili (mpl) ipotetici paper profit

utili (mpl) netti net earnings *or* net income

utili (mpl) record record profits

utili (mpl) societari corporate profits

utilità (f) *[beneficio]* usefulness *or* benefit (n)

utilizzazione (f) utilization

utilizzo (m) della capacità produttiva capacity utilization

Vv

vacante vacant

vaglia (m) [mandato di pagamento] money order

vaglia (m) postale postal order

valere be worth

validità (f) validity

valido valid

valido: essere valido be valid *or* be in force

valigia (f) case *or* suitcase

valore (m) value (n) *or* worth

valore: in base al valore di ad valorem

valore (m) attuale present value

valore (m) contabile book value

valore (m) di mercato market value

valore (m) di riscatto surrender value

valore (m) di sostituzione replacement value

valore (m) dichiarato declared value

valore (m) massimo peak (n)

valore (m) mediano median

valore (m) nominale nominal value *or* face value *or* par value

valore (m) patrimoniale asset value

valore (m) patrimoniale netto net assets *or* net worth

valore (m) totale della fattura total invoice value

valorem: ad valorem ad valorem

valuta (f) currency

valuta (f) bloccata blocked currency

valuta (f) convertibile convertible currency

valuta (f) debole soft currency

valuta (f) di riserva reserve currency

valuta (f) estera foreign exchange *[currency]*

valuta (f) solida hard currency

valutare value (v) *or* evaluate

valutare [stimare] estimate (v)

valutare i costi evaluate costs

valutato estimated

valutazione (f) valuation; evaluation; estimate

valutazione (f) approssimativa rough estimate

valutazione (f) dei costi costing

valutazione (f) del mercato azionario stock market valuation

valutazione (f) della prestazione performance rating

valutazione (f) delle scorte stock valuation

vantaggioso economic *or* profitable

variare [estendersi] vary; range (v)

variazione (f) variation; variance

variazioni (fpl) [scala] range (n) *or* variation

variazioni (fpl) stagionali seasonal variations

vario [miscellaneo] various *or* miscellaneous

vecchio old

vecchio: di vecchia data long-standing

vecchio: di vecchia istituzione old-established

vecchio: più vecchio senior

veicolo (m) vehicle

veicolo (m) per merci pesanti heavy goods vehicle (HGV)

veicolo (m) articolato articulated vehicle

veloce fast (adj)

velocemente [rapidamente] fast (adv) *or* rapidly

vendere sell

vendere [commercializzare] market (v) *or* put on the market

vendere a minor prezzo di un concorrente undercut a rival

vendere a termine sell forward

vendere al dettaglio retail (v)
[goods]
vendere all'asta auction (v)
vendere sotto costo discount (v);
undersell
vendere tutto *[esaurire]* sell out
[all stock]
vendersi be sold; move
vendersi a retail for (v) *or* sell for
a price
vendibile saleable
vendibilità (f) saleability
vendita (f) sale (n) *or* selling
vendita: in vendita for sale
vendita (f) a domicilio
house-to-house selling
vendita (f) al dettaglio retailing
vendita (f) all'asta sale by auction
vendita (f) coatta forced sale
vendita (f) con carta di credito
credit card sale
vendita (f) con possibilità di resa
see-safe
vendita (f) di merce sotto costo
distress sale
vendita (f) di realizzo bargain
made (n) *[on stock exchange]*
vendita (f) diretta direct selling
**vendita (f) diretta tramite
corrispondenza** direct mail
vendita (f) per contanti cash sale
vendita (f) porta a porta
door-to-door selling
vendite (fpl) *[fatturato]* sales
vendite (fpl) a termine forward
sales
vendite (fpl) basse low sales
vendite (fpl) interne domestic sales
**vendite (fpl) nazionali o vendite sul
mercato interno** home sales
vendite (fpl) per telefono telesales
vendite (fpl) presunte estimated
sales
vendite (fpl) previste projected
sales
vendite (fpl) record record sales
vendite (fpl) registrate book sales
venditore (m) salesman; seller *or*
vendor

venditore (m) a domicilio
door-to-door salesman
venditore (m) di assicurazioni
insurance salesman
venditori (mpl) sales people
venduto: essere venduto be sold
or change hands
venduto con possibilità di resa
sale *or* return
venire a un compromesso
compromise (v)
ventiquattrore (f) personalizzata
personalized briefcase
verbale verbal
verbale (m) *[di assemblea]*
minutes (n) *[of meeting]*
verbalizzare *[mettere a verbale]*
minute (v)
verde: al verde broke (informal)
verdetto (m) *[decisione]*
judgement *or* judgment; verdict
verifica (f) *[controllo]* verification;
control (n) *or* check
verificare verify; audit (v)
verificare i conti audit the accounts
verificato: non verificato
unaudited
vero *[autentico]* genuine *or* true
versamento (m) d'acconto down
payment
versare denaro deposit (v)
vertenza (f) di lavoro labour
disputes
vertenza (f) operaia industrial
disputes
veto (m) veto (n)
veto: porre il veto a una decisione
veto (v) a decision
vetrina (f) shop window
vetrinetta (f) display case
vetta (f) (cima) top (n) *or* highest
point
vettore (m) common carrier
via (tramite) via
viaggio (m) d'affari business trip
viaggio (m) di ritorno homeward
journey
vice amministratore (m) delegato
deputy managing director

vice direttore (m) assistant manager *or* deputy manager
vicino a close to
videoscrittura (f) word-processing
video-unità (f) display unit
vie (fpl) legali legal proceedings
vietare *[interdire]* ban (v)
vigilanza (f) *[supervisione]* supervision
vigore: essere in vigore rule (v) *or* be in force
vincere un contratto win a contract
vincolante binding
violare la legge break the law
violazione (f) dei regolamenti doganali infringement of customs regulations
violazione (f) di garanzia breach of warranty
virgola (f) decimale decimal point
visita (f) visit *or* call (n)
visita (f) a freddo cold call
vista (f) sight
vista: tratta a vista sight draft
visto (m) consolare visa
visto (m) consolare di transito transit visa
visto (m) consolare multiplo multiple entry visa
visto (m) d'ingresso entry visa
vita (f) ciclica di un prodotto product cycle
viziare *[rovinare]* spoil
viziato *[privo di validità]* defective *or* not valid
voce (f) item *[of information]*
voci (fpl) straordinarie extraordinary items *or* exceptional items
volantino (m) leaflet
volere *[richiedere]* take (v) *or* need
volo (m) flight *[of plane]*
volo (m) a lunga percorrenza long-distance flight
volo (m) a lungo raggio long-haul flight

volo (m) charter charter flight
volo (m) di coincidenza connecting flight
volo (m) di linea scheduled flight
volume (m) volume
volume (m) *[grande quantità]* bulk *or* mass
volume (m) d'affari sales figures *or* turnover
volume (m) degli scambi commerciali volume of trade *or* volume of business
volume (m) delle vendite sales volume *or* volume of sales
voluminoso bulky
voto (m) decisivo casting vote
voto (m) per delega proxy vote
vuotare empty (v)
vuoti (mpl) a rendere returned empties
vuoto empty (adj)
vuoto (m) *[spazio]* blank (n)
vuoto *[in bianco]* blank (adj)

Zz

zero (m) *[nulla]* zero *or* nil
zona (f) *[quartiere]* zone; area *or* district *[of town]*
zona (f) commerciale shopping precinct
zona (f) di libero scambio free trade area
zona (f) di libero scambio free trade zone
zona (f) franca free zone
zona (f) industriale industrial estate

Business correspondence

La corrispondenza commerciale

Sample Curriculum Vitae

CURRICULUM VITAE
Giuseppina Cataldo
Via Colfosco 15
00151 Roma
Tel: 00 44 20 8868 9854   Cellulare: 00 44 7914 248553 E-mail:
giusecaldo@scalinet.it

Interessi
Assunzione con ruolo direttivo e di capo squadra di un ufficio personale,
all'interno di una affermata società di informatica

Esperienza lavorativa
1999 ad oggi
Costello Commerci Marittimi srl |Genova
Consulente per le Risorse Umane
Ha lavorato come consulente in questioni di politica del personale. I suoi compiti
comprendevano l'amministrazione della politica delle relazioni e del tirocinio del
personale. Ha collaborato all'ideazione e l'implemento di nuove strategie
all'interno della compagnia, su territorio italiano.

1996 - 1998
Costello Commerci Marittimi srl |Genova
Consulente per le Risorse Umane nel campo marittimo, navale e d'aviazione
Ha lavorato come consulente per tre reparti della compagnia a livello globale:
prodotti marittimi, spedizioni marittime e spedizioni aeree. Ha coordinato diversi
processi d'assunzione, dalla fase di richiesta di personale al momento delle
selezioni dei candidati.

1993 - 1995
Costello Scavi Petrolifici srl |Genova
Consulente per le Risorse Umane nel campo dell'ingegneria petrolifica
Fra le altre cose, ha offerto consulenza in un importante processo di trasferimento
della compagnia.

Studi

1999 – 2001	Diploma di specializzazione in Relazioni Umane
	Università della Sapienza - Roma
1996 – 1998	Diploma di specializzazione in Risorse Umane e Sviluppo
	Istituto di Ricerca delle Risorse Umane e
Sviluppo	
1990 – 1993	Diploma di Laurea in Psicologia Sperimentale
	Università di Bologna
1982 – 1990	Conseguimento di diploma di maturità scientifica
	Liceo Scientifico Statale G.B. Morgagni -

'rototipo di Curriculum Vitae

CURRICULUM VITAE for Ms. Josephine Catterall
5A, Hanton Street, London, SE13 1DF
Tel: (020) 8868 9854   Mobile: (07914) 248553   E-mail:
jfcatterall@hotmail.com

Objective:

To become a professional HR manager with a team-leader role within a blue-chip company. Future positions to involve managing employee relations on a UK or global basis.

Work History:

Dec 1999 – present   GP International Trading and Shipping Company Ltd.,   London
Human Resources Policy Adviser
Provided professional advice on all HR policy matters including employee relations and training. Developed UK policy and implemented policy changes within the business.

May 1996 – Nov 1999 GP International Trading and Shipping Company Ltd.,   London
Human Resources Adviser: Marine, Shipping, and Aviation
Provided recruitment advice to 3 departments of the Global Businesses group: Marine Products, Shipping, and Aviation. Coordinated several internal and external recruitment processes through all stages from advertising to candidate selection.

Sept 1993 – April 1996   GP UK Exploration and Production, Southampton
Human Resources Consultant: Oil-well Engineering
Provided advice on a range of issues, including helping to manage a large-scale company relocation.

Education/Qualifications:

1999 – 2001	MSc in Employee Relations, *University of Westminster, London*
1996 – 1998	Graduate of the Chartered Institute of Personnel and Development
1990 – 1993	BA (Hons) Experimental Psychology (Class Iii), *University of Bristol*
1982 – 1990	'A' Levels: Biology (A), French (A), German (B), *St Stephen's School, Ely, Cambs*

Sample covering letter for job application

Antonella Grimaldi
Vicolo Marino
00 160 Ostia   25 marzo 2003

Gentile sig.ra Gianna Stefanelli
    Ufficio Assunzioni
    Infodati spa
    Via Merlo 1
    20 122 Milano

    Gentile signora Stefanelli

Riscontro all'inserzione da voi pubblicata su Repubblica del 20 marzo con
l'offerta di un posto di Capo Area Vendite presso la Infodati spa.

In merito, essendone interessata, mi preme segnalare che, in qualità di Vice
Direttore Vendite presso la Promedia spa, ho personalmente prodotto un
incremento pari al 15% sul valore delle azioni del passato anno.
Dal vostro resoconto annuale, secondo i dati della vostra web-site, risulta che
anche le azioni della Infodati spa hanno goduto di un incremento per cui si è
decisa una programmazione di rialzo delle azioni per il nuovo anno finanziario.
Sono certa che, con la mia esperinza e le mie qualifiche, potrei collaborare alla
realizzazione di quanto da voi programmato.
Come da vostra richiesta, allego copia di mio curriculum completo e aggiornato.

Sperando di essere presa in considerazione per l'incarico offerto, in attesa di
gentile riscontro invio distinti saluti

Antonella Grimaldi

Prototipo di lettera per domanda di assunzione

Adrienne Griffiths
20 Shakespeare Road
London
SE18 2PB

Jane Stevenson
Senior Personnel Officer
DataTech Ltd
Botley Road
Oxford
OX2 1ZZ

25 March 2003

Dear Ms Stevenson

I am very interested in the position of sales manager at DataTech Ltd as described in your advertisement of 20 March in the Guardian newspaper.

In my current position of deputy sales manager for Parker Smith Plc I have helped to increase our market share by 15% in the past year. I see from your website and annual report that DataTech have also increased their market share this year and are aiming to do the same in the next financial year, and I feel my track record and qualifications would fit in well with these plans for growth.

As requested in the advertisement, I enclose a copy of my CV which gives full details of my qualifications and work history. I would be very pleased to be considered for this position and I look forward to hearing from you.

Yours sincerely

Adrianne Griffiths

Encl.

Sample letter making a job offer

Infodati spa
Via Merlo 1
20 122 Milano

10 aprile 2003

Gentile sig.ra Antonella Grimaldi
Vicolo Marino
00 160 Ostia

Oggetto: conferma assunzione a Capo Area Vendite

Gentile signora Grimaldi

Facendo seguito al nostro ultimo colloquio, sono lieto di comunicarle la sua assunzione presso la nostra società, con l'incarico di Capo Area Vendite.

Il signor Davide Merlo, nostro Direttore Vendite, sara il suo interlocutore diretto.

Per l'incarico da lei svolto, le sue spettanze ammonteranno € 18.000 annuali, che saranno revisionate in occasione del primo rinnovo contrattuale.

I termini di assunzione le verranno puntualizzati in sede.

Auspicando una proficua collaborazione, le invio distinti saluti

Gianna Stefanelli
Direttore del Personale
Infodati spa

Prototipo di lettera d'offerta di lavoro

DataTech Ltd
Botley Road
Oxford
OX2 1ZZ

Ms Adrianne Griffiths
20 Shakespeare Road
London SE18 2PB

10 April 2003

Dear Ms Griffiths

Re: Post of Sales Manager

Further to your interview last week I am pleased to be able to offer you the post
of Sales Manager, reporting directly to David Wardlock, our Company Sales
Director.

Your starting salary will be £29,635, with an annual salary review on the date of
your joining the company. Other terms and conditions will be as outlined in the
interview.

If this offer is acceptable to you I would be grateful if you could send me
confirmation in writing. We can then finalize details of your contract and starting
date and discuss any relocation expenses you may have to claim.

Best wishes

Yours sincerely

Jane Stevenson
Senior Personnel Officer
DataTech Ltd

Sample reply to request for information

Emilia Del Fosco
Direttore Vendite
Infocarta spa
Via di Donna Olimpia 8
00 151 Roma   10 aprile 2003

       Egregio signor Luigi Volpe
       Via Albaro 18
       16 124 Genova

       Egregio signor Volpe

Facendo seguito alla nostra conversazione telefonica odierna, ho il piacere di inviarle il nostro catalogo con tutte le informazioni da lei gentilmente richieste, dove troverà una lista dei nostri prodotti disponibili e relativi costi.

Per ulteriori informazioni, non esiti a contattarmi al seguente indirizzo e-mail: info@scalaro.it.

Nel ringraziarla sentitamente per essersi rivolto a noi, le invio i piu distinti saluti

                        Emilia Del Fosco
                        Direttore Vendite

Prototipo di lettera di richiesta informazioni

---

12 Smith Street
Manchester
M90 1AA

Customer Sales
New DIY Ideas Ltd
Butler Industrial Estate
Manor Park
Manchester SE12 8NU

24 June 2003

Dear Sir or Madam

I recently saw an advert for your new range of DIY products in my local paper
and would be very interested to have more information on prices.

Could you send a copy of your catalogue to my home address above?

Thanking you in advance.

Yours faithfully

James Fox

Sample letter of complaint

Eleonora Giordano
Via del Tuorlo 22
00 153 Roma   20 marzo 2003

      Gentile sig.ra Silvia Rossi
      Computer & Accessorii
      P.le Aurelio 15
      00198 Roma

Oggetto: Malfunzionamento della stampante a getto (modello A1234)

      Gentile signora Rossi

Giovedì 13 marzo, presso il suo negozio, ho acquistato una stampante a getto modello A1234 (allego fotocopia della ricevuta).

Purtroppo la stampante risulta difettosa, e i vostri due tecnici non sembrano essere in grado di individuare il problema.

Chiedo pertanto il rimborso immediato della spesa da me sostenuta nell'acquisto della suddetta stampante.

La prego di contattarmi all'indirizzo sopraindicato così da potere fissare un appuntamento a perché lei venga a riprendere la stampante.

Nell'attesa le invio distinti saluti

                                Eleonora Giordano

Prototipo di lettera di reclamo

47 Highfield Road
York
YO2 3BP

Ms H Naughton
The Computer Shop Ltd
123 High Street
York
YO1 7HL

20 March 2003

Dear Ms Naughton

Faulty inkjet printer (model number A1234)

I purchased an inkjet printer (model number A1234) from your shop on Thursday 13 March (copy of receipt enclosed). Unfortunately, the printer appears to be faulty, and two engineers from your shop have not been able to isolate the cause of the problem. I would, therefore, appreciate a full refund on the faulty printer at your earliest convenience.

Please contact me at the above address so that we may arrange a time when the printer can be picked up and returned.

I look forward to hearing from you.

Yours sincerely

Elizabeth Kendall